many families, many literacies

many families, many literacies

an international declaration of principles

EDITED BY
DENNY TAYLOR

HEINEMANN TRADE
PORTSMOUTH, NEW HAMPSHIRE

The names of some of the participants in the family literacy programs discussed herein have been changed at their request.

HEINEMANN
A division of Reed Elsevier Inc.
361 Hanover Street
Portsmouth, NH 03801-3912
Offices and agents throughout the world

The author and publisher wish to thank those who have given their permission to include material in this book: "What Is a Family? What Do All Families Share?" by The Seven-Eights, The Manhattan Country Day School appears in *Keepsakes: Using Family Stories in Elementary Classrooms* by Linda Winston (Heinemann, A division of Reed Elsevier Inc., Portsmouth, NH, 1997). ■ "Some Perspectives on the Family" by Hope Jensen Leichter. Reprinted by permission of the publisher from Hope Jensen Leichter, *The Family As Educator* (New York: Teachers College Press, © 1972 by Teachers College, Columbia University. All rights reserved.), pp. 1–3. ■ "Oral and Written Language: Functions and Purposes" by Ken Goodman originally appeared in a different version in *Ken Goodman On Reading* by Ken Goodman. Copyright © 1996 by Kenneth S. Goodman. Adapted and reprinted by permission of Scholastic Canada Ltd. ■ "Family Literacy Programmes and Home Literacy Practices" by David Barton originally appeared in a different version in *Challenging Ways of Knowing in English, Maths and Science*, edited by D. Baker, J. Clay, and C. Fox. Copyright © 1995. Published by Falmer Press, London. Reprinted by permission of the editors. ■ "From Untapped Potential to Creative Realization: Empowering Parents" by Marla Hensley originally appeared in *Practicing Anthropology* 17 (3) (Summer 1995). Reprinted by permission of the publisher. ■ "Family Literacies: What Can We Learn from Talking with Parents?" by Helen James was originally published in *Language Matters*, CLPE, 1993/94, No. 3. Reprinted by permission of the author. ■ "Family Treasures" by Jean Bruce. *Family Treasures*™ is an outreach project of the Canadian Museum of Civilization. ■ "Learning Through Play at the Public Library" by Sandra Feinberg. This article is based on a program initiated by Mrs. Feinberg at the Middle Country Public Library and is fully described in *Running a Parent/Child Workshop: A How-To-Do-Manual for Librarians* by Sandra Feinberg and Kathleen Deerr (New York: Neal-Schuman Publishers, 1995). ■ "Debating Intergenerational Family Literacy: Myths, Critiques, and Counterperspectives" by Audrey N. Grant is adapted from "Debating Intergenerational Family Literacy: Myths, Counterperspectives and Metaphors." Copyright © by Audrey N. Grant. Reprinted by permission of the author.

Library of Congress Cataloging-in-Publication Data
Many families, many literacies : an international declaration of principles / edited by Denny Taylor.
    p.   cm.
Includes bibliographical references.
ISBN 0-435-08130-6
    1. Literacy.   2. Family literacy programs.   3. Literacy—United States.   4. Family literacy programs—United States.   I. Taylor, Denny, 1947–   .
LC149.M27   1997
379.2′4—dc21   97-7124
                                                                                                        CIP

Printed in the United States of America on acid-free paper
00 99 98 97 **OO**   1   2   3   4   5   6   7   8   9

What Is a Family? What Do All Families Share?

A group of people that share a home together and food.
People who love each other.
People who care about each other and listen to what each
    other say.
People who share a room with each other and other things.
People who get married and might have kids and raise them.
A group of people who are related.
People who share toys.
A family is something that keeps going on and on.
The family keeps getting shorter and getting bigger because
    people die and children are born.
It's like telling a story over and over again.

—*The Seven-Eights, The Manhattan Country Day School*

contents

acknowledgments

Many people shared their hearts and minds to make *Many Families, Many Literacies: An International Declaration of Principles* such an extraordinary publication. Individuals from around the world came together to support families, to recognize communities, and to work for equality and social justice. They invested both their time and their energy, and they paid their own way. In response to their extraordinary generosity, any royalties that are received from the sale of the book will be used to support family literacy research and program development in many different countries.

While it is impossible to thank everyone who participated in the development of the declaration, there are people whom I would like to mention individually. First my thanks go to Debbie Smith and Joanna Morasco, who are working on their doctorates in the department of language, reading, and culture at the University of Arizona. Neither Debbie nor Joanna thought it strange when I suggested that we hold a forum on family literacy, even though we didn't have any money to pay for conference facilities. In those first few weeks they worked around the clock exploring the possibilities and trying to obtain funds. Other graduate students joined them, until in the last hectic weeks Alan Flurkey, Terry Greene, Debra Jacobson, Prisca Martens, Janelle Matthis, Pamela Rossi, and Jesse Turner were all working to make the forum a success.

My sincere thanks go to the participants at the international forum in

Tucson who came together in October 1994 to share their personal experiences of family and community life and to use their educational expertise to build the foundation for the seven sets of principles that are the foundation of the declaration. Their vision took the forum from a local meeting to an international event, and the declaration from a small pamphlet to a full-sized book.

Special thanks goes to Toby Gordon for sharing the vision and agreeing to give us an advance, which we used to pay for the conference facilities. Also to Richard Ruiz, the chair of the department of language, reading, and culture at the University of Arizona for providing funds for the administrative costs of the forum. Without his support we would have been hard pressed to complete all the arrangements. I am especially grateful to Ken and Yetta Goodman, who provided funds after the forum for graduate students to assist me with the organization of the documentation. Also to Shirley Thornton and Richard Figueroa, who arranged for funds from the University of California. These funds were used to provide small travel stipends to participants, especially those traveling from other countries.

As I began the long task of developing the preamble and the seven sets of principles, many other graduate students came to my assistance. Melanie Uttech transcribed audiotapes before she left to do her doctoral research in rural Mexico. Then Gretchen Owocki took her place, transcribing, analyzing, and organizing, until she too left on the completion of her doctorate. Karen Onofrey filled her shoes and also provided me with invaluable administrative assistance. Alan Flurkey became involved again, providing me with much needed support as he reformatted all of the disks from individual authors and used them to produce a megadisc to match my hard copy of the manuscript. I am doubly grateful to Alan because he performed this task twice—the first time, just as he was nearing the completion of the task, his computer crashed, and he spent several days and nights reentering the individual articles and juxtaposing them with the seven sets of principles.

And there were others who left their mark. The educators whom I am about to mention have both my admiration and respect. Special thanks goes to David Bloome for arranging for a second forum held at the University of Massachusetts. Terri McCarty deserves similar thanks for inviting me to speak at the conference for Native Americans that she organizes each summer at the University of Arizona. My gratitude also goes to Susan Lytle, for arranging for me to speak at the University of Pennsylvania, and to JoBeth Allen, who invited me to speak at the National Conference on Research in Language and Literacy. They are a constant inspiration to me.

These presentations, together with presentations made at the International Reading Association Convention, the Annual Conference of the National Council of Teachers of English, the National Reading Conference, and the Whole Language Umbrella, were all influential in the development of the declaration. To all those who read drafts of the document and gave me their comments I am extremely grateful.

Eventually, the five-hundred-page manuscript was delivered to Alan Huisman at Heinemann, who is the finest copy editor with whom I have ever worked. I am always impressed by his attention to detail, but most of all by his sense of humor. Alan can make me laugh even when I am lost in a morass of paper, and I was lost many times during the production of this book. So my thanks go to Alan for his good-humored notes that championed the cause of brevity, and for accomplishing the impossible by turning a stack of crumpled pages into such an impressive-looking book. Joanne Tranchemontagne was also instrumental in this accomplishment. I enjoyed my conversations with her and I am particularly grateful to Joanne for the amount of time and care she took to ensure the cover reflected the spirit of *Many Families, Many Literacies*.

Finally, I want to thank David, my husband, for not batting an eyelid when our telephone bill was peppered each month with calls to places as far away as South Africa and Australia, and for rushing out to get copy cartridges that always seemed to fade just as the "final" version of the manuscript was printing out. Whatever book I write—or in this case edit—David is there beside me, talking through the issues, reading drafts, drinking tea, and working late. We laugh a lot, but we also enjoy grumbling together—which is a good quality to have in a relationship if you ever try to edit a book.

the history of
the declaration

DENNY TAYLOR

On Wednesday, March 13, 1996, I transferred the last of the individual files of the essays for *Many Families, Many Literacies* onto the megadisc for Heinemann. I decided to take a break and went into the kitchen to get a cup of coffee. While the coffee brewed I turned on CNN. There were reports from Scotland, that in a little town called Dunblane, thirteen children had been killed in a primary school. There were pictures of parents running. The reporter said that the children were five and six years of age. In the next report the newscaster said that sixteen children have been killed and that their teacher was also dead. In Scotland life stopped, and in England and in Wales. Here in the United States friends called, teachers like me, who had at some point in their lives, taught five- and six-year-olds. What had happened was incomprehensible.

On Thursday, in the House of Commons during the Prime Minister's question time, the members of parliament who have turned nineteenth-century agonistic debate into an unruly twentieth-century fracas put aside their scathing sarcasm and injurious wit to express their deep regrets to the families who lost their children. On Sunday at 9:30 AM, the time of the massacre, the BBC and commercial radio went off the air. TV stations were silent as they broadcast pictures from Dunblane. At Heathrow Airport landings and take-offs were suspended and planes turned off their engines. In the terminals passengers and airport personnel stood in silence. At fourteen main railway stations, trains stopped moving and people stood still. For a brief moment there were no contentions. The frictions of everyday life were of no importance as a nation came together to remember the children of Dunblane and their families.

I kept thinking of the way an entire nation stopped, of the deep political divide in the House of Commons that was bridged by the members of parliament who share an unwavering commitment to families. My thoughts returned to *Many Families, Many Literacies*. It is a deeply caring, passionate book that is argumentative and provocative as well as thoughtful and informative. It is a book with an "attitude," a positive attitude towards families. But that does not mean that those who disagree with the arguments presented in this book do not care. Whatever our philosophies, our theoretical orientations, our political persuasions, we would all stand together and hold hands for the children of Dunblane. We share our commitment to families, and I believe that it is because of that commitment that we can disagree. From this perspective I encourage you to read *Many Families, Many Literacies* with a pencil. It is truly a work in progress, and the principles are open to examination and reinterpretation. Reinvent them. Participate in the conversation. Let your voice be heard.

The International Declaration of Principles presented in *Many Families, Many Literacies* has a long history. For many years, educators in countries worldwide have been concerned by the "treatment" of families in the media and educational publications.

In the popular press, such well known figures as Carl Sagan and Ann Druyan (1994) tell readers of American Sunday newspapers that "if you are preoccupied by the absence of basic family support or dropped into a roiling sea of anger, neglect, and self-hatred, you might well conclude that reading takes too much work and just isn't worth the trouble." Sagan and Druyan go on to state, "Survival comes first. Growth comes second. In this nutritional triage, the body seems obliged to rank learning last. Better to be stupid and alive than smart and dead."

In educational publications there is talk of the disappeared parent and of families who will have to change cultures if they want to become literate and help their children learn to read and write. Illiteracy is portrayed as a family problem, and it is clear from the rhetoric that many believe it is the family that must be fixed.

Negative images of both parents and children are a part of our everyday lives. But when a private organization develops "national" standards for family literacy programs that include "well-designed induction activities and friendly intake procedures," it's time to act.

The urgency is underscored by the complexity of the process by which other education standards have been developed. It took three and a half years for the National [U.S.] Council of Teachers of English and the International Reading Association to develop national standards for the English language arts. Thousands of teachers and curriculum supervisors reviewed multiple drafts of the standards and thousands upon thousands of hours were spent conceptualizing, planning, discussing, and drafting the document. The result is a series of standards designed to be a beginning not an end, a starting point for discussion and action within states, districts, and individual schools across the United States.

This is not the case with the standards developed to evaluate such federally funded family literacy programs as Even Start and Headstart. In 1994 the National Center for Family Literacy (NCFL), a private organization whose "national" status is self-bestowed, announced the development of family literacy program standards and rating scales. An NCFL newsletter stated that the standards instrument would include ratings of the following "indicators" relative to the evaluation of family literacy programs: relevant content/individualized instruction; prior knowledge and transfer of learning; appropriate, balanced learner assessment design; systematic assessment/instruction design; friendly intake procedures; established orientation procedures; and well-designed induction activities. The operative words in the document appeared to be *intake*, *induction*, and *retention*.

Concerned that a private group was arbitrarily imposing "national" standards on publicly funded family literacy programs, I set about organizing a forum on family literacy (the forum eventually took place in Tucson in October 1994). With the help of some extraordinary graduate students in the department of language, reading, and culture at the University of Arizona but *without* any funds, I began calling members of the educational community. The response was overwhelming. Those whom I telephoned not only said they would come, but also agreed to pay their own expenses. One prospective participant suggested another, and within a short time a diverse group of people, including teachers from Alaska and family literacy practitioners from New York City, were making plans for a trip to Tucson.

The challenge was to ensure that we represented as broad a spectrum of professionals as possible. Classroom teachers, special educators, university professors, librarians, directors of community family literacy programs, policy makers from local, state, and national governments, even a college vice president and a television executive from the Children's Television Workshop, all promised to be there.

It quickly became evident that the issues surrounding the development both of family literacy programs and of the standards by which to evaluate them were of international concern. I called educators in the United Kingdom, Canada, and Mexico, asking them to join us, and I received calls from educators in Australia. News of what had become an international forum grew by word of mouth, and more and more people made arrangements to attend.

To prepare for the forum, we asked participants to send us a brief summary of their concerns about the family literacy movement and the development of national program standards. Our request hit a nerve. We were deluged with print. Alan Flurkey, one of the graduate students, reviewed the texts we were sent and came up with ten recurring critical issues. We decided to organize the forum around those ten issues. When participants arrived at the forum they were asked to join one of the ten working groups that would address these issues.

The forum began with presentations by David Barton, from the United Kingdom; Bram Fisher, from Canada; Audrey Grant and Julie Spreadbury, from Australia; and Judith Kalman, from Mexico. Then a number of American educators spoke: Elsa Auerbach from the University of Massachusetts; Shirley Thornton, who at that time was with the California State Department of Education; Klaudia Rivera, the director of Programa de Educacion de El Barrio in New York; Luis Moll from the University of Arizona; and finally, Jennie DeGroat, from the University of New Mexico and the Navajo Nation. After that, we rolled up our sleeves. Participants met in their working groups, which were charged with the task of developing a series of international principles that could be used to guide the development of family literacy programs. At regular intervals each group reported back to the entire forum and received feedback from the participants of other groups.

We shared our diverse experiences of working with families and studying literacy, argued the critical issues, aired concerns, and built frameworks. The energy level was high, the discussions memorable. Graduate students from the University of Arizona documented the discussions by means of notes and audiotapes. The first draft of the preamble and the seven sets of principles were based on this documentation.

The Tucson international forum was followed by other conferences. In June 1995, David Bloome arranged for a family literacy miniconference at the University of Massachusetts. On a rainy Sunday, family literacy practitioners, teachers, and researchers from universities and schools crowded into a classroom in the school of education for a spirited dialogue. Marilyn Antonucci, Lucille Fandel, and Sharon Smith each went back to family literacy programs in their communities and wrote articles with participants. Their stories are now a part of this book.

Later that month, I presented the preamble and principles at a summer institute for Native Americans that Terri McCarty organized at the University of Arizona. At the end of the session, everyone was asked to write about their reactions; the notes I received helped me edit those principles focused specifically on indigenous languages.

Later drafts were presented and discussed at the Whole Language Umbrella Conference in Windsor, Canada, in July 1995, and at the National Reading Conference in San Diego, California, in December 1995. More changes were made. Then, in March 1996, Susan Lytle, from the school of education at the University of Pennsylvania, organized a family literacy seminar for teachers from Philadelphia and the surrounding area. Again, changes were made.

Finally, the preamble and the seven sets of principles were mailed to some of the participants in the original Tucson forum and to other educators worldwide who had expressed interest in participating in the development of the declaration. *Many Families, Many Literacies: An International Declaration of Principles* is the result of this enormous collaborative effort, but it is important to emphasize that what we developed is *an* international declaration, not *the* declaration. Like the standards for the English language arts, it's a beginning, not an end.

Many Families, Many Literacies is a book of critical appraisal. Elsa Auerbach deconstructs the rhetoric of the National Center for Family Literacy, and Audrey Grant, of LaTrobe University, has written a companion paper in which she deconstructs the language of the family literacy movement in Australia.

Other articles broaden our understanding by bringing us other world-views of family literacy. Letta Mashishi writes of family literacy in Soweto and Elvira Souza Lima shares with us an article on literacy as a human right in Brazil. Other articles present exemplary programs such as the truly extraordinary Programa de Educacion de El Barrio in New York City. Klaudia Rivera writes about El Barrio and Antonia Tapia and Lucia Vega, who are participants in the program, are both authors in the book.

There is a discussion of ethical issues and principles for the assessment of family literacy programs. Sharon Murphy asks, "Who's reading whose reading?" and Peter Johnson explores standardized tests in family literacy programs. Practitioners are ever present in the book. Helen James, who is deputy head teacher in Tower Hamlets, London, writes of reaching out to the families of the three- to five-year-olds who attend Bangabandhu Primary School, and Marla Hensley, who teaches in Tucson, writes about the ways in which she incorporates the life experiences of her students' parents into her curriculum.

Members of communities whose voices are silenced by family literacy programs are also present. Practitioners who have lost their jobs speak out. One writes: "I believe that funding issues are what have left me powerless in this state—for I have not been silent nor compliant. But I have often been alone or at least jobless and at this point unable to find steady work." Another reminds us: "As professionals it is important for us to keep sight of the real nature of family literacy and where the power lies."

Family literacy is not one-stop shopping. The adverse effects of a monocultural perspective are emphasized by Jennie DeGroat, who, at the international forum, put her hand on her heart and said, "Too bad people don't see *me* as documentation." It is important that we listen to Jennie, because the "national" family literacy standards are now being used to evaluate families who are members of the Navajo Nation. She writes in *Many Families, Many Literacies*: "The people are never asked about their perspective to solve their own problems. Instead of meeting standards, educators should be concerned with helping families construct knowledge and share in the learning process.

To assist individuals in understanding their own history, to understand why things are the way they are today."

Indeed, this is the purpose of the International Declaration of Principles. The intent is to:

1. Support families.
2. Emphasize that the opportunity to become literate is a human right.
3. Provide alternative ways of thinking about and working with families that are not based on deficit talk.
4. Provide a point of departure for open dialogue within communities, schools, government agencies, and for-profit agencies engaged in family literacy work.
5. Provide respectful and collaborative models of family literacy programs.
6. Encourage families and communities to create their own community-based family literacy activities.
7. Support educators who participate in family literacy initiatives.

We hope that *Many Families, Many Literacies: An International Declaration of Principles* will provide organizations and local communities with the information they need to question the development of inappropriate family literacy assessment procedures and that it will provide guidance in developing policies and practices that recognize the need to build on the funds of knowledge—the languages, literacies, and complex problem-solving capabilities—that *all* families bring to *every* learning situation.

Reference

SAGAN, CARL, and ANN DRUYAN. "Literacy—The Path to a More Prosperous, Less Dangerous America." *Parade Magazine*, March 6, 1994, 5–7.

Why a declaration?

In many industrialized countries the increasing emphasis on deficit-driven family literacy programs for "undereducated" adults and their children raises fundamental ethical issues and questions of social justice that have yet to be addressed. The potential for human rights violations is considerable as the demands of advanced technological societies collide with the needs of families whose lives are perceived to be in conflict with this rapidly changing informational age.

These difficulties are compounded when affluent, technologically advanced countries export family literacy programs to countries that are less industrialized or less technologically advanced. The situation becomes particularly dangerous when these programs are not supported by the understandings of literacy learning that have emerged from the years of research that has taken place in many different countries around the world.

The intent of *Many Families, Many Literacies: An International Declaration of Principles* is to address these ethical issues and human rights concerns, to honor families, to support family members of all ages as they continually develop and share their literacies, and to shift the discourse away from deficit-driven family literacy programs. Illiteracy is not a "disease," illiteracy does not "breed" illiteracy, and a "dose" of some prepackaged family literacy program will not "cure" those who are poor.

What can we learn from family literacy research?

Descriptive studies of families and literacy in many different countries with many different cultural traditions have changed narrow preconceptions. These studies show that each family is an original, that there is a seemingly infinite variety of patterns of cooperation and domestic organization, and that flexible household arrangements are often an adaptive response to an uncertain world. Within family settings there are both multiple literacies and multiple literacy practices. In cultures in which the indigenous languages do not have a long written tradition, the indigenous languages are as sophisticated and complex as in cultures that do have a long written tradition. And families living in multilingual communities evolve new literacy practices that reflect but do not replicate literacy practices in either the first or second language tradition.

Unfortunately, these complex understandings of families and the multiple literacies that are a part of their everyday lives are not reflected in the prescriptive "family literacy" programs that have been established in the past few years. In many such programs, the measurement of "literacy" and "illiteracy" has become an issue complexly tied to the socioeconomic status of program participants. Inherent in the political context of this situation and the public discourse that supports it is the premise that there is a causal link between "illiteracy" and poverty.

What are the problems with the dominant approaches to family literacy?

The premise that a lack of facility with literacy is causally related not only to poverty, but also to underemployment, low educational achievement, crime, the breakdown of the family, and the decline of moral standards is the result of faulty reasoning that enables us to abdicate responsibility and blame families for these societal problems. The recent focus on family literacy that is seemingly designed to bring more literacy to parents and children is an effort to shift the blame for poverty and underemployment onto the people least responsible for and least able to struggle against the systematic inequalities of modern societies.

Too often, we are told in the family literacy literature, educational attainment is actively discouraged by family and friends. The argument is made persuasively. The seeds of school failure are planted in the home, and we cannot hope to uproot the problem by working only within the schools. We must approach it through the family.

In the United States it is not enough that we have blamed public schools, we now blame families and foist upon them the unsuccessful educational practices that fail many children by the time they enter high school. We have moved the same faulty assumptions about language, literacy, and learning—the same destructive systems of evaluation, remediation, and compensatory education—into the home without taking into consideration the complex ways of knowing and the many funds of knowledge that are inherent to family life.

In Australia, Canada, and the United Kingdom, family literacy programs are supposedly designed to stop children from repeating their parents' underachievement. As in other industrial countries, there is a general belief that social hierarchy is related to ability and that illiteracy is passed from one generation to another. Family literacy programs are claimed to be designed to "break the cycle." Families are told that hard work and increased skills and abilities lead to success and well-being. However, there are many closed doors along the way. Race, gender, and socioeconomic status are all factors that critically affect whose "literacy" counts. There seems to be a limit to how much success there is to go around, and not all types of knowledge or ways of knowing are recognized.

In many industrialized countries, when children enter school great attention is paid to organizing and measuring the success of one group of students against another. The dominant approach to family literacy is similarly structured. The danger inherent in such narrowly defined versions of family literacy is that they bring the same sorting mechanism into the homes of families whose own funds of knowledge do not count in this assessment of skills. The cultural and language resources of families are not recognized, and the families themselves often recognize that the programs they are "encouraged" to attend are family "il-literacy" programs for "disadvantaged adults" and "poor children," which is why many avoid them.

How can we redefine family literacy?

Literacy efforts that focus on families must take into consideration the cultural and language resources of the families who participate in them. There are many kinds of literacy and many kinds of families, and the use of reading and writing within family contexts does not necessarily reflect the teaching of reading and writing in classroom settings. In many societies, children are encultured into the most common and evident forms of literacy in their homes and communities before they even begin school. The accumulated ways of knowing and funds of knowledge of family members—their local literacies—are complexly structured and are intricately woven into their daily lives.

We need to shift the discourse that focuses on families and literacy away from the current deficit-driven pronouncements and negative stereotypes of families who are excluded from full participation in the social and economic life of both industrialized and less industrialized societies. To this end we offer here a redefinition of some of the key issues—such as the relationship of literacy to poverty, the notion of socioeconomic status, and the concept of "disadvantage."

Rather than ask about the relationship between illiteracy and poverty as if they are two isolated phenomena linked in a causal or correlational relationship, we prefer to ask: By what institutional arrangements is there a consistent and seemingly easy-to-measure relationship between the reading and writing that family members have to do and the activities in which they engage in order to put food on their table, clothe themselves, and find shelter for themselves and their children?

Socioeconomic status is often taken to be a description of persons and the characteristics they develop in various socioeconomic contexts. However, we consider socioeconomic status more a description of the structural opportunities afforded to family members as they seek employment and as parents try to take care of their children. Given that socioeconomic status is not the property of family members but is instead a reference to their opportunities for social and economic participation, it is important that the seemingly independent variables such as income, education level, and literacy level be used only to refer to the access structures of the wider community and to society in general, not to families in particular.

Although the term "disadvantaged" is often used to describe the learning potential of family members, including individual children and their parents, we prefer to understand "disadvantaged" as a name for the process by which one group of persons—the "advantaged"—suppresses another group of persons, disadvantages them, and then blames them for their degraded situation.

By this redefinition, a family literacy program for the "disadvantaged" would not so much deliver skills to those who are considered to be without them as it might organize the advantaged and the disadvantaged to read, write, and do other kinds of work together to increase the opportunities available to all, or at least help equip the disadvantaged to struggle against those who would call them "illiterate."

What can family literacy programs do to support all families?

It is essential that literacy programs recognize and honor not only the diversity of literacies that exist within families, but also the communities and cultures of which they are a part. No single, narrow definition of "family literacy" can do justice to the richness and complexity of families, and the multiple literacies, including often unrecognized local literacies, that are a part of their everyday lives. The process of defining "family literacy" cannot be left in the hands of those outside the families and communities that are affected by the decision-making process. The culture of the community and the experiences of the families who live in the community are an essential part of all literacy programs. This implies that program developers should respect local definitions of problems, needs, resources and preferred courses of action.

In literacy programs designed to foster social justice, family members should be full participants in the organization, implementation, and evaluation of their projects. Examples of such family literacy endeavors can be found in Australia, Canada, England, and the United States. But equally important examples can be found in countries that are struggling with their own economic development. In Brazil, for example, one of the basic assumptions that underlies recent literacy efforts is that literacy development depends on culturally relevant pedagogical practices. Another basic assumption is that the types and uses of literacy supported in literacy programs must go beyond the demands of socioeconomic development. For literacy workers in Brazil, this positioning of themselves alongside the participants in their programs suggests that they consider the work they do together primarily a matter of social and cultural development.

As we prepare to enter the twenty-first century, literacy should be considered a human right. And yet we know that literacy practices are specific to their political and ideological contexts, and that the consequences of such context-specific literacy practices vary according to the situations in which they occur. Some of these literacies have become powerful and dominant, while others have been constrained and devalued. The problem is not so much a lack of literacy, but a lack of social justice. Local knowledge is not always appreciated and local literacies are not always recognized.

Literacy is not always liberating, but it could and should be. Under the present political conditions, working for literacy necessarily involves becoming a part of the struggle for social justice. The resulting product is not some artificial measure of more "literate" parents and children, but more people working together, grandparents and parents, sons and daughters, sisters and brothers, aunts and uncles, friends and neighbors, celebrating their own literacies while at the same time using the many forms of literacy available to them to find their own solutions to the problems they face within their families and communities.

principles about families

Families have the right to define themselves.

❑ Families have members of all ages and should not be narrowly defined as "undereducated parents and their children."

❑ Families are both biological and social. They span the generations from great-grandparents to great-grandchildren. They bring together people who want to spend their lives together; sometimes there are no children.

❑ Definitions of family need to include the men, women, and children who are separated from their families because of political, social, or economic reasons—family members who are refugees, those in political exile, and those who work as migrants in other countries to support their families at home.

❑ Such definitions also need to include children who might be living away from their biological parents in foster care, on the streets, or in institutionalized care.

Families share the social, cultural, economic, and political contexts of their everyday lives.

❑ Families' funds of knowledge and ways of knowing are complexly structured and highly dependent on the cultures to which they belong, the languages they speak, and the social, economic, and political circumstances of their daily lives.

❑ Such a view of family life may be thought of as processual—in process—and evolutionary as well as dynamic and developmental. A processual view of family life shifts our thinking away from abstract notions such as "normative states."

❑ Simplistic statements about families that do not take into consideration the complexities of their everyday lives—such as "low levels of literacy are the result of poor parenting"—cannot be supported and should not be made.

❑ The voices of family members are important. "Experts" should not speak for them, own the talk, or write family literacy programs in which their voices are not heard.

Families are the primary literacy resource for their children.

❑ All families should be given support in their important role of initiating and maintaining their children's literacy.

❑ Once we take into account the cultural and linguistic complexities of family life, the ways of knowing, and the funds of knowledge that families share, we can no longer assume that living in a low-income community means that a mother or father cannot read and write.

Racial and ethnic identity should not be used explicitly or implicitly to suggest that families live in households that lack social and intellectual resources.

❑ We should resist the pressure not to recognize the rich resources of some families simply because they are socially, educationally, and economically disadvantaged.

❑ We also question whether some families have fewer job opportunities and educational opportunities because they are denied such opportunities by the dominant society.

❑ When families experience racism and prejudice they often also experience hopelessness and despair. Economic hardship, poor health, and the lack of adequate housing all take their toll, and sometimes leave families unable to cope with the problems that they face in their everyday lives.

❑ Many families who speak multiple languages and have complex literacies still live in poverty, their lives disregarded or considered a burden by the society in which they live.

❑ When all families are valued by society all of society benefits.

❑ ❑ ❑ ❑ ❑

Literacy Is Ordinary: A Family Against the Labels
Ray McDermott

My father turned eighty in 1984. "I learned something about myself this week," he told me at the party we gave him. "I am a dropout." He had quit high school sixty-four years before to go to work, and he labored most of his life as an elevator mechanic. He was not a dropout in 1920. He was a worker, eventually a husband, a father, a grandfather, and for his last ten years a retired worker. These were all labels he liked. "Work will save us," he always said, often to no one in particular.

By the late 1970s, the United States was going through a "dropout crisis." Anyone who did not finish high school for any reason but early death, so says the governmental agency that counts such things, was called a dropout. By the numbers, the country had too many dropouts, and they were going to cost the next generation money. They, them, those kids, those problem kids, had become something to worry about, count, build policy for, and remediate. And so it come to be that my father had been reclassified. What had been a normal and responsible act had become exactly the wrong thing to do.

"So Dad," I asked, "how long have you been a problem child?" Never one to answer a question directly, he should have replied with one of the double-edged, mostly true half-jokes with which he kept us organized, something like, I was so busy taking care of you guys, I never had any time to have any problems of my own. But I had missed his mood. Instead, he was more serious, and said, as he had rarely said before, "If I had it to do over again, maybe I would do it all different." For sixty-four years, he read every New York City paper but the *Times* every day, voted in every election, and hardly missed an opportunity to work hard, but, on his eightieth birthday, none of that counted. He had been reading about the dropout problem in the newspaper, and, for a moment, he knew himself as only and perhaps totally a dropout.

My mother had to leave the same high school a year before my father did, and she has been furious about it every day since. Soon to be ninety-three, she could be heard last week teaching my nine-year-old child how to say *Nadia en mi casa*. She remembered it from her ninth-grade Spanish class from 1918–19. She also remembers the lines from her class play that year. Between then and now, she has read parts of thousands of books in five-minute spurts. From 1932 to 1946 she had a child every other year, and she was hideously busy for the next four decades. Six of the children lived, they all finished college, five took master's degrees, three finished their doctorates, and so did a fourth, almost. They brought thousands of books into the house, mostly philosophy and religion, but also history, anthropology, biography, and who knows how many novels. She didn't read all of them, but she tried.

She had no desire to know everything—that trick of the oppressor being the downfall of her children—only the desire to understand people and have lots to talk about. She read faster than the rest of us, and to the extent that she could tell others about what she read, she would remember it in great detail. It would be impossible to tell that she left school after nine years. On the rare occasion when my father would read a book—maybe one of his kids had an article in one—he would hold it at arm's length as if he were reading a paper on the subway. He had an unpedantic relationship to print, and we rarely heard about what he read, although we knew we could always ask him questions and get answers. Mom, on the other hand, while never flaunting what she knew, would earnestly use her reading. "Did you ever read Thomas Merton," she would ask, hoping someone could tell her something she hadn't heard before. "A wonderful personality." she would say, "but I have my reservations. He could be very intolerant."

Their literacy stories are as similar as they are different. My father had more facts, my mother more stories. My father had more opinions, my mother more ideas. My father's literacy brought him peace and quiet, my mother's kept her involved in more conversations. Differences in style aside, their literacies were identical in being simply part of what they did. They did not have dropout literacy. They did not need remedial literacy. They had ordinary literacy in the best sense of the term. They used literacy as an ordinary part of their life.

My father did his job, and his literacy did its job. Together they worked, read newspapers, raised kids, and defined the demands on a good person. The responsibilities came first, long before any talk of skills. His advice was right: "Work will save us." Neither my father nor his literacy needed to be classified as a public menace in 1920, and neither of them should have been so classified in 1984. My father was a remarkable person for his relentless and generous attention to ordinary life, and his literacy and his culture, like everyone else's, were ordinary. We should appreciate people for what they do and ask of their literacy only that it serve their efforts to do the right thing.

My mother did her job, and her literacy did its job. Together they worked, read books, raised intellectuals, and defined the demands on a person concerned with the good of all. The people came first, long before any talk of their skills. Her question is worth a life's focus: "Why do they have to have it so hard?" Neither my mother nor her literacy needed to be classified in 1919. My mother is remarkable for her relentless concern for ordinary life, and her literacy and her culture, like everyone else's, is ordinary. We should appreciate people for the ways they care about others and ask of their literacy only that it serve their efforts to help.

❑ ❑ ❑ ❑ ❑

The Rich and Multiple Literate Environments of Three Families
Lucille Fandel

Even Start is a federally funded program for parents with preschool children. Usually the parents receive basic adult education while their children participate in a preschool program. Here in Springfield, Massachusetts, Even Start is a collaborative program that brings the community together. The library provides the adult education program—Read/Write Now—while the public schools provide the preschool program.

In Read/Write Now, we found that the varied environments of learners, coupled with a wide spectrum of family issues, have consequences. Staff members need to be alert to the literacy materials and practices used by various members of a student's family, and alert to where help may be needed. On a given day, a parent may come in and want help reading or writing something, and they may need that help right away.

Families have to negotiate the social service and health care systems almost daily. In the present climate of "welfare reform" participants have to deal with regular (and seemingly arbitrary and unexpected) notices that benefits of one sort or another have been reduced or cut off. Such notices are the occasions of multiple visits to various offices, reading many bits of paper, filling out forms, etcetera. The work of obtaining health care, including counseling services, involves another whole group of literacy practices.

Some of the parents in Read/Write Now have been active in their children's schools or in neighborhood organizations. Gladys, for example, was made secretary of her daughter's Head Start parents' association. She sometimes brought minutes from meetings or a letter to parents to work on during writing time. Elsie, another parent, has been the moving force in her local housing development, getting other parents together to provide a basement recreational facility for their children. She has also gotten the local police involved with the residents' meetings, in an effort to access whatever community resources might be available to fix up the nearby park facilities for the children.

The following are a few vignettes out of two years of what has become, for some, an Even Start family. I hope they will show that while "family literacy" needs to be critically examined within the shifting United States educational climate, there are a lot of us out there trying to do family literacy in a way that recognizes that most learning takes place in the family and that literacy development becomes a natural part of the teaching-learning process in a family.

A lot of us see family literacy as a way toward helping families act as subjects of their own education and helping parents find ways to enhance their interactions and relationships within the wider community.

Gladys Rios's motivation in joining the program with her daughter, Patricia, included her need for a community as well as her desire to work on her learning goals. She is a single parent, who, since leaving the program, also has a full-time job outside her home. This is a poem she wrote to her daughter:

Part of Growing Up

When I carried you for nine months
I always was thinking about what
you would look like if you were
a boy or a girl.

When you were born, I was so excited
that you were so tiny and with little
white spots on your nose.
When I took you home I put you in
your new crib.
When you were 6 months old it was
great watching you trying so hard
to crawl.
When you were 1 year old, learning
how to walk on your own, you didn't
want me to help you.
When you were 2–3 years old all I
heard was "mine."
Now that you're 4 years old I see
you and just seeing your expression
on your face tells me that you love
me, and that you're happy.
As long as I live I will protect
you from the bad and wrong.
I will always be there when you
need me.
I know that there will
be mistakes. No matter what they
are I'll try to be understanding
about it.
Always remember there'll be good
times and bad times but the important
thing is that you have a mom
and a friend that will always love
you no matter what.
When you are full grown I will show
you trust and never nag.
Whenever you have a problem
or you're ready to make good decisions
I will support you in anything.
When you're ready to go on your own just remember
I'll always be there for you.

Affordable, up-to-code housing is in short supply where Gladys lives. The problem is compounded by the level of street violence (shoot-outs). Several Read/Write Now participants have worked on letters to the local housing authority in search of a better apartment, in an effort to get lead paint taken care of, to report violations, or to register a complaint about the unresponsiveness of the housing authority itself. Gladys used her class time one day to prepare the letter below.

To who it may concern:

I Gladys—who live at 2752 Main St., 4R—had an incident Friday, October 29, 1993. It happened at around 10:20 pm while I was in the living room with my daughter and neighbor. We happened to hear noise of fighting, screaming with a lot of people. Then, I heard three gun shots. After an hour passed my daughter was asleep on the floor in the living room. I went to her bedroom to put the window shades down when I noticed that the window was broken from a gun. I called the police. They gave me a written report of the incident.

I had an appointment with Hap Housing Authority with Ana Maldonado on November 2, 1993. I went to her with the police report. I found that she acted unprofessionally in her job. I, as a mother, was concerned for my daughter. This person doubted the police report. Furthermore, she doubted just because I live on the 4th floor. In fact, a bullet was recovered from my daughter's bedroom.

My point that I am getting at is this person, Ms. Maldonado, was not helpful. I didn't feel any empathy from her. I know that I went to the right place and the right person to talk to. Instead, I felt she wasn't doing her job right, helping, counseling or pointing out what I can do in a situation like that. She just wasn't helpful at all even though that's why she's there.

It is her profession to try to do her best at her job to try to help the people. I hope this letter is taken seriously for in the near future somebody could come in and ask for help. That person should be heard and not be judged.

Sincerely,
Gladys Rios

This journal entry shows Gladys grappling with the violence to which her family had been subjected the month before:

Today I am not really feeling that well. Last night it happen again. There were a lot of gun shots from two different gangs. I just heard them. I picked up Patricia and headed to my bedroom. And I just hold my daughter as close as I can. Until everything stopped. I think I am getting sick of my nerves. But I'll just wait until they get me another place.

I am looking forward for the place. I know Patricia would be happy. But I am a little nervous.

Elsie Rivera and her husband, Miguel, live together with their three children—Miguel, who will enter fourth grade this fall, Maria, who will begin

Elsie Rivera and her two youngest children

kindergarten in September after two and a half years in Even Start, and Mariluz, who is not quite old enough to join the program but who comes along with her mom. Elsie attended class regularly the whole while she was carrying Mariluz. She delivered, missed one day of class, and was back— with the baby! Here she writes about telling stories to her children:

The Pirate and the Princess

When you tell stories to your children, your children will love you. I begin like this. "Once upon a time, there was a fairy princess. Her name was Maria and she had a brother and a sister."

They love to listen to me tell stories and they laugh. Sometimes they cry too. I talk about mysteries and they act like the floor has monsters. The children are afraid they will get them but, after, they know it's imaginary and laugh at it. Sometimes I tell them about pirates and they want to pretend and I help them dress up like pirates. They find it funny and have lots of fun doing different things.

They love me for being different than other parents. That's what my son said to me. I cried but I'm glad he thinks of me like that because sometimes he hates me too. When that happens, I know he is just upset with me. I let him rest for a while before I talk to him.

In the journal entry below, Elsie ponders the death of her nephew, one of several young people gunned down in gang-related violence.

Why?

Why did it have to happen to him? Carlos was a happy boy and went to school and worked. All he got he spent on his mother. When his daughter was born he spent on her too but most was for his mom. He always went from school to work but he lived with his mom. He had a car and rode to school, to work and to different places with his family.

Carlos had friends and his mom knew some of them. It was wonderful when they had a picnic. His friends would surprise their parents and have a big picnic, all of them. There was love all around. It was wonderful because they forgot all the bad things and had lots of fun.

You have to think of it like he is with God and safe and happy. We will see him again, some day. We will all be happy again. So, for now, we have to keep going with our lives. It doesn't stop for a minute. It keeps on going all the time. So, we have to keep on going too.

Sonia Carrasquillo is a twenty-six-year-old single mother of two young children. Her daughter, Jennifer, five, is autistic and prone to prolonged seizures. She requires constant care and supervision. Sonia's son, Benno, is four. He and Sonia have been part of Even Start for two years now. Sonia's primary learning goal has been to improve her English.

At one point, Sonia was forced to leave her apartment because lead paint had been used on the walls. She and the children lived in a family shelter for several months while she tried to find another apartment that was on the first floor (so that Jennifer wouldn't have far to fall if she threw herself out a window) and near to a hospital (and so it could be reached quickly when Jennifer had a seizure). "We Are Kids" was written in the voice of her children, and reflects Sonia's frustration with a social service worker sent to help her.

We Are Kids

We are kids,
only kids.
We don't know
about danger or safety.
We need a good person
like my mom,
to take care of us.

Photograph by Bill Hughes

Sonia Carrasquillo and her son, Benno

Not everybody
can take care
of children with
disability or even without a disability.

We are the special kids
for my mom.
For this reason
We love my mom.
Our mom is a special person too.

Our mom wants
the best person to care for us.
We want a person
who works with love
but not for money.

We are little kids.
Right now we need safety
not danger.
But that doesn't mean
we don't feel
when someone is working without love.

We and all kids
we feel love quickly.
We need a person to care
for us with love and safety.
In other words not lazy lumps.

In the journal entry below, Sonia recounts a typical day:

Last Friday

I was in the Legal Aid Office for an appointment with my "lawyer" about my housing case. I was in the office about 3 hours. When it was the end of the appointment, I went to McDonald's to get food for Benno because he was hungry.

After that, I went to my Aunt's home. When I entered from the door my grandma said "from the school called you because Jennifer is in the hospital in the emergency room." I thought "Jennifer have a seizure?" I ran to the hospital quickly.

My aunt said "She not has nothing" and I asked her "What she has?" She was better, my aunt said. When she entered from the hospital door Jennifer said "Ahh. Ay." My aunt told me that and she smiled. After that Jennifer was fine. My conclusion was that Jennifer needed to see the hospital because she is always happy, very happy in the hospital!

Sonia was recently honored by the State of Massachusetts for being an outstanding advocate for her children. She wrote this piece chronicling her experience:

Boston

The One Thousand Families is a nomination from the Department of Mental Retardation. The 1,000 families are people who advocated for their own family or community. These families are outstanding from other families. There was a meeting in Ludlow. It was beautiful. The meeting room was full. All the families there received an award in recognition of their advocacy.

In Boston, on March 27, 1995, I received a cup and a book with my name and what I did. In the ceremony, the Commissioner of the Department of Mental Retardation, Philip Campbell, said some words. The Governor of Massachusetts, Weld, spoke too. He gave an award to five families. Among these families, Josefina Castillo was nominated. She's a family advocate. She words for MCS.

We, the Hispanic families, make a demonstration to demand more services. After that, Josefina Castillo and I went to Senator Linda Malconian's office. She knew about my case for one year or more. She didn't work on my case. On March 24, 1995, I had spoken with her by phone and she told me I can work because my English is very good and my daughter can live on the second, third, or fourth floor. She spoke about "the rules" [concerning housing]. When I was in her office on March 27, I said to her "You remember when I spoke with you by phone and you talked about 'the rules'?" She didn't know who I was. She pushed my coat to see my name tag and she said "Oh, you're Sonia Carrasquillo!" Josefina said "The same person!" She couldn't believe I was in her office! When we entered her office, I told her I needed the "rules" she was talking about on the phone last Friday.

Wilfreda Rivera told me they can't help me because I need a first floor apartment and they didn't have one available. After he told me that, he tried to help me. Then, on the bus, on the way home to Springfield, Josefina spoke to Steven Bradley, the Director of the Department of Mental Retardation. He knew about my problem. He said "I can help her" and he told me that I just need to find an apartment and they would do the rest. I have known Steven Bradley for about one year, at DMR meetings.

I looked for an apartment but when the news was in the *Union News* on March 28, 1995, about our trip to Boston it said something about Josefina Castillo and she said "Some people still need the services" and she discussed my situation with Steven Bradley. When the news was published, everybody called me and called Josefina too. The New England Farm Workers Council told Josefina they helped me but it's not true. One week later I received a letter from Linda Malconian. It said "Congratulations because you're nominated in Boston."

Now, I finally have an apartment on the first floor—just what I wanted. I only need to move. The papers are all ready.

❍ *Children of poor, undereducated families often fail to achieve a solid grounding in basic skills. Their schools, in urban ghettos and isolated rural areas, offer remediation, but special services may come too late for children from unstable homes and violent neighborhoods who have already given up on themselves as learners. At best their home environments provide neither the literacy tools nor the personal supports which might enable them to make up their skill deficits. Too often educational attainment is actively discouraged by family and friends.*

—Sharon Darling

□ □ □ □ □

Some Perspectives on the Family

Hope Jensen Leichter

From a seminal paper entitled Some Perspectives on the Family As Educator, *first published in an edition of* The Teachers College Record *devoted to the family as educator. These papers (which included one on the role of grandparents, by Margaret Mead) were then published by Teachers College Press in a book entitled* The Family As Educator, *which is out of print.*

The family is an arena in which virtually the entire range of human experience can take place. Warfare, violence, love, tenderness, honesty, deceit, private property, communal sharing, power manipulation, informed consent, formal status hierarchies, egalitarian decision making—all can be found within the setting of the family. And so, also, can a variety of educational encounters, ranging from conscious systematic instruction to repetitive, moment-to-moment influences at the margins of awareness. Moreover, since almost everyone has had profound experiences within one or more families, judgments of the family are often deeply felt and charged with emotion.

The importance of understanding the family is widely recognized by present-day educators, their interest deriving in rather specialized ways from a concern with contemporary social problems. A central focus has been the attempt to determine the family's contribution to the outcomes of schooling. Much of this current interest has been associated with the effort to uncover sources of educational failure, particularly those associated with poverty, social disadvantage, or "cultural deprivation." Not surprisingly, a good deal of heated debate has surrounded these issues. One hears the charge that the sources of failure lie in deficits that children bring with them to school and the countercharge that the sources of failure lie in the school. The "cognitive deficiencies" of the lower-class home are contrasted with the "hidden curriculum" of the middle-class home. As complex as these issues are in their own right, they are compounded by issues of women's roles, community control, and the rights of parents in the determination of educational programs.

A good deal of current interest has also been associated with the search for educational deficits within the home. Particular aspects of family relationships, such as the extent of the mother's verbal fluency or absence of the father as a role model, have been examined as possible sources of educational deficiencies, especially in the homes of the poor. Indeed, deficits of the lower-class home have sometimes been viewed in extreme terms, with Banfield actually proposing that the solution to the problems of poverty lies in selling the children of the poor to qualified bidders who can offer them a "normal" family environment. Evaluations of middle-class families are often strikingly different from those of lower-class families. Thus, one hears in almost the same breath assertions that welfare mothers should not receive funds that would enable them to stay home to care for their children but that professional women who leave home during the early years of child rearing will inevitable damage their children's psyches.

Granted these controversies, the assumption that the family does exert a significant impact on the outcome of the child's education has been sufficiently strong in recent years to stimulate a wide variety of intervention programs. Some of these have attempted to modify education within the home, while others have attempted to supplement the child's education outside the home or to remove the child from the home at an early age.

Stepping back from these specifically contemporary concerns, one can see that the family is always a setting in which important educational encounters occur. Furthermore, the way in which the educational functions of a society are allocated among institutions varies from one time to another. Cremin has referred to the tendency of educational institutions at any given time and place to relate to one another in what he calls "configurations of education." Periods of social change often entail fundamental shifts in the character of educational configurations and in the relation of various components to one another. At such times, questions about the allocation of educational functions, among the family and other institutions, are likely to rise to the level of explicit policy concerns. Thus, for example, Dewey argued in *The School and Society* that because of the move away from the agrarian household, where much of the adult world stood directly revealed before the eyes of the child, the school needed to re-create versions of the adult world to teach what the child had formerly learned in the household.

Beyond the question of the way in which educational functions are divided among the family and other institutions, there is the possibility of extending our knowledge of education in general by examining the richly diversified educational encounters that occur within the family. The problem is to address the family as a setting in which education invariably takes place with questions that are posed in broad and basic terms, and to pursue those questions with methods that enable one to hold emotional reactions and personal values in abeyance when necessary. Ideally, it will be possible to understand the special features of education within the family while at the same time using this understanding to enlighten and extend our fundamental theory of educational encounters as they occur over the entire range of educative institutions and settings.

References

BANFIELD, EDWARD C. *The Unheavenly City*, pp. 229–31. Boston: Little Brown, 1970.

CREMIN, LAWRENCE A. "Notes Towards a Theory of Education." *Notes on Education*, June 1973, pp. 4 and 5. (Published by the Institute of Philosophy and Politics of Education, Teachers College, Columbia Univeristy.)

□ □ □ □ □

 [Family literacy] means changing attitudes, values, and in some cases cultures.

These parents do not know the joy of reading to their children, and their children do not reap the documented benefits of being read to.

When they are asked to help with schoolwork these parents are likely to push their children away.

Often without a job, a spouse, or a support network of close friends and relatives, these disappeared parents are likely to feel cut-off, boxed-in, devalued. Under this strain, many can't provide the emotional and economic support their children need.

Slowly, the children's enthusiasm for learning is throttled, and they begin to look for satisfaction outside of school. They become sexually active at a tender age; they have children before they're emotionally ready: they drop out, ready to begin the cycle anew.
        —National Center for Family Literacy, *Spreading the Word and Planting the Seed*

□ □ □ □ □

We have learned from the families [with whom we worked] that the difficulties that confound their lives are shaped into personal configurations of poverty. . . . Inadequate housing, the lack of essential services, poor schools, limited access to higher education, and restricted job opportunities all have an impact on their daily lives. Society has placed them on a collision course which, despite the odds, they survived. Then instead of recognizing their efforts we blame them for the "inadequacies" of their survival. We say, "It is your fault that you are poor. You should work harder. Take care of your children. Stop taking advantage of the welfare system." We do not hear when Jerry says, "I'm a producer. I can produce," or Tanya says, "People tell me all I can do is hope for the best. I think if I give it my go I think that my kids will turn out fine. I'm hopeful. . . . There's no reason why my child should be standing out there on the corner. I'm not going to have it."
        —Denny Taylor and Catherine Dorsey-Gaines

□ □ □ □ □

In low-income communities where many family literacy programs are targeted for African American and other families of color, the programs address only a small and, for some participants, relatively unimportant part of the problems facing them, problems that they see as centered in the ability to obtain employment. The appearance, if not reality, of a declining economy and labor force have been evidenced in low-income communities through increases in layoffs, the reminders of "last hired–first fired" for many people of color, a growing crisis of labor-force participation among African American males, and crime and hopelessness that appear in tandem with or shortly after economic hardship and crisis.

—Vivian Gadsden

❑ ❑ ❑ ❑ ❑

A Letter from Tomás Enguidanos

September 1994

International Forum on Family Literacy
Tucson, Arizona

Dear Denny:

I have been struggling with the issue of family literacy for my entire life. I come from a family who values education. My father was a professor at the University of Texas in Austin when I was born in the late 1950s. I was born into a family, Spanish and Puerto Rican, that spoke only Spanish at home. We were read to in Spanish. As a little boy I watched my older siblings go to a school where they were not allowed to use our language.

Later when we moved to Indiana I had learned conversational English from my siblings. I had seen the struggles between my parents' values and the ones that my siblings brought from school. So I was probably for that reason very suspicious of school right from the start.

Yet I did want to learn. When my teachers would teach about the world from their cultural point of view, I tried in earnest to share my family's point of view. This outspokenness was seen as rebellion and I was often scolded, ridiculed, and sent to the office for expressing an opposing view.

The way I see it now is that I learned from these struggles that we must value the language and cultural viewpoints of all people. That is true multicultural education. A bringing together of ways of being and creating, and viewing the world. I know my family could have contributed much more to the school community if that school community would have honored us.

Tomás

□ □ □ □ □

The Wind That Blows North:
Families in a Mexican Migrant Community
Melanie Uttech

Claribel's sun-faded *rebozo* covers her graying hair and encircles her prematurely wrinkled face. Her plump figure bespeaks a fat-laden diet as well as the stress of having given birth to ten children. The darkness of the soot-covered brick kitchen, a separate building from the rest of the house, partially obscures her features. But the corncob fire in the far corner, normally used for cooking tortillas, counters the darkness enough to let me see the feeling behind her words and her wisdom. Her arm is elbow deep in an old lard bucket now used for making cheese. She gently and reflexively stirs the formless substance as she shares with me stories of her life.

In another home, Rosa sits on a tiny throw rug with her dry, bare legs curled to one side. She speaks quietly as she nurses her three-month-old baby. The contrast between the newborn's skin and the overworked hands cradling him is stark. The room is empty save for a refrigerator and a double bed, one of two this family of nine shares in their two-room house.

Both Claribel and Rosa live in rural Mexico. They live in a *municipio* that deceives the passerby on the only "highway" into thinking the area consists of fertile agricultural land. Beyond the highway, however, the pavement and the irrigation systems end. The rich soil turns to a dry powder that can only be planted three months out of the year. There are no carrots, no broccoli, no tomatoes, no strawberries, growing in Claribel's and Rosa's community. That luxury is for the rich landowners a world away from theirs. Beans and corn, life's staples, are the only inhabitors of their earth, and then only when the rains come.

The village where Claribel's and Rosa's families live is small. There is no drainage system, although running water (from outdoor spigots) and electricity are in place. A preschool and a three-room elementary school are the only buildings aside from the modest homes. Claribel, a woman in her mid-fifties, had no access to these schools or any others as a child. Rosa, age forty-two, had attended through second grade only, all that existed at the time. Presently, all but the eldest of Claribel's children, ranging in age from seven to thirty-seven, and Rosa's children, ages three months to nineteen years, are either enrolled (or will enroll) in the multigrade school in the community or have completed their education there. They leave school with a sixth-grade education.

These families take full advantage of what the system offers them, but it has not offered them much. The children would attend *secundaria*, the equivalent of U.S. middle schools, if there was one nearby, but the nearest school is five kilometers away. This is but one of several problems related to access. The government promotes education in the *secundarias* as free and obligatory. The neighboring middle school for these families, however, is a *telesecundaria* (where classes are taught via television), and the children must buy their books. They must also buy uniforms, notebooks, and pencils, and pay *cooperaciones* that schools request for maintenance and supplies. Additionally, parents worry about the trip the children must make each day. They do not want their daughters to walk alone, but neither can they afford the fare for their children to attend a *telesecundaria* on the bus route. In short, middle school is too far and too expensive, and the trip too dangerous. Few can attend.

Armed with a second-grade or even a sixth-grade education, adults are not prepared to enter an extremely competitive job market outside their community. Children thus learn the skills their parents pass on to them. Females assume family leadership roles in the home, and males learn to work the fields or become manual laborers in construction. With these skills, community members have little hope of moving beyond the struggle for basic survival. The land is arid and generally only provides what the family consumes; there is precious little left to sell. Men—both young and old—seeking to provide a better life for their families begin to think about the work possibilities in the United States—*el Norte*. They do not want to leave their families behind to enter a country where they know they are not always welcome, where they will assume physically challenging or even dangerous jobs and live in degrading and unsuitable housing conditions for nine months of the year (or longer). They do, however, yearn for the subminimum wage they may be paid to send home to their wives, mothers, and children. Claribel's husband and two sons have elected this option. Rosa's husband has not.

The recent barrage of media attention placed on the beatings of the undocumented workers who crossed the border into California, along with the news coverage of a group of Mexicans who were killed when their car crashed while being chased by the U.S. Border Patrol, has filled the women in this community with anxiety. In Rosa's words, "I'd rather die of hunger than have a family member come back in a box." In the same breath she comments that often it is a struggle simply to provide tortillas for her family. Her husband, a construction worker, has not been employed for the past year. Throughout the week he and their two oldest daughters travel long distances to search for and collect wild fruits, edible flowers, and firewood in an effort to provide life's essentials.

Claribel's situation is different. Three family members work in the United States. Two send money home periodically, which helps supply primary needs. Although the family is still poor, they have more than those who elect not to go. It is difficult for the women whose husbands are away to wait for money that sometimes does not come as often as is hoped. When there is a delay, the women grow uneasy about what might have happened to the loved one so far away and apprehension sets in about how to provide for their children.

Despite these concerns, this is not a village of women who do nothing more than worry. They are strong, both physically and emotionally, and carry out all familial responsibilities. They rise at the crack of dawn to begin making tortillas, a process that can take two hours as they winnow the corn, cook the *nixtamal*, wait in line at the *molino* to grind the mixture, finish the grinding process at home, press the tortillas, and then finally cook them. They wash their clothes by hand in outdoor tubs. They must find firewood to be able to cook. Both Claribel and Rosa also raise animals. Claribel uses the milk from her cows to make cheese, which she markets in a neighboring village. Rosa raises goats and hogs to sell. The job of tending animals is not easy; their food does not come from a store-bought bag. The animals must be herded and watched as they forage over vast areas in search of food. Sometimes children help their mothers with these and other responsibilities, occasionally missing classes to do so.

The children enjoy school and recognize the value in attending. They want to learn. These children are often their mothers' eyes when it comes to reading. They read announcements in stores when they go to town. They read medical information and instructions, bills, official notices, and most important, letters from those living afar. But the children want to learn more than just how to read. I asked a sixth-grade girl who is about to graduate from elementary school if she wanted to go on to *secundaria*. "Sí," she answered. I asked her why. She said she would like to be a teacher or a nurse. "And do you think you will be able to go?" I asked. She lowered her head. Her eyes swelled with tears. I gently wiped them away and asked her what the main reason was for not attending. "*Porque no tengo dinero*," she whispered. She does not have the money. She tells me she could live with another family in a nearby village where there is a *secundaria* and she would not have to walk the long distance; but the "free" education is just too expensive.

The stories of Claribel, Rosa, and others in this rural community are not isolated ones; they share features that are familiar to many families living in rural areas of central Mexico. They are caught in a system, a web of economic, political, and societal factors influencing their lives, that they cannot control and without more skills cannot even modify.

Each succeeding generation learns a little more as schools are built and expanded. The community members in Claribel's age group and older had no access to school; "*Ni conozco la 'O'*" [I can't even recognize an 'O']," she says. Younger mothers attended through second grade, and of those, most can sign their names when necessary. Their children generally attend only through sixth grade.

Will their children's children have access to a complete education? In addition to recognizing their needs and desiring a better life, will they be prepared to take action and overcome some of the adverse situations confronting them? Even with a full education, will the young adults be able to enter the overburdened system or will they remain unemployed or underemployed as so many university graduates in Mexico do today?

These questions remain unanswerable for the present, but the hope is alive for more schools, for critical education, to help produce a new generation of participants in a society where policy changes could influence economic growth, where little girls' dreams of completing school could come true, and where children not only learn to read words but learn to read reality with new eyes and promote changes for a more just society.

❑ ❑ ❑ ❑ ❑

An Invitation from Aimee
DAN MADIGAN

I met Aimee for the first time in 1990 as she escorted her grandson Paul through a crowd of people and into a building where Paul and his classmates (authors who had just published an anthology of their writings) were being honored by a university audience. As Paul rushed to meet his friends, Aimee and I stood in a gentle rain. She spoke briefly. "I'm very proud of Paul," she said. "Sometime we should talk. I like to write too."

I remember at the time I was caught off guard. I had just begun working as a guest teacher in an urban neighborhood school with Vicki Rybicki and her fourth graders. Together we were building a writing workshop in the classroom called The Writers Community, a place where children would be supported in their efforts to become writers. However, as thoughtful as we had been in developing our community workshop, and as much as we counted on parents to support our efforts as teachers and their child's efforts as literacy learners, we had never really considered the role of family members, like Aimee, as literacy learners who impact how a child comes to think about literacy purposes.

As Aimee slipped into the back of a cab and disappeared in the morning traffic, I was determined to follow up her invitation to share in her literacy experiences. I had suddenly realized what Vicki had been trying to tell us all along, that is, we as teachers too often narrowly define the meaning of community and its role in a child's learning. Aimee's brief invitation reminded us that we needed to rethink our definition of our Writers Community. We needed a broader definition that emerged from an understanding of the literacy experiences families engage in outside of school—literacy experiences that often converged and intersected with the literacy experiences and needs of the larger communities in which our children and their families lived, went to school, and worked. Aimee's offer to share the literacy experiences that helped shape her life was an invitation I couldn't pass up.

After our brief encounter on that rainy morning, Aimee and I met many times to discuss her literacy experiences. The narratives that follow this introduction describe both explicitly and implicitly how Aimee, as a child and later as an adult, came to understand the power of literacy, particularly how literacy functioned as a way to change her life. This theme—literacy for change—has become most significant to us as teachers and researchers of literacy in that it represents similar themes that we have discovered in the literacy narratives of other adults we have worked with and in the writings of the children of some of those adults whom Vicki and I have had occasion to teach in The Writers Community. Literacy for change is a theme that makes sense for the literacy learners we have had the opportunity to work with. Literacy for change is not limited to literacy for the purpose of attaining a better position in life but includes the notion of literacy for the purpose of changing the world in whatever way is important for the literacy learner at the time. Such notions have tremendously influenced how we as teachers and researchers have come to think about community literacy programs for both children and adults.

I share these narratives with Aimee's support and encouragement. It is Aimee's and my hope that readers learn as much from these stories as Aimee has in telling them and I have in listening to them. Occasionally, I have interrupted Aimee's stories with an explanation that I hope makes clear the purposes of reading and writing for Aimee. Following Aimee's last story, I offer a brief comment on how Aimee's stories gave my colleagues and me an insight into how to forge new relationships and collaborations with the parents and guardians of the children we were teaching.

I can remember an incident when an insurance agent came to the house. My uncle had had this insurance policy for years . . . and [the agent] called my uncle "uncle" and my uncle said, "I am not your uncle. I am Mr. Wells. To you and everybody else. And if you want to continue to be my agent, this is how you will address me." And my uncle did not have an education . . . but he was very smart. . . . And I taught him to draw his name. He was using Xs before I went to school to learn to write. . . . I taught him enough so he could be understood. So he had been Xing his signature for all those years. And I told him he could learn to write his name because I was eager for him . . . 'cause I knew how proud he was.

He was strong in the male cause. . . . Sometimes the black people— it was segregated—would get out of order and if Mr. Mike Duffy, the white sheriff, couldn't handle 'em he would come get my uncle. And he would talk to them . . . solve things out. Because he knew how to write, it gave him respect in his community.

He was very proud and good—very proud. At first he was embarrassed and ashamed. I said, "Oh no. We can do it together, just you and I." . . . And he learned . . . and he was always eager to sign his name. If someone in church would say, "Well, who would like to volunteer to work on this?" he said, "Oh, I'll sign my name! I'd be willing." So there was no programs to teach people to learn. . . .

[His secretary] would be right there, and he would say it and she would write it. And they learned to understand that he was not a good reader. And they accepted that gracefully, 'cause he had so many other good things going on. They would say his words in writing.

In commenting about the preceding story, Aimee explained that she suspected at an early age that literacy could be a powerful tool, but she did not understand the full potential of that tool until she had an opportunity to teach her uncle. Learning to write, even minimally, enhanced her uncle's status in the small town in which he lived. Yet even after her teaching experience, Aimee was hesitant to use literacy to promote change in herself. Her status was not enhanced even though she could write and read much better than her uncle. Sometime after she taught her uncle to write, Aimee found herself struggling with her own literacy learning.

I didn't read well and write well at school because I was afraid that I might be wrong. And anytime we would do anything wrong . . . my aunt would punish us. . . . So I was afraid. Maybe I could read but was afraid to let it be known. I was afraid to even pick up a book to try to read, because I was afraid that I wouldn't be able to read it. . . . If I misread a word or misspelled a word, then I'm gonna be hurt. And I don't like being hurt. I could pick up a paper and read it . . . but I couldn't understand it enough to be able to write like I wanted. My spelling wasn't always good. I spent over half my time in the dictionary trying to learn how to spell.

Throughout her childhood and into her adult life, Aimee never received the same support from others for her own literacy learning that she had given her uncle. She was confused. She responded by holding back her feelings about the potential of literacy to change herself. Discouraged, she lost herself in raising a family until finally, at forty years of age, she was motivated to act on her feelings about the importance of literacy learning for herself.

I knew there was something inside of me that was there and would not leave me alone. I had to just keep on exploring it. I always wanted to be a person with a good education, to get a good job, and earn money, and make it comfortable for my children and my family. And I just knew I could do it, but didn't know how to do it. So I withdrew. . . . [My husband] was good in spelling and reading and math, and I would ask him to spell some words for me and help me. He would cut me down, so I stopped asking. I would get up at three in the morning to study, learning how to write better and building a better vocabulary. If I was studying, he would find something to bitch about. My socks, my food, or my anything. 'Cause, I don't know, I assume as long as I'm like down to him, he can control me. So I learned to just go on to bed, be passive, and get up when everybody's sleeping, and study. And I used the dictionary to learn to spell and read better. That's what I do now. . . . I bought myself encyclopedias.

In interviews following the preceding story, Aimee revealed to me that she eventually wrote and read her way out of an abusive relationship that had lasted for more than twenty years. Writing and reading more proficiently gave her the confidence to succeed. After taking her GED, Aimee went on to a community college, where she earned enough credits to qualify her for a job in social services. Yet, a better job was only part of what Aimee received when she taught herself to read and write at a more proficient level. She also gained the courage to articulate her feelings and ideas about many important issues. At sixty, Aimee had just begun to take a role in her church that required her to speak to large audiences concerning community issues, and she successfully challenged the school district that her grandson attended because they wanted to put him in a special education program. Aimee based her written and verbal arguments to keep her grandson in a mainstream academic program on the fact that he had been denied the opportunity to learn (because he had missed a lot of school) when he was a first and second grader. He had never been given the chance to learn and succeed in school, she argued.

What is significant about Aimee's argument is that she paralleled her own experience as a literacy learner to the experiences of her grandson and used both their experiences as a framework to build an argument that eventually persuaded the school district to return her grandson to a mainstream classroom. Aimee knew that as a fourth grader Paul had written a story entitled "Enslaved." It was a story in which Paul expressed an interest in changing how things might be if everyone worked toward eliminating the kinds of slavery that are still prevalent in our society today. *A child needs to be given the opportunity to learn*, she said to the school district, *and if he is, he might change the circumstances in which he lives.*

Aimee and Paul have taught my colleagues and me that both children and adults share similar ideas about the potential for using literacy as a means for change in their community. Knowing this, we have begun to build a writers' workshop for children that encourages them to work with others in their community, including adult family members, and to use writing and reading and other communication skills to bring about the kind of change they feel is necessary for their growth and the growth of other community members. Rather than disconnect family literacy events from school, we are now seeking to make connections and to rediscover the political, social, and historical implications of language use by our students and their families.

❑ ❑ ❑ ❑ ❑

Mostly I'm Busy. But Every Chance I Get, I Try to Read.
SHARON W. SMITH

The stories below reveal just a few of the ways in which the families of students at the Bob Steele Reading Center in Hartford, Connecticut, have had an impact on their learning to read and write and vice versa. The stories also show some of the ways in which loyalty and obligations to family take priority over learning to read and write.

I came to know the authors of these stories through my volunteer work as a literacy tutor. These stories are not unusual. There are many others like them. Anyone who hears or reads these stories will be hard pressed to continue seeing adult literacy students as deficient parents, students, or human beings.

Circumstances have made life difficult at times for these students and their families. Personal problems have also taken their toll. In spite of all this, in trying to meet the needs of their families while drawing on resources provided by their families—and their own inner resources—these students have accomplished much of what they set out to achieve.

The following are excerpts from an interview that college intern Allison Gruner conducted with student George Brice:

> I used to have my own business. Painting. I messed up. I couldn't read. I don't have it any more. I lost it. . . .
>
> I had a fear to go for my driver's test. I didn't want to go because I knew I had to read before I could drive. But lately I went for my test. I passed it. . . .
>
> I'm starting over now with bills. I've had a hard bit of luck. I kept on letting friends pay them. You give them money and they say they paid them, but they never did. . . .
>
> I want a little business, carpentry, something like that. I'm good with my hands. . . . Mostly I'm busy. But every chance I get, I try to read. I'd like to go for my GED, if possible. I want to get to know what real edu-

cation is. All these years I've been trying to fake it, pretending I was reading. None of my family knew I didn't know how to read! I was trying to hide it. I was trying to find a way to get out of it. Reading, going for a job, filling the application out, I always tried to find a way to get somebody to do it for me. I always tried to find a way. I'd been doing it for years and I got away with it.

In my job now, I have to write out contracts. Now I can do the billing myself. Before, I didn't know what to put on the paper. I just gave it to the people, and I didn't know what was on it; I say, Write on it. But now I can do it myself.

Maria is a mother who has stopped coming to the center because she is now working two jobs. When she was working with me, she shared some of her history:

I like to work with machines. I don't know why, but I always loved to work with machines. So, I . . . joined metal machine training. I took the training. I had my diploma. I don't know how I made it, but I did. I studied. I learned all the parts [of metal machines] and everything. I made it there. There wasn't much reading, but there was math. I love math because I'm good at it. But reading and writing, it's terrible for me. So, I went there. I took a test and they said, "Okay, Maria, let's start class." The class started at seven o'clock in the morning. I had to punch in by seven o'clock. And I would get up at three o'clock! You couldn't miss any days. I mean, they were strict! And then, after that, I got a job. That was after I had the kids.

I got training and I went to work. I only worked there for two weeks. Two weeks! I had good training. It was a good job but the problem was I didn't have a baby-sitter. When you've got kids, and you can't find a baby-sitter, you can't do you job. So after that, I got [another job], and I stayed there for two weeks. So the baby-sitting trouble came again. I quit. I told them I loved the job. I was making good money and I could support my kids. They said, "Maria, don't leave us." I said, "I have to because my kids come first."

Elaine became a nurse's aide while participating in the center program. Here, Elaine talks with George Demetrion, the Reading Center's director:

Elaine: When I stay at home, I read just about every night. I get library books, anything.
George: So you like to read for enjoyment, is that right?
Elaine: Yes. Anything I can do to get my reading higher. I try every little thing.
George: How about reading and taking care of bills, taking care of mail, those kinds of things? Is that pretty easy?

Elaine: Yes, because I used to do it before.

George: What about reading with your son. Does reading help you with his school?

Elaine: I don't have to help him. He's bright. He's an A student.

Brenda Hall talks with George Demetrion:

George: Do you have to do anything with bills or letters?

Brenda: Yes, I do my bills myself.

George: Could you read letters before?

Brenda: No.

George: Do you read material from your child's school?

Brenda: Yes. Before I couldn't read it, now I can.

David Moses grew up in Guyana. As a child, he helped his mother farm and could not attend school on a regular basis.

> Mostly, I had to work all the time. I went to school two or three times a week. The next two days, I had to plant crops on the farm. We had to help our mother because she couldn't do all the things by herself.

William grew up in the rural South and came North during the "Great Migration":

> I guess I started farming for my momma when I was six, seven years old. I started farming, I would hit turf; the plow would knock me down, I had to turn the mules all the way around. The white guy owned the mules, I think. Yeah, I only went up to the second. And after that, you know, I went and got me a real job. You see, why I had to work, I had to help my mother and work. She was farming at that time. Most of [the school] was black. Yeah, it was, like, we had our own school.
>
> After the old man died, she didn't farm no more. She would go down and work, you know, all the kids were grown by then. . . . She went and worked for the white people, you know, clean up and stuff like that, like a maid. I didn't have too many jobs. I worked to the tobacco warehouse, selling tobacco. I left there, went hauling pulp wood. So I left there, quit that. You know, I've done one thing or another that could make me a buck. I'd make it, you know. . . .

Sarah came to the center when her children were young.

> I think I probably went to school when I was about seven years old. I leave when I was about fifteen, same time I leave my father. (My father was an angry man, a very angry man. We had a lot of tension.)

School, first couple of years, it wasn't too good for me. . . . It was kind of difficult, actually, going to school. Too much chores at home, I was exhausted. Actually, we used to skip school pretty often [because] sometime, you know, the smaller ones got sick. We have to stay home and take care of whoever got sick since I was the oldest one. . . .

Before my son was born, I worried about day care. . . . I became a day-care worker because I wouldn't have to go out and look for a job and worry about my son and my daughter like I did before, I was good to those kids and the parents respected me a whole lot. I gained respect for myself. I didn't have to get up in the morning anymore to work for this and that person, shouting at me as if I'm a child. The parents [in day care] come mostly from the Islands and actually look for someone from the islands to take care of their children. . . .

❏ ❏ ❏ ❏ ❏

The piling up and extending out of literacy and its technologies give a complex flavor even to elementary acts of reading and writing today. Contemporary literacy learners—across positions of age, gender, race, class, and language heritage—find themselves having to piece together reading and writing experiences from more and more spheres, creating new and hybrid forms of literacy where once there might have been fewer and more circumscribed forms. What we calculate as a rising standard of basic literacy may be more usefully regarded as the effects of a rapid proliferation and diversification of literacy. And literate ability at the end of the twentieth century may be best measured as a person's capacity to amalgamate new reading and writing practices in response to rapid social change.

—Deborah Brandt

❏ ❏ ❏ ❏ ❏

We're Doing Literacy Around and Around the Clock

MARILYN ANTONUCCI

I worked with six families who were enrolled in an Even Start family literacy program. It was a part of my job as a family literacy teacher to go out to the parents' homes to teach them ways of interacting appropriately with their children and to give them a repertoire of activities that would help prepare their children for school. I brought with me school materials to help me teach a particular lesson I thought would be appropriate for the age and interests of the child(ren) in each family. I also modeled activities that parents and children could do together at another time and brought art materials, books, puzzles, and games from the program lending library and left them in the home. But I never anticipated the variety and kinds of literacy activities that were occurring in these homes.

As the families and I grew to know each other, we were able to move away from the prescribed home-visit model and share authentic, meaningful literacy events. This sharing is important because it reveals complex ways of knowing and provides evidence of family members' funds of knowledge. The following pieces are excerpts from the personal stories written by two sisters, Mary Anderson and Pat Peguese, who have taught me much about literacy and life.

Here's Pat Peguese:

> I was born in Durham, North Carolina. I am the mother of one daughter and the grandmother of three grandchildren. I like to write and bake and cook with my granddaughter, Shatoria. I also like going to church. I have a big family. I have six sisters and three brothers. I thank God for my life and family. I like to write. I know if I keep on writing maybe, one day, I will get good at writing. Who knows? I might write a book one day!
>
> I went to more than one school. The first school I went to was called Shaw High School. I went to Shaw High from first to fourth grade. When I was in first grade, I did not like to go to school. When I got to fourth grade, I liked school, but I had to walk a long way to catch the bus. One year, my sister and I were in the same classroom. I would cry for Kathy to do my work in school and she would do it for me. One day, the teacher saw Kathy doing my work in class. She told my mother about it. Then she put Kathy in a different classroom. When I was in school I did not have lots of friends. When it was time to go outside, I would stay inside. I did not get into trouble in school because my grandmother would punish me by taking her belt to me. I stopped school to help my grandmother.
>
> On September 21st, 1993, I started school with my granddaughter and I was so happy to be coming to school with her. She was so happy to be coming to school that she could not go to sleep. I was so excited. When I was in the Read/Write Now program I liked it, but I know I will like Even Start too because my granddaughter and I will be coming to school together. I love doing things with her. Now I can work toward my GED and get my license for my car. Then my granddaughter and I can go to church on Sunday or just out.
>
> When I was a little girl I always dreamed one day I would finish school. But I did not finish school. I had to help my grandmother who

Pat Peguese and two of her grandchildren

was a very sick person. I went to school sometimes. Most of the time I would be home with my grandmother. She wanted me to finish school. One day my biggest dream is to see my grandchildren finish school. I know dreams do come true.

I Am the One
Pat Peguese

I am the one who hates for children to cry.
I am the one who makes food ideas.
I am the one who loves my family.
I am the one who makes cupcakes for my kids.
I am the one who feels empty inside.
I am the one who got a lot on my mind.
I am the one who tries to be there for my sister.

I am the one who hates to make a mess.
I am the one who loves my sisters and brothers.
I am the one who wories about my daughter.
I am the one who loves to keep my grandchildren.
I am the one who likes to read to P.J.
I am the one who can do it all.
I am the one who can not say no.
I am the one who likes to feed my fish.
I am the one who likes to color.
I am the one who loves my church.
I am the one who thanks God for my church.
I am the one who thanks God for my life.

Mary Anderson provided the title for my contribution to this book. When I asked Mary, "When are you doing literacy?" she quickly responded, "Why, we're doing literacy around and around the clock!" Here she shares a little of her life:

I am married. My husband is Willie Anderson. We have three children, two boys and one girl. I am a grandmother too. I have six grandchildren. I knew I had to go to school if ever I wanted to read and write. I know that I have to stay in school. Now I'm in the Even Start program, together with my granddaughter Latasha.

Have you ever had something happen to you that changed the direction your life was going in? Yes. Let me tell you about my life plan. When I started back to school I got sick. Then I became a grandmother. It looked like I could not get my GED. But things began to look better for me. When I started to go to school I knew I had a chance to get my GED. I knew that I couldn't give up.

Life can get you down. Through it all we can all bounce back. Anyway, God is our help. If you believe you can, you can be anything. I am a strong believer that you can make it if you are determined to go through. Take me for example, I have been in school for the last six years, off and on. I am determined to get my GED even if I am ninety-five years old! I know I may be low, but I know with God's help I'm gonna make it.

Mary's husband, Willie Anderson, died recently. She is now a single mother and grandmother, parenting her teenage daughter and her four grandchildren. She is involved with each of her children's school activities, attending all conferences and school events. Mary recently passed the driver's test and has also carried out her husband's dream of buying a house. When the family moved, she drove the truck herself!

❑ ❑ ❑ ❑ ❑

Mary Anderson and her granddaughter Latasha

Photograph by Bill Hughes

Family Literacy: Questioning Conventional Wisdom
MICHELE FOSTER

Conventional wisdom holds that poor African American families are incapable of providing their children with the kind of literacy experiences that facilitate school success. For their part, educators have done little to alter this conventional wisdom. For in seeking to understand how the community, home environment, parental behavior, and attitudes are linked to early literacy experiences, educators often dismiss African American families as being limited in their ability to provide nurturing settings for the development of their children's literacy. Nor for the most part have educators been attuned to the literacy activities that are embedded in the everyday practices of African American homes and community institutions. The following story, collected as part of a life-history study of African American teachers, captures the literacy practices in the family and community life of an African American family. The narrative not only describes literacy practices in one African American family, but also underscores the affective relationships that underpin learning, highlights the role of the church in African American communities in promoting literacy, and demonstrates how a literacy event—copying—that is often meaningless when disconnected from purposeful activity can become meaningful when embedded in family activity and practiced in the service of community life.

Lillian Lancaster, one of nine children, was born in Haskell, a small town in northeastern Oklahoma. Her father was a minister who preached in several local country churches in the area. Her mother played the piano and led the choir. Although neither of Lillian's parents attended college, all of her siblings have gone on to lead productive adult lives. One of her brothers has a medical degree and a Ph.D.; one of her sisters also has a medical degree; another has earned a Ph.D. A third sister is a speech therapist and a fourth is studying to be a pharmacist. One of her brothers is a minister, another owns his own business, and the youngest is in college. Until she began high school, she lived on a forty-acre family farm five miles from town. She began school in a one-room schoolhouse and later attended Booker T. Washington School, a segregated combined elementary and secondary school in Haskell, from which she graduated. She received a bachelor's degree in secondary education with a certification to teach English from Langston University in Langston, Oklahoma. The summer after graduation, she worked for the *Oklahoma Eagle*, a black-owned and -oriented weekly newspaper that was published in Tulsa. She enrolled in a master's degree program at Kansas State University and had completed all of the requirements for a degree in English except one course when her two-year teaching assistantship ended. Her first teaching position was in Cleveland, Ohio, where she taught between 1966 and 1972. After relocating to Orlando, Florida, with her husband, she began teaching in a public junior high school. In 1975, she transferred to Oak Ridge High School. Named teacher of the year in 1988, she was serving as English department chair. The interview took place over a two-day period in October 1988 at her school and at her home.

> I got very excellent training from Mrs. Harrison, who's someone that I visit occasionally when I go home. She taught me in a one-room school. I remember going there and being not even six yet because my birthday is in October and we started in August, so I was still five. My fondest memory was that she held me on her lap; I remember her holding me on her lap. She must have taught me to read that way. I vaguely remember a book and being held on her lap. I would have been the only one in that age range. I don't remember if she taught me phonics or what, but what I remember in essence is that I was always an excel-

lent reader. I could always read; I started reading early. I don't know what her techniques were, but that is a good memory.

Momma always directed the choir. We didn't have songbooks. They didn't have any money for songbooks. So she would order one songbook. At the time I was the only one who could write because the other children were younger. She and I would sit at home before choir practice night on Thursday, and we would hand copy enough copies of the songs—there were maybe only seven or eight people in the choir, so we would produce seven copies by hand of all the verses of all the songs in the *Gospel Pearl* or the *Hymnal* or the *Martin Gospels*. So I was learning all those songs, and not knowing I was learning all of them. Because now, in any church, almost anything that people sing, if it's something that's older than a few years, then I know all the verses. That's why. I know all of them because of doing this activity as a child with my mother. That's something that just sharpened my memory.

principles about language and literacy

All languages have an equal potential to convey the full range of human thought and experience.

❑ All languages have the potential to be written down.

❑ In cultures in which the indigenous languages do not have a long written tradition, the indigenous languages are as sophisticated and complex as those in cultures that do have a long written tradition.

❑ The division between oral and written language has come to be questioned. Older views claimed that literacy was unique in that it allowed meaning to be represented autonomously, without reference to context.

❑ Recent studies have shown that there are many features of what has traditionally been thought of as oral discourse in written language, and that many people can best demonstrate their understanding of written language in oral forms and vice versa.

A fundamental right of every family is to be literate in the language of their choice.

❑ Family members, both adults and children, should have an opportunity to become literate in their home language.

❑ Literacy in the home language can enhance literacy learning in a second language.

❑ Conversely, ignoring the home language and/or literacy in the home language has the potential to delay literacy learning in a second language—often the dominant language of the society.

❑ The acceptance of a diversity of languages and cultures can lead to tolerance, understanding, equity, and a celebration of creativity.

❑ Literacy is important to the issue of disappearing languages in that writing down a language can be a way of valuing that language and a way of extending its uses.

Like all language, literacy develops in response to everyday needs.

❑ Literacy is not a neutral technology. It is never a fixed or static structure. Like family life, both language and literacy are processual—continuously in process—and evolutionary as well as dynamic and developmental.

❑ In all societies family members, including children, are involved directly or indirectly in literate activities.

❑ In many societies, children begin the development of the most socially common and evident forms of literacy before they begin school.

❑ Literacy is embedded in everyday activities that are a part of family life. The use of complex symbolic systems is an everyday phenomenon constitutive of and grounded in daily lives of family members. Literacy is not usually the focus of attention. The primary focus is on the accomplishment of the task in which the use of literacy plays a part.

❑ Lived experiences of literate activities in everyday life vary in many ways. They depend on the context of the situation, the purpose of the literacy event, and the needs and desires of the participants in the event.

❑ These activities may not be those most valued by schools or by the self-appointed arbiters of what people "should" be reading and writing.

Families continually develop and share their literacies—including marginalized and often unrecognized local literacies.

❑ The development of new literacy uses by family members usually follows rather than precedes changes in life views and circumstances.

❑ When family members take hold of a new form of literacy, they transform it for their own use.

❑ Families extend the uses of literacy, developing their own personal and shared local literacies.

Literacy is embedded in different ideologies, in different political perspectives, and in different political agendas.

❑ Literacy practices are specific to their political and ideological contexts, and their consequences vary situationally.

❑ Ever present in the background of the lives of families are the literacies that are intrinsic to the political life—local, national, and international—of the societies in which they live.

- [ ] The increased powers accorded to literacy have sharpened the need for families to have a broad spectrum of literacies.

- [ ] Literacy in and of itself does not promote cognitive advancement, social mobility, or social progress.

- [ ] The notion of "functional literacy" is frequently artificially defined to support political and ideological agendas.

- [ ] Similarly, literacy is often erroneously equated with intelligence, and charges of "il-literacy" are used to attack the poor and cultural groups who are marginalized in different societies.

- [ ] Literacy is commercialized by those working within the dominant ideological and political frameworks and sold in aberrant forms to families who are often struggling to feed and clothe their children.

- [ ] Often literacy is marketed across international boarders. Literacy learning should not be a product to be bought and sold.

❑ ❑ ❑ ❑ ❑

Oral and Written Language: Functions and Purposes
KEN GOODMAN

Adapted from Ken Goodman on Reading *(Richmond Hill, OT: Scholastic Canada, 1996).*

There was a time, not so long ago, when most scholars studying language paid little attention to oral language and gave their attention only to written language. I suspect that's because it lays there seeming to be so passive. But it's also because written language tends to be used for the more sedate and elegant language functions while oral language is used for all kinds of things, some of them quite mundane—even vulgar. (Not that you can't be vulgar in written language.) Then linguists, quite correctly, shifted the focus to oral language, which, they pointed out, comes first and is used a lot more than written language by most people. However, this preoccupation among linguists with the primacy of oral language led to a strong tendency to see written language as secondary not just in the sense that it comes later, but as being not really language but a way of recording the real language—speech. My research on reading leads me to believe that written language is neither less nor more important than oral language. And written language is not just a way of representing oral language: it is language. Oral- and written-language processes work in much the same way and they are learned in much the same way.

So what is language?

Language is a human personal/social invention. People as individuals in social groups invent language because they are capable of symbolic thought; that is, they can let symbols represent experiences and ideas. Also, humans are born dependent on others for survival and remain interdependent throughout their lives. It is this combination of symbolic ability and social need that makes language universal across human societies.

But language is not just a *collection* of symbols. It is a *system* of symbols—a semiotic system. It must be systematic because it not only names things, actions, experiences, but it represents the way all these essences interact and all the subtleties of our experiences and interactions with each other and the world.

Oral/aural language (oral for the mouth but also aural for the ear) uses sounds as its unitary symbols. But these sounds occur only in syllables—we can't produce strings of uniform distinct sounds, nor can we hear them apart from the syllables in which they are found. One or more oral syllables compose *morphemes*, the smallest unit of language that can carry part of the meaning or grammar. A word may include one or more morphemes; one or more words may be in a phrase, a word group, a clause, which in turn are found in sentences, dialogues, texts. But language cannot be sliced thin or thick like a salami, with each piece retaining all the characteristics of language: if we dissect language we kill it as a dynamic entity. In any linguistic sense each smaller unit exists only in the larger ones.

Furthermore, language exists only to express meaning; so we must always see everything in language in its relationship to meaning. And we must understand that listeners and readers can only make sense of language if they bring meaning to it.

Written language shares all the characteristics of oral language except that it's visual rather than aural. We perceive it with our eyes, not our ears. So we use a system of graphic symbols, patterned marks on a two-dimensional surface. These graphic symbols may be pictorial representations of the experience or idea. But they are more likely to be more abstract than that. Characters, individually or in combination, may represent things (icons or pictographs), they may represent words (logographs), they may represent ideas (ideographs), or they may represent the sound system of the oral language (syllabary, alphabetic). Even if the last is true, that the written language represents the oral in some way, it also represents meaning. And it's not only possible but efficient for readers of alphabetic language to go as directly as possible to the meaning without going through the oral language to get there. As you read this you have the sense of "seeing through" the print on the page directly to meaning. That's because perception of print, like perception of oral language, is controlled by our need to make sense of language. Like oral language, written language is also shaped by situations in which it must be used.

Oral and written forms of a particular language, English for example, share wording, grammar, and meaning. When there are differences in any of these, it is either because of the different functions each is used for or because the semiotic system imposes different constraints. Written language tends to be more formal in many of its uses than oral language. That influences grammar and word choice. But there is formal oral language (as in speeches) and informal written language (as in notes and diaries). Perhaps written language seems more formal to us because we don't think about phone messages, personal notes, billboards, and signs as examples of written language. Grammar in oral language is more complex than that in written language because oral intonation makes it possible to disambiguate complex clause sequences that punctuation can't handle in written language.

Oral language appears first in human societies because it serves here-and-now functions universal to human communities. But speech, at least before the electronic age, was limited to immediate uses. There are limits to how far the voice can reach. So speech is not very useful over large areas of time and space. Written language develops when oral language is insufficient for meeting the language needs of a society. For legal purposes we want things written down on paper, which can be preserved for future reference (though courts are now recognizing videotaped wills).

People have used various devices to extend aural communication over space. Some societies developed elaborate drum signals. The loud deep tones could be used to transmit a limited number of important messages. Mountain people in Europe and elsewhere developed special uses of their voices such as yodeling to speak from mountaintop to mountaintop. In biblical times, ram's horns were sounded from hilltop to hilltop to initiate holy-day celebrations. Polynesians used conch shells similarly. And in the Moslem world holy men sing out from minarets in the mosque to call the faithful to prayers, much as church bells are used in the Christian world. (I was startled to find, on a visit to a mosque in the Middle East, that the voice that called the faithful to prayer was on a tape recording broadcast through a loudspeaker from the minaret.) Sailors at sea use whistle tones aboard ship. Powerful foghorns warn them of danger.

Written language becomes necessary when societies and their cultures become sufficiently widespread and complex that they require communication over time and space. When the culture needs written language, it invents it. That is, the people who share the culture invent written language. Sometimes written language is invented anew. More often in history an existing writing system is adopted and adapted to fit the needs of the culture.

Differences in the use of written language from country to country or culture to culture depend on how much the culture needs literacy and what it uses it for. People and societies are literate to the extent that they need to be. Even in industrialized societies, the need for universal literacy is only a generation or two old. The monks of the Middle Ages were literate for their societies. They copied and stored the books, interpreted them to others, and even served the secular needs of their governments for recording important events and documents. Today in many third-world countries public scribes sit at tables in the villages and great cities, reading and writing for their neighbors. It's ironic that some countries with a long history of literacy, are among the nations with the highest rates of illiteracy.

Let me bring this all back to one central premise: reading is language, no less and no more than listening is language. People learn both in the same ways and for the same reasons.

❏ ❏ ❏ ❏ ❏

In the case of Ambedkar Nagar in Delhi, the discourse of literacy has been located in the superficial context of reading bus numbers or avoiding being cheated at the ration shop. Why is it not located in . . . the real living conditions of the poverty-stricken people of Ambedkar Nagar—highly restricted milk supply which seems to regulate their daily timetable, lack of sanitation, proper drainage and medical facilities and highly limited and irregular water supply. It does not make much sense to say that these problems will be looked into in the post-literacy stage. There is obviously an underlying assumption here that the acquisition of literacy will automatically resolve these problems. The evidence in this direction is nonexistent. The whole enterprise of literacy needs to be located in a struggle to eliminate these problems which those in power have created for the powerless.

—R. K. Agnihtri

❏ ❏ ❏ ❏ ❏

Literacy As Human Right: Literacy Practices in Brazil

ELVIRA SOUZA LIMA

An analysis of the history of education in Brazil shows that the most prevailing concept of literacy in the country is that it is a fundamental tool for the cultural development of human beings and that it is the right of every citizen. Literacy has been historically understood as a form of human activity to which all human beings are entitled; thus it goes beyond being an exclusively central issue in schooling and a factor in economic development.

Educational movements in Brazil have been the result of social movements in which different sectors of society have participated. Unions, community organizations, churches, political parties, private educational institutions, have all been very active in developing literacy, both in and out of school. Literacy programs (most of them for adults) that take place outside schools are common and affect how literacy development is seen in institutional settings.

The last decade has been one of upheaval in education, with a strong emphasis on developing pedagogical actions within the schools that integrate the experiences of popular education and adult literacy programs. This pedagogy envisions the empowerment of people through the appropriation of formal knowledge and the development of forms of action incorporating funds of knowledge and culturally developed behaviors already available in the community. It is a pedagogy that integrates the cultural development of students and teachers into the teaching/learning process.

Two main assumptions underlie many of the recent literacy practices developed in Brazil. The first is that literacy depends on culturally appropriate pedagogical practices; the second is that literacy is considered primarily a factor of cultural and social development, not economic development.

Pedagogical practices coherent with those assumptions are those that combine an investigation of literacy practices in the community with language development in the classroom. Uses of oral and written language found in the community can thus be integrated into the classroom. For example, when keeping and sharing a journal or a little book of reminders is a major way in which language is used in the community, the teacher may use this form to introduce literacy practice in the classroom, moving on later to more scholarly uses of written language such as taking notes.

Another aspect is the development of literacy connected to its use as a tool for learning other subjects. Thus there are a number of initiatives that articulate literacy in history, literacy in the sciences, literacy in math. Language is nonetheless seen as a subject in itself, which means that the structure of language as well as the broadening uses of literacy has to be revealed to the students. All forms of working in, reporting on, and reflecting on other subjects also become part of literacy development.

To approach literacy as a process of cultural development has an important consequence: since literacy is socially constructed, both participants in that construction—student and teacher—are equally important pieces of the process. Thus adults/teachers are simultaneously agents for literacy development and subjects of the literacy-oriented action. Rethinking their role in the process may be a major difficulty for teachers, since they have been educated to think that they act to foster students' knowledge acquisition, not that their pedagogy acts upon themselves. To focus on literacy as empowerment and/or to adopt the premise that construction of meaning is facilitated by culturally based pedagogy prompts teachers to reason, to think critically.

Seeing literacy in this perspective—empowerment through culturally based pedagogy—raises the issue of teacher education. Urgent changes have to be made both in the curriculum and the methodology of teacher education programs. Teachers need to be prepared for dynamic classroom action that involves a series of decisions about language and language uses. They must also learn to think about themselves as literate people within a process of cultural development. Recent educational reforms in Brazil have revealed some intriguing aspects of cultural development in relation to the awareness that can be achieved through written language. Especially interesting is the role of writing. Journals and stories can be powerful tools for understanding one's own concepts about children and one's attitudes toward social classes, cultural behaviors, and ethnic and racial diversities.

Through the more active and inclusive nature of our literacy practices, we in Brazil have advanced from the "pedagogy of the oppressed" to the "pedagogy of the excluded," to use Florestan Fernandes's terminology. Comprehensive literacy development has become a priority for many Brazilian educators. And this comprehensive approach means thinking of literacy as a multiple form of human activity.

❑ ❑ ❑ ❑ ❑

It is not just that literacy is spreading but that certain beliefs about literacy, certain ways of teaching and assessing, ways of evaluating writing, and very particular practices are being spread along with the language.... English becomes an imported literacy bringing its own practices with it and consequently stifling indigenous or local literacies.... (W)herever there is a literacy programme there is a world language close by: that behind any literacy programme there is a world language.... (T)here are many historical examples where the spread of literacy has been related to the standardisation of the language.

—David Barton

❑ ❑ ❑ ❑ ❑

Rewriting the Written

KAI ALLEN, ELIZABETH J. CANTAFIO, OLIVIA MILAGROS CHABRAN, AND SUSAN L. LYTLE

This is a brief excerpt from "On the Borders: Women's Literacies in Contrasting Communities," an unpublished paper exploring the relationships among four women: Susan Lytle, a university professor, Elizabeth Cantafio, a graduate student/community college faculty member, and Kai Allen and Olivia Milagros Chabran, who were homeless. With Kai and Olivia, Elizabeth had been reading all of the articles and books she was assigned in her graduate classes, including one in which Susan was the instructor. Although Kai and Olivia could not read or write in conventional ways, they initiated a dialogue with Susan about issues of representation emerging from their concerns about the ways in which the stories and experiences of adult literacy students like themselves were positioned in several articles she had written. Elizabeth brought Susan what she, Kai, and Olivia had written in response to Susan's work. In the written dialogue below, Kai and Olivia are responding to Susan's synthesis of research on the literacies of adult learners.

We are not present in these articles in any form other than the thing examined—we are not the one who talks *or* who is listening, since you're not talking to us either. We wondered what it would look like to have our words and ideas literally juxtaposed with yours . . . to dialogue in writing, to be located, named, present. We took the "synoptic perspective list" [assumptions about learners, literacy practices, and learning] from your article and *wrote* each of the ten parts on separate sheets of paper. Then, one by one, we interacted with each idea. We put your words in all caps; our words follow:

1. THERE IS CONSIDERABLE EVIDENCE THAT THE COMMON-PLACE IMAGES OF INCOMPETENCY AND MARGINALIZATION OF ADULTS WHO ARE WEAK AND EMBARRASSED DO NOT MATCH THE ADULTS WHO ACTUALLY COME TO LITERACY PROGRAMS, BRINGING WITH THEM SELF-CONCEPTS, INTERESTS, AND LITERACY ABILITIES AS VARIED AS THOSE IN ANY GROUP IN THE POPULATION.
Yes, there are many lies told and believed about us—that we are stupid, mindless, lazy, slow, worthless, hopeless, pathetic, lacking in ideas, motivation, and will, that we are without a sense of self or community or reality. But we are as different and necessary and complicated and textured as the fall leaves in all their color and fullness.

2. ADULTS OFTEN OPERATE WITHIN COMPLEX SOCIAL NETWORKS, OFFERING SKILLS OF THEIR OWN IN EXCHANGE FOR THE LITERACY SKILLS OF OTHERS WITHIN THEIR NETWORK.
Yes, we do what we can to survive, to keep our jobs, our homes, our families. Our trades and compromises can be fair, like you help me fill out the welfare form or write a letter to my brother or read to my children and I'll make you some cornbread, show you how to make jewelry, teach you some Spanish. They can also be unfair—you find out that I can't read and hint that you'll fire me; I sleep with you to keep my job. The fairness of the exchange depends on the power relationships.

3. MANY SO-CALLED ILLITERATE OR LOW-LITERATE ADULTS DEVELOP LITERACY SPONTANEOUSLY, OUTSIDE OF FORMAL PROGRAMS, BY WORKING COLLABORATIVELY TO ACCOMPLISH A RANGE OF TASKS.
We're not sure what this means, what you mean by spontaneously, what you mean by range of tasks. We tried to figure it out, but we just don't get it. So

we have to skip it. How would it feel to have this point omitted from your framework? Isn't there something important here that needs to be said? Is it possible that it can be best said by you? Isn't it also possible that there are some things that can be best said by us?

4. THERE IS A NEED TO LOOK FOR LITERACY AND LEARNING IN A WIDE RANGE OF CONTEXTS, INCLUDING FAMILIES, WORKPLACES, UNIONS, STORES, CHURCHES, COMMUNITY OR-GANIZATIONS, ETC.

Sometimes it is easier, more supportive, more fruitful to work in and among those we know, environments we're familiar with, comfortable in, rather than on strange turf with strangers. Sometimes it would be nice to find you coming to the places where we are rather than always having to come to you.

5. BECOMING MORE LITERATE IS NOT NECESSARILY CHARAC-TERIZED BY AUTONOMY. INSTEAD, THERE ARE DIVERSE ROUTES INTO LITERACY AND IN DIFFERENT CULTURES OR SO-CIAL GROUPINGS THESE PATHS MAY REVOLVE MORE AROUND JOINT WORK AND INTERDEPENDENCE THAN INDIVIDUAL INI-TIATIVE.

We need to know that there are others like us who share our experiences, that we can work together, intimately. That we can give and receive help, that we are worth knowing and talking with. That it is not necessary that we can do every part alone. That we need each other.

6. LITERACY PRACTICES DIFFER FROM GROUP TO GROUP WITHIN A SOCIETY AS WELL AS FROM SOCIETY TO SOCIETY.

Yes, and they vary within groups as well.

7. INDIVIDUALS CAN BE EXPECTED TO VARY GREATLY IN THEIR PURPOSES FOR READING AND WRITING AS WELL AS IN THE CONTEXTS FOR PERFORMANCE OF READING AND WRIT-ING ABILITIES.

Yes, and we should be treated by you as though we are capable of making these decisions for ourselves, that we don't need you to tell us what is or isn't important.

8. LITERACY CAN BE VIEWED AS A PROCESS OF INTERPRETING THE WORLD AND DEVELOPING A CONSCIOUSNESS OF VAL-UES, BEHAVIORS, AND BELIEFS AS SOCIALLY CONSTRUCTED.

Yes, and also to explore and construct and create and support the possibilities and potential for alternative ways of valuing, acting, and thinking.

9. LITERACY PROGRAMS DIFFER DRAMATICALLY FROM EACH OTHER. THERE ARE OFTEN STRIKING DISSIMILARITIES WITHIN PROGRAMS AS WELL, AS TEACHERS AND TUTORS BRING THEIR

OWN PRIOR KNOWLEDGE, ASSUMPTIONS, AND EXPECTATIONS ABOUT LITERACY AND LEARNING.
Yes! Why didn't you say more about this? In a way, you talked so much about us and for us that you never really got around to saying who you are, what you want, how this perspective is good for you—as teacher, researcher, writer, thinker.

10. PROGRAMS REFERRED TO AS "PARTICIPATORY" PROVIDE OPPORTUNITIES FOR DEVELOPING LITERACY WITHIN THE PROGRAM AS AN ORGANIZATIONAL AS WELL AS AN INSTRUCTIONAL SETTING, AND THUS REGARD ADULTS' PRIOR EXPERIENCE AND ESTABLISHED PATTERNS OF SOCIAL INTERACTION, OFTEN IN ORAL SUBCULTURES, AS CONTEXTS AND RESOURCES FOR LEARNING.
Yes, and they can become a place where we can challenge what exists, question, change, revolutionize, tear down, build. And validate and demand legitimacy for other ways of seeing, reading, writing, talking, living. "Participatory," though, is a kind of condescending term, a pat-on-the-head term. We like equality better, we like equity. We'd like a program where the learners can invite and the researchers can be "participatory."

After writing through this dialogue there is something else we want to draw attention to before moving on. The ideas [in the article] are not what is in question for us here, it's the words and who they belong to. This is the most unsettling part about having someone speak *for* you—the possibility that they might do it well and then say, Hey, what's the problem? We represented you accurately, didn't we? We didn't tell lies about you. And we'd have to say, Yes, this is true. But the issue for us is who's informing who? How does who gets to speak the ideas, whose name is in parentheses, reinforce unequal power relationships?

❑ ❑ ❑ ❑ ❑

Sr. Gonzalo and His Daughters: A Family Literacy Tale from Mexico
Judy Kalman

In Mexico, as in many other places, the widespread view of literacy in educational spheres and other social circles is based on a normative and prescriptive understanding of reading and writing. I recently heard a television news commentator in Mexico City note that from his point of view one of the barriers to development and democratization was the fact that Mexico was a nation of nonreaders. He then cited a recent statistic that Mexicans read only 2.5 books a year per person. His argument linking literacy to national development and political participation is not new; it dates back at least to the previous century and has been very popular since minimum literacy criteria were put forth by UNESCO and other international agencies in the 1960s.

My uneasiness with his remarks is not so much in the data but in the implications. It may be true that on the average, adults in Mexico read only 2.5 books a year. However, in selecting this particular statistic, he is excluding many widespread literacy practices that include using reading and writing in a variety of ways (dealing with newspapers, comics, party invitations, street signs, forms, and labels are just a few examples). In doing so, he also excludes the people who use those practices. Furthermore, it is not clear whether people do not read books because they cannot or for some other reason. (At a time of severe economic crisis, when a single paperback book usually costs more than twice the minimum wage for a full day's labor, buying a book is not a high priority for many Mexican families.) The facile use of a statistic such as this one has more than one drawback: on the one hand it can lead people to conclusions that are erroneous (adults in Mexico cannot read) and on the other it can opaque other issues (adults in Mexico cannot afford to buy books).

The French philosopher Michel Foucault once wrote that whoever is able to disseminate and impose his or her version of reality has power. The idea that reading books is synonymous with being or not being a reader is an example of what Foucault had in mind and connotes a hegemonic image of literacy that limits written language use to a few elitist practices and disqualifies everything else as "not literacy." In a portrait such as this one, nothing else fits.

As far as I can tell, the only way to counter such a narrow definition of what is or is not reading, and by extension, what is or is not literacy, is to present an alternative view, a different version of reality. While the notion that literacy is a multiple construct and not a singular phenomenon has been well accepted by many researchers and educators as an important theoretical contribution of the 1980s, it seems that this idea still has not made its way into other spheres. Therefore, I want to contribute a different reading of literacy: a case study of one man's use of literacy in his everyday life. This case is particularly interesting because the protagonist, while he has had only three years of formal schooling, has an ample repertoire of literacy practices, built up over years of using reading and writing for a variety of purposes. He reads recreationally, does crossword puzzles, keeps a personal notebook and directory, reads several newspapers, researches information, and follows written instructions. He also reads books, but this is not his main literacy activity. For him, other uses of reading and writing are more essential.

Literacy and Sr. Gonzalo

Sr. Gonzalo is a retired driver for the municipal government. He is in his early sixties and currently works as the personal chauffeur and handyman for a family. He is not originally from Mexico City; he was born in the neighboring state of Morelos, where his father fought as a Zapatista in the Mexican Revolution and was one of the few who actually carried a gun. At some point in his early childhood, around the age of seven, his family moved to Mexico City and he began to work in a gas station, washing windows for tips and draining oil out of cars. At eleven he began to learn to drive cars around the gas station.

Sr. Gonzalo did not go to school as a boy, as many of his generation did not. But in his late teens he did what is called the *servicio militar*, a mandatory one-year stint of weekends in the army. When he entered the service it was discovered that he could neither read nor write, so he was required to sign up for night school. He stuck with it until he reached the equivalent of the middle of the fourth grade, when he could no longer afford to go. He got his driver's license when he was in his early twenties.

At about this time, he met his future wife María and began to court her. He was working as a laborer laying streets, and María would meet him near his work site each day, or as often as she could sneak away from her parents' strict supervision. They could only see each other in passing, so Sr. Gonzalo had very little opportunity to woo her. To further his cause, he would periodically visit a street scribe and dictate a letter. He would walk by where María was waiting and slip the envelope in her hand. He explained to me that he told the scribes, "I want the letter to say, you know, this and that, and I love you and all that stuff. Then they would write it."

Sr. Gonzalo and his sweetheart eventually married, and they have ten daughters, now ranging from fifteen to thirty-eight years of age. While working for the city government, Sr. Gonzalo was assigned different jobs within the city crew—driving a truck, working as the personal chauffeur for one of the engineers, laying pavement.

The chart in Figure 1 summarizes some of Sr. Gonzalo's principle uses for reading and writing, divided according to the domain in which he uses them. As with many classifications, this one is somewhat arbitrary. The literacy practices could just as well have been classified in terms of Sr. Gonzalo's purposes: reading for pleasure, reading for information, reading for learning, writing to be reminded, writing to keep records, writing to communicate from a distance, etc. When Sr. Gonzalo reads or writes something, it is usually on his own initiative: many of the ways that he uses reading and writing at work, for example, have been his idea. He also collects and uses many of the implements that go along with literacy: clipboards, pens and pencils, scratch paper, portable files, folders, calendars, date books, address books, and so on.

DOMAIN	LITERACY PRACTICES
Work	Keeps notes on things to do
	Keeps running account of petty cash expenses
	Keeps files (receipts, pickup slips, documents for vehicles)
	Keeps log book on car maintenance and purchases
	Does bookkeeping of daily expenses
	Consults traffic laws
	Makes measurements, drawings, and diagrams
	Reads maps
	Looks up information in phone book
	Organizes documents by dates
	Organizes itineraries
	Writes and receives messages
Recreation	Does crossword puzzles
	Reads *Reader's Digest*, illustrated texts (comics, fotonovellas), novels, stories, and sports journals
Church	Reads Bible and prayers
Home	Administrates family budget and keeps records of expenses
	Maintains family file of official papers, files, forms, bills, and identification documents
	Looks for information in phone book and TV guide
	Uses how-to manuals for building and gardening projects
	Writes and receives messages
School	Does homework with grandchildren
	Reads stories to grandchildren

Figure 1: Sr. Gonzalo's uses for reading and writing

An interesting aspect of Sr. Gonzalo's literacy is that not only does he use reading and writing for multiple purposes, he also invents ways of using written language as a way of organizing his life. For example, when his daughters were younger, he created a petty cash accounting system for them. Each week he left a certain amount of money in a jar for them to use to buy minor supplies they needed for school. When one of them spent some, they were supposed to fill out a slip that he kept near the jar. He told them to write down their name, the date, how much they spent, and what they spent it on. Then they were to put the slip in the jar. At the end of each week he would add up all the slips to see if the exact amount of change remained. If it did not, he would call his girls together and go over all of the slips and figures with them.

Sr. Gonzalo's story defies many widespread expectations about literacy: UNESCO documents state that a person must have at least five years of formal education for literacy not to be lost, yet Sr. Gonzalo did not have that much education. There is also the view that "low literacy" is passed on from generation to generation. Sr. Gonzalo also breaks this "rule": of his ten daughters, one is a physician, another an accountant, another a translator. His youngest daughter is now in high school.

In Sr. Gonzalo's story we observe a continual gain in literacy across generations. His parents were unschooled and it is very likely that they were not literate. In the early 1900s, when his parents were young, only a fraction of the population had access to reading and writing. Sr. Gonzalo had not even four years of schooling but was able to use reading and writing in a variety of ways. At least three of his daughters have a postsecondary education. His grandchildren are going to school, are doing well, and are expected to continue past the sixth grade.

How did Sr. Gonzalo pick up these amazing abilities, what were the circumstances in which he developed and diversified reading and writing practices? I cannot be absolutely sure, but I would like to make an educated guess. During Sr. Gonzalo's life, at least four factors favored his construction of literacy practices. First, he confronted situations at home and at work that required reading and writing. Second, he interacted with people who were readers and writers, which allowed him to participate in literacy events in different ways. When he worked as the chauffeur for a city engineer, he would frequently drive his boss's wife where she needed to go. When she knew that he was going to wait for her a long time, she would give him things to read, mostly novels and newspapers. He was also expected to keep track of his daily expenses and give an exact accounting of the purchases he made and the fees he paid during working hours. This is the third factor: being lent a novel or a newspaper, using pencil and paper to keep track of his expenses, made literacy materially available to Sr. Gonzalo. He might not have been able to afford to buy books to read, but if they were lent to him he would make the effort to read them. Sometimes in the car he had the opportunity to talk about the books with his passenger. Each interaction around written language and each situation that required Sr. Gonzalo to read or write allowed him to diversify his uses and understanding of written language. The fourth and final factor has to do with ownership: in many of Sr. Gonzalo's uses of literacy, he decides how to organize documents, when and what to read, what to file and what to throw away.

Sr. Gonzalo's tale is a story of reading and writing deeply embedded in the context of his daily life, one more piece of evidence that literacy practices are constructed in response to communicative need. His story defies widespread and long-held ideas about literacy—what is needed to get it and keep it and how it is (or isn't) passed on between generations. A single statistic could never portray the place of written language in Sr. Gonzalo's life, and we must not allow it to misrepresent him.

□ □ □ □ □

Instead of conceiving of literacy as involvement with written language that is the same everywhere and involves some fixed inventory of capacities, we began to think of literacy as a term applying to a varied and open set of activities with written language.

—Sylvia Scribner

□ □ □ □ □

Multiple Roads to Literacy
YETTA M. GOODMAN

There is no single road to becoming literate. As I read the work of those who have studied the literacy development of children in many places in the world, as I consider the kids (my own children and grandchildren among them) who have informed my literacy development research, I am convinced that it is extremely important to legitimatize the concept of multiple roads to literacy. There is a tendency in the popular press, in schools, and in family literacy programs to consider that all people become literate in the same way. In much of the literature about how children learn to read and write there is an undue emphasis on the idea that the major or only road to literacy learning occurs when children are read to by their parents. This suggests to the society at large—and the suggestion becomes embedded in the culture—that being read to is the only aspect of literacy that counts as an influence on children's literacy development.

Such a belief places a heavy responsibility on families who do not read aloud regularly in the home; they often accept the notion that since they do not read books aloud to their children, they are irresponsible and the cause for their children's lack of literacy. I want to dispel that notion: not to diminish the importance of reading aloud as one road to literacy development, but to document that there are many ways, equally important but different, in which children are immersed in literacy events that positively influence their development. It is unreasonable and, I believe, actually dangerous to expect all families to follow the same prescriptions for literacy learning.

Those who speak to families and communities about literacy development, who plan literacy curriculum for schools, or who publish literacy materials must be knowledgeable about the literacy events that occur in a wide range of households. As the variety of literacy experiences in different homes are acknowledged and respected, families come to believe that the literacy events they experience in their homes are legitimate roads to literacy learning. Schools and publishers must also respond with sensitivity to and respect for the many different ways people use literacy. The materials they publish and the curricula they develop should help parents and communities appreciate that they can involve their children in the cultural literacy events of their homes and communities and at the same time support literacy development.

Certainly, being read to by parents, grandparents, teachers, siblings, and other caregivers establishes one kind of context in which children are engaged and immersed in becoming full-fledged members of a literate community. But immersion in the connected discourse of children's books is not the only road to literacy. Connected discourse takes many other formats and occurs in many other genres. Reading newspapers and magazines is a ritual in many households, and children see, hear, and often participate as family members share news and advertisements, decide what movie to attend, or decide where to do the family shopping that evening. Some families read comics, while others share notes or letters from family members or friends. Some families read the Bible regularly, often including their young children in the oral reading and the discussions that follow.

The writing roads to literacy development occur simultaneously with the reading roads. Families write letters, notes, and special-occasion cards, sometimes in more than one language, to family members in distant places. Since we now understand that literacy in any language is helpful to literacy learning in another language, the bi- and multilingual nature of writing (and reading) in the home takes on an importance heretofore often unappreciated. In households, phone messages are taken and people leave notes on pillows, on tables, or on the refrigerator door. Children see homemade posters and signs. Children are often encouraged to be part of the writing experiences that take place incidentally and daily in the home and in community settings.

Within the home and in the community there is also the survival road to literacy—all the reading and writing related to health care, business transactions, and the general "goods and services" necessary for the well-being of the family. This may include reading the warnings on cleaning materials or medicines and collecting and organizing coupons or trading stamps. People who are job hunting, paying bills, or applying to schools are all involved in important literacy transactions. While shopping, family members may read and write lists and scrutinize labels to discover the best buy or the healthiest ingredients. And their children are often at their side, observing and sometimes playing at or participating in the same kinds of experiences. In bilingual homes or homes of new immigrants, children are often the "culture brokers" who are asked to read and interpret official letters and proclamations that parents or the extended family believe they are not understanding.

The playing-at-literacy road is another undervalued road to learning.

Children love to pretend to do the things adults do. Children pull pencils and pens from their parents' purses or pockets to write bills, receipts, menus, or recipes. They write tickets for the plays they perform, writes faxes to send for business purposes, and sometimes even make worksheets while playing school. When parents and teachers allow children to have easy and open access to reading and writing opportunities in their play, literacy learning expands.

Environmental print is another road to literacy. In my print-awareness research with very young children, I discovered that by age three (and often much earlier) children are attending to and are aware of the functions of the print that is an integral part of their home and community environments. When I ask teachers and graduate and undergraduate students to reflect on their personal literacy biographies, I find that many of them are consciously aware of the impact print, in a variety of contexts, had on their early reading. Some remember being intrigued by the print in supermarkets or malls. Others vividly remember a particular street sign because it made a connection with their name or a billboard that made some other connection with an aspect of their life.

Colleen, an adult working-class avid reader, whom I interviewed extensively about her literacy learning as a child, was on the move often as her parents drove from place to place looking for work. Her early reading memories include sitting in the front seat of the car helping whichever parent was driving search for small towns on maps and then finding the appropriate signs that led them to their next destination.

Colleen also reported that seeing others read (and write) was significant to her literacy history. I call this the demonstration road to literacy. Colleen remembers clearly that her mother was always reading mysteries and other novels. The messages about literacy in this family were loud and clear. Not only did reading serve important functions for daily survival, it also was an engaging and pleasurable activity that people often did silently and alone. Colleen is herself such a reader, never without a book, often taking a break to get in some reading between her chores as a housekeeper.

Marilyn, an undergraduate preservice teacher, was aware that her mother and her older brother and sister were annoyed whenever they had to read to her, so she began to read in self-defense. "I knew that if I could read by myself, I would be able to enjoy books like my mom did. She was always immersed in a book. Even in the kitchen she would be reading and beating eggs at the same time." Everyone in her family breathed sighs of relief when Marilyn was reading on her own before she went to kindergarten. This road to literacy involves actively observing others read and write in ways that demonstrate the value independent silent reading or writing serves. The personal literacy histories of university students and working-class readers alike often include comments like this: "My mother reads so much." "My father had to have quiet to read the newspaper, then he would sometimes share the news with us at breakfast." "My dad was always at the computer writing letters but mostly stories, which he read to us if we played quietly at his side."

The technological road to literacy includes all the written language that family members deal with when using computers, playing video games, and watching television. New information networks are adding to the literacy learning of the growing numbers of people who have access to technology. (This brings to mind a bus ride I took during a trip to a rural mountain community in Colombia. The bus was filled with *compesinos* traveling to sell their produce at the marketplace of the next small town. Observing this scene, I formed a picture of an earlier time in the history of American transportation. Yet, tucked into the front corner of the bus was a TV set playing videos of commercials, the news, and other programming.)

Family literacy traditions are another road to literacy learning. Families who gather around a musical instrument with songsheets or books to sing together, who read the Bible at regular times at home or in church, or who participate in acting out comics every Sunday morning are engaging in family literacy traditions. In some families, people write stories or keep diaries together. In my family, the children and grandchildren anticipate when they will read from the Hagaddah (written in Hebrew, English, and Yiddish) at Passover. At age three and four, they learn their parts for oral presentations that they read from the script during the family Seder. Such literacy traditions are integral to daily family and community life, and children and adults simply take for granted that they will participate as literate members of the culture—usually without conscious thought as to its impact on literacy development.

There are many unique and personal literacy experiences that also provide roads to literacy. Each household has unique literacy experiences of which schools and researchers are often unaware. One woman remembers learning to read with her dad as they were cooking. He would have her read the recipes with him; when she was successful, she got a piece of dough to make her own cookies. A working-class reader remembers fixing the car with his father and looking up car parts in a mail-order catalogue. A number of research reports document such individual literacy experience. David Hartle-Shutte tells of a Navajo fifth-grade-proficient reader who learned to read by watching the on-screen words in TV commercials and the credits at the end of movies. Gertrude Hildreth documents a boy's literacy development in her longitudinal study of his train drawings from two and a half to eleven years of age. Although her study focuses on art as a symbol system, Hildreth also examines how writing becomes embedded in Philip's drawings. His writing increases over time, as he uses it not only to label features of his drawings but to provide instructions and narratives to accompany them.

Careful documentation of literacy histories of people from a range of socioeconomic backgrounds, from students in teacher education programs, and from children reveal these various roads to literacy development. Each road—being read to and participating in reading from books and other forms of connected discourse, writing alone or with others, playing at literacy events, making appropriate use of technology and environmental print, watching others read and write; observing family and personal literacy traditions, and becoming involved in sign systems other than written language— becomes part of the literacy history of our highly literate society. Most literate people travel more than one of these roads to literacy and in doing so become successful readers and writers who learn to use literacy in a range of ways for work or for pleasure. These multiple roads to literacy are accompanied by shared discussions among family members and friends. Flyers are questioned, letters from teachers and principals are explained, and memos and prescriptions from medical centers are thoughtfully discussed.

Many of these roads to literacy are taken for granted by members of a literate society. We don't consider their importance to the literacy development of both the children and adults in a community. In fact, we have a tendency to give credit for literacy learning to more academic events such as being read to, writing stories, or being taught to read and write in school settings. When the range of literacy events that occur daily, often incidentally, in homes and communities are recognized as important aspects of the literacy learning of that community, then it is likely that members of that community will come to realize that these reading and writing experiences are rich reservoirs for literacy learning.

The reason conscious acknowledgment of and legitimacy for multiple roads to literacy is important is that the same roads to literacy that influence the literate members of society are also responsible for the attitudes about literacy learning held by those children and adults who do not see themselves as successful literate members of society. Some children have literacy experiences that lead to uneasiness with the processes of literacy. They may not be "good" readers as measured by standardized reading tests and therefore do not believe that the literacy events significant in their lives are of any academic importance. Often their parents and teachers corroborate their beliefs through a variety of talk and actions. There are children who participate actively in literacy events while watching TV, playing video games, fixing cars, cooking, responding to environmental print, etc., who never value their literacy because no one helps them perceive that they are indeed already readers and writers. There are children who use literacy as a peripheral event to activities such as hiking or other sports, musical ensembles, drama, or art who seldom recognize that these rich literacy events are a subtle but integral part of their life experiences. Too many parents tell tragic stories about children who have been eagerly reading and writing at home only to cease these activities when they enter school and learn that reading and writing are narrow literacy practices limited to lesson routines or specific writing formations. Such children often come to believe they are not valued by the literacy establishment and that what they read and write does not count as literacy.

It is therefore necessary to help each individual recognize and value her or his unique literacy experiences, and teachers can play an important role in doing so. Parents and community members can also be helped to recognize and value the myriad of literacy events unique to their cultures.

In closing, let me share a story. Often when I fly to conferences or consultancies, the people sitting next to me become interested in the children's book I am reading or the manuscript or journal article I am responding to. Finding out that I am interested in how people learn to read and write, many of them admit they are not readers and writers. These confessions often come from successful business and professional people: I've been told this by, among others, a nuclear engineer and a neurosurgeon. The latest such confession came from a very successful jeweler. He was very loquacious, and I quickly learned how successful he is at creating unique jewelry and how proud he is of his success. He gets his customers to make sketches so that he can incorporate their visions and interests into his creations. But he kept telling me that he could not read or write. He said that his employees write his letters for him and that his wife keeps his financial records. As we talked, I became aware that he was a well-read person. He talked about the influence of Robert Heinlein's books on his view of life, about the Christian concepts he has been exploring with his pastor in a Bible study group, about the latest black hole theory he had read in *Omni* magazine, and about the insights he was gaining from chaos theory. When I pointed out all the reading and writing he was doing—labeling jewelry designs, organizing information about gems for his customers to read, knowing the technical and common labels for a wide range of gems and metals, reserving hotel rooms and purchasing airline tickets for himself and his family, and discussing theories about the world that came from books and magazines he was reading—he said repeatedly that he knew he was creative but he was not a capable reader or writer. Even when I asked him how he got a master's degree in psychology without being able to read and write, he said, "I think they wanted me to get the degree because they recognized that I was creative. They overlooked how I wrote papers and a lot of my spelling problems."

In this highly literate society, this creative artist actively participates in literacy events all the time, but his many roads to literacy have not been made visible to him and have not allowed him to perceive or define himself as literate. He does not count the reading and writing that he does as literacy. He does not appreciate them as important aspects of his literacy learning, and these beliefs influence his attitude about himself as being nonliterate.

In order to understand fully the importance of legitimatizing the multiple-roads-to-literacy concept, we have to take into consideration the attitudes about being literate that are articulated by people like the jeweler, the physicist, the surgeon, and the children and adolescents who are struggling because they see themselves as not being functioning readers and writers.

The lack of appreciation for the multiple-roads concept helps explain how the same phenomena, sometimes even in the same contexts, when experienced by different readers and writers, produce people who consider themselves differently literate. It is not because people do not learn that they do not value their own literacy and literacy learning. *It is what and how they do learn* that leads them to this view of themselves. Those of us concerned with family literacy are in a unique position to demonstrate for each family the possibilities that exist in their daily lives and to help them see how these experiences define them as literate members of society.

References

HILDRETH, GERTRUDE. *The Child Mind in Evolution.* New York: King's Crown Press, 1941.

HARTLE-SCHUTTE, DAVID. *Home Environment Characteristics of Successful Navajo Readers*, p. 229. Unpublished dissertation, University of Arizona, 1988.

❏ ❏ ❏ ❏ ❏

Literacy Education As Family Work
JEROME C. HARSTE

To appreciate the wonders of literacy I recommend parenthood and a doctorate in language education. That's what I had, and my mouth literally hung open in amazement as I watched my son, Jason, grow in literacy. There was a downside, however, and that was schooling. In Jason's case, schools didn't value what he knew. We both found the experience extremely frustrating. Jason, because the schools were always nagging him to do his worksheets. Me, because I was an educator and "a member of the dominant culture." Schools supposedly not only served children of the dominant culture, but served them well!

From birth on Jason loved cars. As a little baby he would spin the wheels on his Hot Wheels cars for hours on end, fascinated by their rotation. At two years of age he had such fine coordination that he could get his Play School Trolley going at top speed and negotiate a right-angle turn into our kitchen that took his parents' breath away. He wore out two Big Wheels during his preschool years. By age five we were sure he was going to be an Indianapolis 500 race car driver and that this was our punishment for deciding to live in Indiana.

Jason also loved the sandbox. If there are doctorates in sand, Jason earned one. He would spend hours in the sandbox, building roads, creating tunnels, having races. And weather didn't bother him. We timed him: he spent eight hours in his sandbox during one of southern Indiana's coldest winter days. Although I, his mother, and the neighbor children spent time with him at various points, he outlasted us all. We have some idea of what he did out there, but he clocked in many hours alone and probably created worlds we only one day hope to see.

Jason also loved to draw. During one memorable period, he and his friend Joe drew war picture after war picture. Often he would tell me about the picture. "This guy got shot in the eye. Don't tell Mom." The sheet of paper was more a stage than an easel. One almost had to be present to make sense of the final product, because each picture was a story in which multiple events occurred. The final product often looked a mess, not the kind of tidy work that would be expected of him in school. He went through reams of paper. A new set of colored pencils would keep him absorbed for hours.

Jason had little time for books. Oh, he would listen from afar and come running to look at a picture if he found the story interesting, but books paled to insignificance in light of drawing, sand, and cars.

Surprisingly, Jason read before going to school. The first word I know he recognized was *Chevrolet*. He read it on the back of a car as we were driving to the mall. I asked him what other words on other cars said and remember being amazed that he knew. In retrospect, it shouldn't have surprised me, it was one of things he was really interested in.

Jason didn't like doing worksheets. He avoided them at all costs. In kindergarten he came home at Thanksgiving, Christmas, and Easter vacations with stacks he was to complete because he never voluntarily found time to do even a single one during choice time. In first grade things got worse: Jason averaged twenty-seven worksheets a week (I kept count). By second grade Jason was on his way to becoming what his teacher said was "a remedial reader." Mary Hill and I worked with him after school, getting him to use his knowledge of letter-sound relations to complete worksheets using invented spellings. When, one day, he came home with only three items red-checked, I said, "See, that works better, doesn't it?" His response was wise beyond his years, "Yeah, I guess, but teacher doesn't like it much!"

I'm pleased to report that Jason is grown up now. Currently he is finishing his undergraduate degree, majoring in fine arts with a special interest in graphic design.

I've always liked Jason. I valued his ways of knowing, even when the schools thought of him as on the brink of failure. While he does things others insist he must, he does them with a bit of disdain and then gets on with what it is he likes. I'm convinced he sees the world differently than we teachers do. He moseys. We stride.

I often wonder why school had to give Jason even that single moment of doubt. What was accomplished by our questioning who he was and what he wanted to be? What would school have been like if a broader definition of literacy were accepted and we saw our task as supporting and extending everyone's way of knowing? A great society needs good plumbers, good lawyers, good teachers, good mechanics, as well as good design artists. What value is great philosophy if the plumbing doesn't work?

Jason raised my consciousness about literacy. He taught me to think in specifics rather than in glib generalizations. He reminded me that even the dominant culture is not well served by the current policies and practices of schooling and literacy. He forced me to define literacy more broadly, to entertain cars as a way of knowing, sand as a way of knowing, art as a way of knowing. His story could, if we let it, help our society's notions of schooling and literacy grow too. Think of him as family. I do. Think of what you do as family work. I do and in so doing glimpse a new future.

Sarah entered kindergarten ... not as a neophyte to literacy but as an experienced reader and writer who was knowledgeable about written language and confident about herself and her ability to invent and solve problems she confronted in making sense in her reading and writing. She entered kindergarten seeking rich, functional, meaningful experiences with literacy to broaden, deepen, and extend her understanding and support her as she continued to refine and sharpen her reading and writing and grow as a citizen in our society.

Unfortunately, those aren't the kinds of experiences she encountered in school.

—Prisca Martens

The models for what families should be doing come from educated, middle-class families, whose relative success in school seems to be reason enough to believe that their family literacy practices are ideal.... Looking more closely at what happens in educated, middle-class families, we may want to reconsider whether these practices provide a workable and desirable model, even for the families who already use them.

—Judith Solsken

□ □ □ □ □

The provision of literacy in the language of the community helps the learners to build on their linguistic experience, to get reinforcement from and in their daily environment, to play with words, to gain better control of the written technology and to express [their] creativity in the school and not in spite of the school.

—*Paul Belanger*

□ □ □ □ □

Biliteracy Development of a Chinese/English-Speaking Child

Nan Jiang

Ty is a native speaker of Chinese. He and his mother came to join his father in the United States when he was four. He is eight now and has just finished second grade in an American school. His parents started to teach him Chinese characters when he was about three, and this effort continued after their arrival in the States. Ty would learn to recognize three to five new characters before going to bed each day. The next evening he would review the characters previously learned and learn the new ones. Copying the characters was his daily homework.

Ty's parents tried to create situations in which Ty could see the relevance of Chinese literacy to his daily life and put his Chinese skill to use. Ty enjoyed listening to stories, so they spent time reading storybooks with him and telling him what the Chinese characters meant. They made every effort to let Ty always have something to read on his own. As his active vocabulary grew, they encouraged Ty to write letters in Chinese to his grandparents in China (with whom he had spent much of early childhood), and his grandparents wrote back to him. At the suggestion of his father, Ty also started keeping a diary in Chinese at the beginning of first grade, which gave him a daily opportunity to practice his written Chinese.

Reading and writing had became part of Ty's life even before he went to kindergarten. By the time Ty came in contact with written English, he was already an experienced reader of Chinese. He didn't feel intimidated by printed words: he had gotten used to them, and his experiences with them had been encouraging and rewarding. He had developed his own strategies for overcoming difficulties faced by a beginning reader, such as ignoring unknown words when necessary or using a dictionary.

However, probably more important, his home-based Chinese literacy education helped Ty develop a strong interest in reading and a positive attitude toward learning. This had a strong positive impact on Ty's literacy development in English. Ever since his kindergarten year, he has been an able and enthusiastic reader of English. He read sixty or seventy books every semester in first and second grade, not including winter and summer breaks, when he usually spent more time reading. This large amount of reading contributed to his rapid English literacy development. Even though he spoke a primary language other than English at home and had been in this country for only two years, he passed the exams necessary to enroll in a gifted-and-talented program.

The books he reads are often ones for students of older ages. He is very accurate in his spelling. In his weekly twenty-word spelling tests during second grade, he missed only two of the approximately six hundred words. The written assignments he did at school, his English diary, and his letters to his pen pal all showed a writing proficiency much above his contemporaries.

Ty's parents are no longer worried about their son's English. Their biggest concern today is his written Chinese. His Chinese literacy development reached its highest level in first grade: he was able to write fairly long letters in Chinese, and his diary entries were getting longer. Then it began to decline. He is now hardly able to write a letter in Chinese. His diary, which began in Chinese and then became bilingual for a period of time, is now exclusively in English. English has become his preferred language in both its oral and written forms. He is using much more English even at home, where using English is intentionally discouraged.

An important factor in his Chinese literacy attrition is the lack of diverse opportunities for him to put his written Chinese to use. Such opportunities are extremely important not only because they allow Ty to practice language, but also because they demonstrate the relevance and importance of the language, thus serving as motivation. As Ty's life becomes more school-oriented and his English proficiency grows, the gap between the effort he has to make to develop his Chinese literacy and its perceived value and usefulness gets wider. Being aware of the cause of the problem, his parents are trying to provide more opportunities for Ty to use Chinese—by asking him to do math problems with Chinese instructions, for example. By doing so, they hope that Ty can at least retain the Chinese literacy skills he still has. However, they feel that what they can do is very limited and that further development of Ty's Chinese literacy has become a goal unlikely to be achieved.

Ty's biliteracy development demonstrates the positive impact of early literacy development in the primary language on later English literacy development of language minority children. It also shows that a key to successful literacy development lies in the connection between literacy and the learner's life.

❏ ❏ ❏ ❏ ❏

All languages have an equal potential to convey the full range of human thought and experience. If that is the case, then language choices in the public domain are essentially political ones and cannot be ascribed to any intrinsic characteristic of a specific language.

—Leslie J. Limage

❏ ❏ ❏ ❏ ❏

ethical principles about family literacy research and program development

Literacy is a universal human right.

❏ It is not a commodity to be bought or sold, researched for profit, prescribed medicinally, or doled out for punishment.

❏ The potential for violation of family rights is considerable, especially when the demands of society conflict with the needs of families.

There is a constant need for family literacy educators to examine their own practices.

❏ Family literacy programs raise fundamental ethical issues because of the power imbalance between program providers and program participants.

❏ Those enrolled in family literacy programs are likely to be at a disadvantage in their relations with family literacy educators and the producers of literacy programs with regard to economics, social status, or power to influence the design of curriculum and instruction.

❏ The possibility always exists that educators might unwittingly participate in the victimization of both parents and children.

❏ Family literacy educators and private corporations producing literacy programs often do derive direct benefit from the work.

It is essential that social agencies and the criminal justice system examine policies that require participation in family literacy programs.

❏ In the United States, participation in family literacy programs is sometimes a prerequisite for social services. Similarly, participation in a family literacy program has become court-mandated for some parents and their children.

❏ In such situations, family literacy programs become a form of punishment and the role of the literacy educator changes from facilitator to corrections officer, a transformation of professional positions that is cause for serious concern.

principles ·69

- Every family literacy educator should be free from external restrictions such as mandated participation, inappropriate standardized assessment, and unrealistic funding requirements, so that the well-being of the participants and their families can be the primary concern.

Researchers in academic institutions should similarly scrutinize their own practices.

- Family literacy research raises fundamental ethical issues of power and profit.

- Questions need to be asked about the extent to which academic research on families and literacy is conducted for personal gain in the form of financial and/or professional advancement.

- Questions should also be asked about the relevance of the research to the everyday lives of the families who participate in literacy studies.

- The family's general well-being and personal needs and interests should always override the personal needs and interests of the researcher.

Policy makers should also hold themselves accountable.

- Blaming the lack of literacy skills for the ills of the society is a national and international form of political propaganda.

- There are many people who have multiple literacies, and some who also speak multiple languages, yet still live in poverty.

- There is systemic denial that the social conditions in which many families live are politically structured. Soweto is symbolic of such conditions, but there are similar situations in many different countries, including the United States.

- The lack of housing, the lack of jobs, and the lack of adequate medical care are often at the root of the difficulties that families face.

- Again, literacy is a universal human right and should not be used as an excuse for racist public policy.

Multinational corporations that are unlikely to examine their commercialization of literacy should be held accountable for the packaging and sale of their literacy products.

- Multinational corporations profit directly when literacy is packaged and marketed both nationally and internationally.

❑ Often their products are sold to families who are least able to afford them.

❑ Families buy such products because of the negative rhetoric—statements about "declining reading scores, escalating dropout rates, and the alarming rise of illiteracy even among many high school graduates"— and because of the unsubstantiated and exaggerated claims of the success of the program.

❑ ❑ ❑ ❑ ❑

Reading Between the Lines
ELSA AUERBACH

Everybody who talks about family literacy supports cultural sensitivity, parent empowerment, and building on family strengths. In fact, now, in the 1990s, it's virtually impossible to have any credibility in the field of family literacy unless you say that you recognize and celebrate diversity. In some ways, this consensus shows how far the family literacy movement has come. In the years shortly after the 1983 publication of Denny Taylor's pioneering book *Family Literacy*, when the term first gained currency, most programs and studies assumed that children with literacy problems came from homes with deficient or inadequate literacy practices and that therefore parents needed to be taught to value and support their children's literacy development; most of these "first generation" family literacy programs focused on transmitting mainstream school literacy practices into the home (teaching parents how to read to their children, help them with homework, etc.). In the late 1980s, however, this approach was criticised as representing a deficit perspective, and alternatives emerged. Now virtually all of these "second generation" family literacy programs claim to oppose deficit perspectives, to embrace family strengths, and to support community cultural practices. The discourse of deficits is out and the discourse of strengths is in.

This apparent consensus has some hidden dangers, and there may actually be pitfalls in all this pervasive talk of strengths, cultural diversity, and parent empowerment. The danger, I think, is that fundamental differences in values, goals, ideological orientations, and pedagogical approaches are obscured. The rhetorical similarities make it difficult to see the differences among approaches. Thus, an important task facing family literacy advocates is to get beyond labels, to look at program practices and implications to see which ideologies they exemplify.

I see three main tendencies within the current generation of U.S. family literacy programs: the intervention-prevention approach, the multiple-literacies approach, and the social-change approach. Briefly, the intervention-prevention model posits that America's literacy problems are rooted in undereducated parents' inability to promote positive literacy attitudes and interactions in the home. Proponents of this view advocate for programs aimed at changing parents' beliefs about literacy and literacy interactions with their children; they argue that intervention is necessary to ensure that patterns of undereducation will be prevented from passing from generation to generation. The multiple-literacies perspective defines the problem as a mismatch between culturally variable home literacy practices and school literacies; it sees the solution as investigating, validating, and extending students' multiple literacies and cultural resources. The social-change approach encompasses all the principles of the multiple-literacies tendency but goes beyond them, placing its emphasis on issues of power as well as culture. The central assumption here is that literacy problems often originate in a complex interaction of political, social, and economic factors in the broader society rather than in family inadequacies or differences between home and school; that is, the conditions created by institutional and structural forces shape access to literacy acquisition. Programs informed by this approach see literacy acquisition as a context for enhancing critical social awareness and challenging conditions or institutions that impede educational, social, or economic equity.

The intervention-prevention approach merits special attention because it informs so much of national family literacy policy and funding in the United States. Its most notable proponent is the National Center for Family Literacy (NCFL), which has taken a leading role in the national family literacy movement. In fact, the NCFL characterizes itself as "the catalyst and driving force behind the national family literacy movement" (NCFL undated brochure) and says that its model "has been adopted and adapted by hundreds of organizations across the United States and has come to define the family literacy movement for many in the field" (Potts and Paull 1995, p. 1). It claims that its model is the single most effective model of family literacy and has recently published program standards for evaluating and validating family literacy programs nationwide according to this model. It has shaped legislation that provides federal funding for family literacy programs across the United States. Because of the NCFL's strong claims and considerable influence, it is particularly important to look closely at its antideficit, profamily discourse.

Claim #1: The NCFL intervention-prevention model is antideficit.

The NCFL literature explicitly opposes deficit perspectives on family literacy and embraces what it calls a "wealth" or "strengths" model of family literacy. For example, NCFL authors state unequivocally, "We rejected the deficit model and developed a wealth model, which views the learner as capable and in possession of healthy traits and prior knowledge which establish a base for learning" (Potts and Paull 1995, p. 5). An NCFL monograph entitled *A Strengths Model for Learning in a Family Literacy Program* argues that all families have strengths that should be the basis for developing literacy skills to address their own needs and goals, stating, "A deficit model reinforces [parents'] fears; a strengths model honors their capabilities" (Potts 1992, p.3). Similarly, the NCFL's *Family Literacy Program Quality Self-Study* (1994) states that quality family literacy programs are characterized by participatory planning and curriculum development; they promote "critical and creative thinking" and "build upon strengths, empower families, incorporate goal setting, facilitate active learning, utilize whole language strategies, and celebrate diversity" (p. 4).

A problem arises, however, when one compares these statements with other NCFL publications. In a widely disseminated paper entitled *Family Literacy: The Need and the Promise* (1992), NCFL president Sharon Darling argues that the pervasive problems of undereducation and poverty in the United States are rooted in family life: "We cannot expect school reform alone to solve a problem which begins in the home" (p.1). She asserts that "excellence in public school education is an empty dream for youth who go home each afternoon to families where literacy is neither practiced nor valued" (p.1) and paints a bleak picture of the home life of children of poor, undereducated families: "At best their home environments provide neither the literacy tools nor the personal supports which might enable them to make up their skill deficits. Too often educational attainment is actively discouraged by family and friends" (p. 3). A *NCFL Newsletter* (March 1994) advocates using passages like the following to make sure the family literacy message is heard:

> The zinging sound snakes behind the bullet as it screams through the air, crashing past the pane of glass and finally slamming into the wall opposite the window. The students, startled at first, gather themselves quickly as someone gingerly peers outside to see what is going on. On any given day of their lives, this is no big thing, this sudden display of deadliness. Here, in this environment, being literate means being able to count to four. (p. 3)

The discourse surrounding this perspective is permeated with metaphors that suggest pathology; the most common is one of disease. One NCFL advocate, for example, describes the homes of low-income children this way:

> No one at home would read books, newspapers, or magazines. There were no library visits or books given as presents. No one even checked on whether the children had done their homework for school. I discovered an intergenerational disease—parents who passed illiteracy and poverty along to their children. (Mansbach 1993, p. 37)

The same author goes on to state, "We can cure the disease of illiteracy, but only if we dispense large doses of family literacy." Darling's own use of terms like *uproot, trapped,* and *break the cycle* suggest images of weeds and prisons; her descriptions of "at risk" and "disadvantaged" children and adults invoke stereotypes of cultural deprivation.

Literacy-impoverished conditions and attitudes in these homes are said to account not only for children's skills deficits, but for poverty itself. In describing teenage mothers, Darling says, "Trapped in the same environment which limited their childhood achievements, most of these young women never manage to pull themselves out of poverty" with the result that "a family heritage of undereducation often perpetuates a cycle of unemployment or underemployment." The ultimate victim, according to Darling, is the nation as a whole; she asks, "What does the American dream mean to these families? What stake do they have in the nation's future? How can we meet the challenges of a global economy with a work force handicapped by Third World–level skills?"(1992, p.3). In other words, not only the problems of children but the problems of the nation itself are rooted in parental inadequacies. Thus, where the traditional deficit model posits that educational problems are attributable to cognitive or cultural deficiencies of individuals or ethnic groups, NCFL literature locates the source of the economic, educational, and social problems facing the nation squarely in the home.

Clearly this discourse stands in stark contrast to that invoked by a "wealth" model; but beyond the contradictory messages, there are deeper substantive aspects of the NCFL model that bear questioning. First, its characterization of the homes of poor families as "literacy impoverished" has been widely challenged. A significant body of research has shown that rather than being literacy impoverished, the home environments of poor, undereducated minority children often are rich with literacy practices and artifacts, even though they may not be the same as those of mainstream families. Although beliefs about literacy and its payoffs vary, undereducated parents generally not only value literacy, but see it as the single most powerful hope for their children; even parents who themselves have limited literacy proficiency support their children's literacy acquisition in many ways. For example, in an article reviewing the literature about home environments conducive to literacy acquisition, Fitzgerald, Spiegel, and Cunningham (1991) found, "There is as much (or more) variation in home literacy patterns within selected socioeconomic levels and/or cultural/ethnic groups as among them" (p. 192). They found that both low- and high-literacy-level parents viewed literacy artifacts and events, in particular interacting with books, as important in the preschool years; the primary difference was that the not-as-literate parents "tend to value the importance of early literacy artifacts and events even more than parents with higher literacy levels" (p. 208). Similarly, an ethnographic study comparing literacy events in low- and middle-income families found that both groups promoted a wide range of activities and experiences (Baker et al. 1995). Interestingly, they found that "low-income parents reported more frequent literate activities undertaken for the purpose of learning literacy than did middle-income parents" (p. 12).

Recent studies also support findings that even parents who have little education and facility with English often contribute significantly to their children's literacy development. Caplan et al.'s 1992 study of the literacy practices in Indochinese refugee families, for example, emphasized the many ways that the parents did support their children despite poverty and lack of English literacy. Likewise, a study of the literacy activities and values of Mexican Americans (Ortiz 1992) also found that parents were very concerned with their children's academic achievement and spent a great deal of time reading and writing with their children. A study by Goldenberg and Gallimore (1991), which examined the relative importance of school- versus home-based factors in the literacy acquisition of Spanish-speaking children, found that although the school staff assumed that home academic support was unlikely, in reality parents wanted their children to do well in school and went to great lengths to help their children succeed academically. Taken together, these studies suggest that blanket assertions that poor homes are characterized by a disregard for the value of literacy and an absence of literacy practices are overgeneralizations that blatantly ignore research evidence.

Claim #2: Intervention is culturally sensitive.

A second problematic aspect of the intervention model relates to the notion of how family strengths are used. The NCFL monograph *A Strengths Model for Learning in a Family Literacy Program* (Potts 1992) contends that every family has "healthy traits," that the way these strengths are defined varies culturally, and that once they have been defined they can become a basis for subsequent change, leading ultimately to parent empowerment. I certainly see many of the features of this model as significant positive steps (for example, the emphasis on validating parents' experiences and beliefs, listening to and learning from families, acknowledging the culture specificity of family-strength norms, and involving participants in goal setting). At the same time, I am concerned that the model ignores research about cultural variability in discourse and literacy practices, attempts to change nonmainstream families to meet mainstream norms, and decontextualizes the problems families face.

This strengths model is informed by the family systems paradigm of clinical psychology, which posits that healthy families have certain core cross-cultural features. The NCFL monograph stresses that in order for lessons to be culturally relevant, students themselves must select the traits that they see as healthy and would like to develop further; it then lists a set of universal traits from which to choose in curriculum development, emphasizing that although no family has all the traits, the one trait that is critical is good communication (p. 6). According to the monograph, family members engage in healthy communication when "they listen attentively and actively to what other family members say, possibly summarizing the message, rephrasing it, or asking for clarification; they write notes to those in the household and letters to those in other places; they own and express feelings, both positive and negative" (p. 8). Additional characteristics include playing games and watching TV together (and discussing program content and applicable "lessons"). Teachers are urged to design action plans with activities and lessons corresponding to each trait; thus, for example, for the "time together" trait, Potts suggests basing lessons on favorite family-restaurant menus (McDonald's, Wendy's, Burger King), Little League brochures, scouting manuals, and TV guides.

The first problem with this model is that it does not take into account the cultural and contextual variability of literacy practices and discourse styles so extensively documented in ethnographic research. For example: expressing feelings openly may be entirely inappropriate in some cultures; writing notes to household members presupposes particular literacy practices and proficiency; summarizing and rephrasing messages is one narrowly culture-specific discourse style. Likewise: playing games across generations may be neither culturally familiar nor feasible (if parents work two jobs, for example); watching TV together presupposes that families have time to watch together. Clearly, McDonald's menus and scouting manuals are culture-specific material. Furthermore, many of the outcomes that the NCFL offers as proof of the "success" of its model are framed in terms of mainstream norms (standardized test scores, parental help with homework, parental involvement with school functions). Taken together, the various descriptors of healthy family traits may in fact be quite culture-specific, value-laden, and prescriptive, leading toward conformity to mainstream Anglo norms and expectations.

The second problem with this model is that its overt purpose and its covert agenda seem contradictory. On the one hand, Potts says that "the objectives of the [strengths] model are to create awareness of healthy family traits and to develop competencies to enhance those traits" (p. 1). Elsewhere, however, the NCFL says that its objective is "to break the intergenerational cycle of undereducation and poverty, one family at a time, by changing the 'messages' communicated in the home—messages related to the value of learning and the expectation of success" (NCFL 1994, p. 3). The underlying presupposition of this statement is that existing messages are flawed and must be changed. Further examination of the strengths model suggests that the purpose of identifying healthy traits may in fact be not so much to enhance them as to correct or modify flawed family interactions. For example, Potts says that enhanced self-awareness prompts parents to question how they are presently conducting their lives and to recognize their own responsibilities as parents. Once they have recognized the need to change their ways, the instructor selects materials for intervention and proceeds to focus on competencies for enhancing family "wellness," instruction in parenting skills, and behavior management techniques. The implicit message that these families need to be "treated" is reinforced by the medical terminology (*wellness, recovery, clinical, health*). Taken together with the NCFL's objective of changing the messages communicated in the home, the underlying purpose of identifying strengths appears to be a pretext for intervening in the internal workings of family life to change behavior.

Again, we need to ask: Who gets to decide what "good parenting" entails? Are there universals of good parenting? Do middle-class academic "experts" know better than low-income African American parents or Cambodian refugee parents how they should raise their children to deal with the challenges of economic survival, racism, or cultural transition? Any program that aims to change values, beliefs, messages, or behavior raises enormous ethical questions; at a minimum, we need to proceed with caution and humility (rather than claiming to know what is best for others).

Claim #3: Family literacy intervention is a solution to personal and national economic problems.

The notion that literacy is the way out of individual poverty and, further, that the family literacy movement will lead to a more prosperous nation, able to meet the challenges of the next century, is another concern. The argument that literacy training will lead to employment and economic advancement disregards macroeconomic factors like recession and unemployment patterns, social factors like job discrimination, and the actual dynamics of hiring and job retention. Census statistics, for example, indicate that race and gender override education as determinants of income and job status (white males with high school diplomas have higher mean incomes than African American males with college degrees or women of any race with graduate degrees). Ethnographic research on the relationship between literacy training and job retention suggests that literacy skills per se may not be the critical factor. A study by Hull (1991), for example, showed that welfare mothers who received job-related literacy training were often forced out of jobs by low wages, hours that conflicted with family responsibilities, intolerable working conditions, and demeaning treatment by their bosses.

I am concerned about any model or rationale that justifies putting responsibility for broad social problems on family shoulders and implies that national economic problems are rooted in family problems. This focus on the unit of the family as the locus of change excludes consideration of social, economic, or institutional forces that may constrain family life and impede literacy development. Even the notion of empowerment in the intervention model is framed in personal, individual terms: power means the ability to transform one's own life through individual effort based on self-esteem and skills; a sense of self-worth will lead to a sense of responsibility; this in turn will lead to making a better life for one's family—a psychological version of pulling oneself up by the bootstraps. Taken to its logical extreme, this argument suggests that if parents change their ways of relating to their children, problems of education, poverty, unemployment, violence, crime, drug abuse, and teen pregnancy will be resolved. The flip side of this argument is that social problems can be attributed to the failures of the family; given demographics and patterns of childrearing, this analysis, in its most simplistic version, could be said to imply that, once again, mothers are to blame (this time for the problems of the nation)! I don't think that it's an accident that funding for family literacy programming premised on this interventionist ideology is one of the few kinds of literacy funding that has not been cut by the current "family values" U.S. legislature. Putting the onus of responsibility for social problems on family shoulders fits clearly into the dominant conservative ideology.

Claim #4: There is one best family literacy model.

The NCFL contends that the most effective family literacy programs are those that are center-based, intensive, and comprise four components: adult literacy for parents, early childhood education for children, a parent education and support group, and parent-child interaction time. In accordance with this model, the NCFL has established program standards by which other programs will be evaluated and validated.

There is nothing wrong with this model as one structural alternative among many; the problem is rather that it is framed as the single best model that all others should strive to emulate. One of the points on which most family literacy researchers agree is that program structures should be context-specific and responsive to the populations they serve and that no single model fits all situations. At a minimum, it is clear that a model that requires an early childhood component is inappropriate for families of older children. Beyond this, having a single model and being responsive to participants are potentially conflicting mandates; some researchers argue that programs focusing on parents' needs and interests independent of their parenting roles can be highly effective. California's Family English Literacy Project (FELP), for example, has implemented a range of models that vary in program structure (parent-focused, intergenerational, and learner-focused), language of instruction (English and native language), and setting (school-based, community-based, and home-based). Clearly, there is no consensus in the field that center-based, four-component models involving both parents and children are superior.

In addition to not being ideal, in many cases the comprehensive model may not be realistic. For many low-budget, small-scale community initiatives (in churches, adult education centers, preschools, etc.), a four-component program is financially and logistically impossible. Nevertheless, it is often precisely in these programs that are struggling to survive where innovative and effective family literacy practices originate. Declaring one model as the most effective may be a way of privileging those who promote that model and disqualifying those who don't (which, of course, has direct consequences for funding). Rather than promote a particular structural configuration as most effective, we need to be as inclusive as possible.

The NCFL quality standards are open to question as well, in terms of both what they include and what they omit. The primary problem here is that the NCFL has represented its particular program qualities as universal uncontested norms. While many of its quality indicators are supported by research (uses learners' prior knowledge and experience, has relevant content), others are widely disputed. For example, in advocating standardized testing as a primary assessment tool, the NCFL completely disregards state-of-the-art research in adult education, which questions the appropriateness of such tests; likewise, proposing equal time for group and individual study is by no means a commonly accepted practice.

Omissions from the list of quality indicators are equally telling. One critical programming area that the quality standards omit entirely is control and governance. Despite repeated talk of empowerment, there are no standards to suggest, for example, that teachers be familiar with the learners' communities, that learners have decision-making roles in program governance, that participant advocacy be supported, or that the learners' communities be somehow represented in an advisory capacity. Also omitted is any discussion of language choice or cultural maintenance. Once again, the danger is that the standards will be used prescriptively, to determine which programs should be funded or how they should be implemented, as a tool for privileging those that support the model and excluding those who don't.

Claim #5: There is a single prime mover in the U.S. family literacy movement.

In describing itself as "the primary source of information, training, and support for the family literacy movement" and "the first comprehensive response to the cycle of undereducation in this country" (NCFL 1994 flyer), the NCFL is attempting to position itself as the leading force not only in the family literacy movement, but in the broader educational reform movement in the United States. There is certainly no consensus among family literacy scholars or practitioners about the NCFL's status or its right to speak for the movement as a whole, as the principles and articles in this volume indicate.

I have no doubt that the NCFL has affected many families lives for the better; any program that opens possibilities that were previously unavailable is important. My aim is not to detract from this good work but rather to question what I see as overblown claims both for family literacy in general and for one model in particular.

The NCFL is quite explicit about its goal of shaping public opinion and public policy. It has orchestrated a sophisticated campaign of marketing family literacy that includes tailoring its message to particular audiences, from policy makers and funders to academics and the general public. Recently, it teamed up with Turner Network News to launch a media campaign marketing the concept of family literacy via a national family literacy day featuring a *Dr. Seuss* production. In its promotional literature for this day, it portrayed family literacy as "a movement that addresses the need of millions of undereducated families across the United States who are trapped in a cycle of poverty, dependency and undereducation" and urged every family to spend ten minutes reading together on that day. Family literacy has become a product to be packaged, marketed, and sold as a panacea for family and national problems.

Of course, this package is being sold not just to the general public but to legislators and policy makers as well. For them, the NCFL emphasizes those aspects of the message that are most in tune with the dominant political climate: "The message to policy makers and legislators, then, is that family literacy can reduce the number of people on government assistance and increase the number of productive citizens" (*NCFL Newsletter* 1994, p. 1). This version of the message is appealing to politicians: it promises to solve problems that even school reform has been unable to solve; it promises to strengthen families in a time when the "family values" solution to national problems is on the rise; it promises to reduce welfare dependency and to make children's literacy the responsibility of parents; it promises to create a more literate work force to meet the challenges of the twenty-first century.

Clearly, no single educational reform can do all this. Further, this message runs the risk of undermining efforts at school reform, potentially pitting support for public schools and adult education against support for family literacy. Even Start (largely based on the NCFL model) was among the few programs that did not suffer significantly in the recent round of government cuts to adult education programming. Certainly, the NCFL would argue that there is nothing wrong with telling legislators and funders what they want to hear if this results in funding for programs that help families, but this raises questions for the field as a whole: Do we want to support a message that plays into a particular political agenda because it secures funding? How do we shape that message to reflect the broad understanding of families, practitioners, and researchers?

Conclusion

The current movement is rich with a range of models and programs; on the surface, many of these programs appear to embrace similar goals. As we enter the second half of the 1990s, the challenge is to see beyond the surface: the danger is that the common rhetoric of "building on family strengths" will mask deficit agendas in order to gain legitimacy in a climate where deficit ideology has been widely discredited. To the extent that this is the case, intervention programs may be dangerous not despite their strengths rhetoric but because of it. By questioning the discourse that surrounds us, we will come closer to shaping a family literacy movement that is a true departure from deficit perspectives.

References

AUERBACH, E. 1989. "Toward a Social-Contextual Approach to Family Literacy." *Harvard Educational Review* 59(2):165–81.

AUERBACH, E. 1993. "Re-examining English-Only in the ESL Classroom." *TESOL Quarterly* 27(1):9–32.

AUERBACH, E. 1995. "Critical Issues: Deconstructing the Discussion of Strengths in Family Literacy." *Journal of Reading Behavior* 27(4).

BAKER, L., R. SERPELL, and S. SONNENSCHEIN. 1995. "Opportunities for Literacy Learning in the Homes of Urban Preschoolers." In L. Morrow (Ed.), *Family Literacy: Multiple Perspectives*. Newark, NJ: IRA.

CAPLAN, N., M. CHOY, and J. WHITMORE. 1992. "Indochinese Refugee Families and Academic Achievement." *Scientific American* 266(2):36–42.

DARLING, S. 1992. *Family Literacy: The Need and the Promise*. Louisville, KY: National Center for Family Literacy.

FITZGERALD, J., D. SPIEGEL, and J. CUNNINGHAM. 1991. "The Relationship Between Parental Literacy Level and Perceptions of Emergent Literacy." *Journal of Reading Behavior* 23(2):191–213.

GOLDENBERG, C., and R. GALLIMORE. 1991. "Local Knowledge, Research Knowledge, and Educational Change: A Case Study of Early Spanish Reading Improvement." *Educational Researcher* 20(8):2–14.

HULL, G. 1991. "Examining the Relations of Literacy to Vocational Education and Work: An Ethnography of a Vocational Program in Banking and Finance." Report to the National Center for Research in Vocational Education. Berkeley, CA: University of California.

MANSBACH, S. C. 1993. "We Must Put Family Literacy on the National Agenda. *Reading Today*, February/March, 137.

National Center for Family Literacy Newsletter 6(1) (March 1994).

National Center for Family Literacy. 1994. *Family Literacy Program Quality Self-Study*. Louisville, KY: National Center for Family Literacy.

ORTIZ, R. 1992. "The Unpackaging of Generation and Social Class Factors: A Study on Literacy Activities and Education Values of Mexican American Fathers." Doctoral dissertation, UCLA.

POTTS, M. 1992. "A Strengths Model for Learning in a Family Literacy Program." Louisville, KY: National Center for Family Literacy.

POTTS, M., and S. PAULL. 1995. *A Comprehensive Approach to a Family Literacy Program*. Louisville, KY: National Center for Family Literacy.

TAYLOR, D. 1983. *Family Literacy: Young Children Learning to Read and Write*. Portsmouth, NH: Heinemann.

□ □ □ □ □

You may see someone who is going to do a research project on a local housing estate in Brighton who says, I am going to look at the causes of illiteracy and how it is connected with cultural deprivation, poor motherhood (that's one of the classical ones) and inadequate working-class cultural norms and values. For them to suggest that this is also a neutral approach to the study, that this is purely a scientific effort, completely disguises the ideological force of what they are saying there about the relationship between working-class life and the professional middle-class world they are coming from. And that of course applies to the kind of culture and imperialism that is involved in a great many of the world's literacy development projects. In fact I would hazard the explanation that the reason for the failure of most of the literacy programmes that have been put forward in the last twenty years, particularly some of the early ones, but they are still failing, is the lack of this understanding. That imparting literacy to others involves ideological contexts over meaning and power and is not simply a neutral giving to people the basics for them to do what they want with.

—Brian Street

□ □ □ □ □

 ### Community Development Block Grant
Federal Year 1994 Application

Describe the impact of the project. What will the project accomplish relative to the stated need?

A. *Parents will have an increased awareness of age-appropriate capabilities of their children.*
B. *Parents will be able to communicate more effectively with their children.*
C. *Parents will view their school as a community resource and will become involved in their children's learning processes at an early age.*
D. *Parents and children will develop and strengthen loving bonds.*
E. *Children will increase their self-esteem and positive self-concept.*
F. *Families will develop informal, community-based support systems.*
G. *Parents and children will create "happy memories" together.*
H. *Children will enter elementary school already comfortable with and cognizant of the school's important role in their lives.*

The project was funded.

□ □ □ □ □

I think about all of the meetings I've attended over the past fifteen years and I want to scream, but what has allowed the dichotomy between Request for Proposals and what really happens in literacy programs to continue is our giving in to "taking what we can from what they offer us." Compliance. I believe that funding issues are what have left me powerless in this state—for I have not been silent nor compliant. But I have often been alone or at least jobless and at this point unable to find steady work.

—Lindy Whiton

□ □ □ □ □

The desire for funding requires negotiations between those who want and those who have money. Obviously, these negotiations do not take place among equals. One group has their hats in their hands, so to speak, and the other not only has the power to fill those hats but the authority to name the problems, to persuade others to modify their ideas, and to enable particular actions.

—Patrick Shannon

□ □ □ □ □

Where the Power Lies: The Colorado Experience
ELAINE DeLOTT BAKER

During my years as an adult educator and family literacy practitioner, I was intrigued by the fact that adults with similar demographic and educational profiles were more successful (as measured by retention and outcomes) in family literacy programs than in adult education programs with no family component. Why was this so? The most obvious reason was children's power to motivate their parents. When I looked at the effort mothers invested in bringing their kids to school with them and at the effort they put into their own studies, I understood the central role played by their determination to give their children "a better life."

Discovering this didn't require great insight. This is what mothers told us, over and over. They were doing this for their kids, and for their kids' futures. We offered parents an opportunity to do something for themselves and their children, something they believed would help their children become more successful in life. In response, they gave us their participation and their trust. Family literacy tapped into the power that connects generations, the power that comes from the dedication of one generation toward the next, and the renewing quality of hope that accompanies this connection.

The heart of family literacy is parent/child interactions around learning, but there are multiple contexts that support these interactions: parents and children getting ready to go to school together, dressing and eating breakfast, riding the bus; a mother reading to a child sitting on her lap, centered on that child and on that moment; a parent dropping off a child for class and then returning to that class later in the day to work on a "literacy" activity. At school or at home, these events form a succession of interactions in the day-to-day flow of time.

Most practitioners, however, would point to elements in addition to parental love and parent/child interactions in their assessment of the dynamics of family literacy. Another key variable is the social context in which learning occurs. Lave and Wenger (1991) describe one such context as a "community of practice," a learning situation in which the members of a group learn new roles and negotiate new identities through their participation in group activity. In Lave and Wenger's community of practice, the learning curriculum is "a field of learning resources in everyday practice viewed from the perspective of learners." The community of practice implies "participation in an activity system about which participants share understandings concerning what they are doing and what that means for their lives and for their communities" (p.98).

Applying the community-of-practice concept to family literacy helped me focus on the importance of parents coming together to identify problems, share resources, and renegotiate their identity as parents in a confusing social world; of their being given the space, time, and professional support to create a community of practice around their commitment to family learning. Whether related to issues of parenting or to issues of skills mastery, it was the participants who helped formulate the agenda of what was to be learned. For parents who were not adequately prepared for their parental roles or who were faced with renegotiating the meaning of being a parent in a society unlike the one in which they were raised, family literacy offered an opportunity to create a community of practice. "This is what parents do, this is what we do; this is how they act, this is how we act; this is how they guide their children, this is how we guide our children." New roles and attitudes emerged from the collective experiences of participants.

One of the most significant implications of viewing family literacy as a community of practice has to do with program design. If the strength of family literacy is related to its operation as a community of practice, then its strength is also related to its ability to create a true "learning curriculum," one that reflects the concerns of learners. It is this learning curriculum that helps parents develop into full participants in a community of practice centered on family learning. From this perspective, program design is not only rooted in community; it is constantly negotiated within that community. In contrast, a program designed and directed from an external source is the antithesis of a learning community's organizing principles and strength.

In Colorado, in the late eighties and early nineties, a number of family literacy programs had begun to develop individualized learning curricula. Financial support for these efforts was modest, coming largely from demonstration grants and foundation funding. Still, several programs were attempting to adapt their program designs and curricula to the characteristics of their learners. Student response was strong; public interest in family-based programming was strong.

A succession of events followed very quickly during this pivotal period. The Colorado Department of Education, aware that family literacy was emerging as a new pool of federal money and a new focus of federal interest, moved rapidly to survey what had been up until then a series of local efforts. Individuals with no prior experience in family literacy were asked to learn about the field and to connect it to the existing infrastructure. In the state adult education office, the homeless coordinator was designated the family literacy/homeless coordinator. On another floor of the state building, jurisdiction for family literacy went to the Title I administrator. The Adult Literacy Commission named a family literacy subcommittee to define family literacy, to survey its programs, and to make recommendations. An educational consultant, commissioned by the adult education office, was asked to draft a report on statewide family literacy efforts, and a halftime family resource teacher was named.

In 1993, the Toyota family literacy effort (administered by NCFL) chose Denver as one of their expansion sites. In a climate of national interest and shrinking educational resources, this new funding source was seen as an exciting opportunity to expand services to families. The Denver program involved three sites, one of which was the program I had worked with as director of a Barbara Bush Foundation for Family Literacy grant. For the agency where I worked, it was a victory in the battle to keep afloat financially, as well as a victory in the battle for prestige. Toyota designation meant money, a blue-ribbon advisory panel, meetings at the governor's mansion, and higher visibility in the education and foundation communities. It also meant replacing the local program design and curriculum with the Keenan model, the model championed by NCFL, a model whose structure dictated a full-day curriculum with clearly designated segments for literacy instruction for children and adults, time for parent-children interaction, parent discussion time, and time for parents to volunteer in their children's schools. Last, it meant out-of-state training in the implementation of the model and nationally defined accountability.

The program underwent significant changes as it adapted to the Toyota designation (I left the agency before the Toyota program was in place, but kept abreast of its progress through colleagues). Prior to the Toyota grant, the program ran four mornings a week, from nine to noon. Under Toyota, this changed to three full days a week, to accommodate NCFL's emphasis on parents' volunteering in their children's schools during the afternoon. The full-day program, which had evolved as a solution to the transportation requirements of rural Kentucky, where the Keenan model was developed, was problematic for our African American and Hispanic urban student body. Schools were not a friendly environment for these students. Most of them had dropped out of school in the not-so-distant past, and their own negative experiences, often laced with self-condemnation, weighed heavily. In addition, no mechanisms were put in place to help students approach the experience in a different way. Parents began to skip the school volunteer requirement. Attendance was down; morale was low. Instead of a full roster and a long waiting list, the program struggled to "make its numbers." Afternoon internships at local work sites were offered as an alternative to school volunteer time, but there were not enough of them, nor were these sites always able to provide parents with support and supervision.

The afternoon segment of the full-day program wasn't working, but there was little room for flexibility. The full day was a keystone of the NCFL design. Where the Barbara Bush Foundation for Family Literacy initiative had allowed local programs to design their own curriculum as defined through grant objectives, there was no such flexibility in the NCFL model. What remained was a committed staff, beleaguered with paperwork, left to figure out how to juggle their understanding of program effectiveness with the demands of the new orthodoxy.

The NCFL model, backed by program dollars and a strong national presence, quickly became the dominant model in the state. In a period of two years, several of the older grass-roots programs found themselves struggling to find support. Programs were given the implicit message that future funding would be tied to their approximation of the NCFL model, already a feature of the Even Start selection process. The state echoed the NCFL sentiment that if you weren't running a program that followed the NCFL definition of family literacy, then you couldn't call what you were doing family literacy. You could claim to be an "intergenerational program," but not a "family literacy" program. It was as if family literacy had been trademarked.

As professionals, it is important for us to keep sight of the real nature of family literacy and "where the power lies." Family literacy is not simply "one-stop shopping" for families, nor does it imply a single model of program delivery. Family literacy is a complex of relationships that center around learning: the relationship of parents and children, of staff and families, of families and communities, of individuals and institutions of learning, and of institutions of learning and the larger society. If we, as professionals, can provide the contexts in which these relationships can flourish, and can work together with families within these contexts to create meaningful learning curricula, then we will have established the groundwork for families' explorations into the ways in which literacy can enhance their lives. In our own learning as professionals, the ability to sustain the creative promise of family literacy may depend on our honest and careful assessment not of family "outcomes" as measured by national standards but of our will, commitment, and skill in serving as resources to families and communities in ways that acknowledge and enhance their strengths.

Reference

LAVE, J., and E. WENGER. 1991. *Situated Learning: Legitimate Peripheral Participation*. Cambridge, UK: Cambridge University Press

❑ ❑ ❑ ❑ ❑

Reconstructing Teacher Views on Parent Involvement in Children's Literacy

TREVOR H. CAIRNEY AND JENNY RUGE

Children move in and out of multiple worlds. They sometimes use different languages, they vary their discourse from one context to another, and they learn to use a variety of literacy practices as they relate to other people. And yet, curriculum in schools often seems to reflect an implicit belief that all learners are the same and need to be supported in the same way.

Teacher assumptions about the role of families in students' education are often impoverished and based on limited perceptions of the vital role that families play in children's education. We need constantly to reread our knowledge of the family backgrounds of our students. We need to reexamine our assumptions about our students in the light of a better understanding of students' multiple worlds.

The dangers inherent in our assumptions, the difficulties in interpreting what we witness, and the benefits to be gained from putting preconceived notions aside are clearly illustrated in the educational experiences of Jan Robinson and her family. Jan is an Aboriginal who grew up in a small town in northwestern New South Wales, Australia. She is raising her two children, Joshua (twelve) and Tina (eleven), as a single parent who can "read a little, but not write at all." Apart from a sister who she sees only occasionally, Jan has no other close family. As Jan expresses it, "It's just us three. It's really always been just us three."

Jan's situation is unusual for an Aboriginal because her culture places such high value on kinship. But Jan has distanced herself from her extended family because she cannot accept some of the common cultural practices of her people. Nevertheless, she maintains her strong sense of Aboriginal identity and seeks to actively introduce her children to Aboriginal culture.

Tina Robinson is in her last year of primary school (grade 6). Her level of school achievement is well below that of her classmates, and she struggles with almost all school tasks. Her difficulties are not considered surprising, considering her home background.

We interviewed Jan and her children, teachers from Tina and Joshua's school, and staff from a family learning centre that Jan and the children attend. We also observed Tina as she engaged in literacy activities in class, at the learning centre, and with her mother. This triad of contexts and informants is important. Jan as a mother is keen to see her children succeed at school and have greater life chances than her own. The children's school is committed to providing quality education for its students and sees parents as having an important role to play in this education. The learning centre is an innovative attempt to bridge school and community, a place where children are supported and parents are involved as coworkers and where support is given to them as well as to their children.

As our study proceeded it became apparent that there are important differences between the views of the staff in the school and the staff in the learning centre. The teachers in the school are constantly looking for ways to support parents in promoting a school-based learning agenda. Their strategies rely on finding ways to get parents to help in the classroom or to support school literacy at home. On the other hand, the family learning centre is attempting to look for common ground between home and school and to support children and parents through a variety of community-based programs.

While it is easy to criticise the school for its limited views on parent involvement in children's learning and for its failure to build on the cultural resources of families and communities, it is working within its own limited understanding of the role of schooling and its relationship to the cultures of those it serves. And teachers' misperceptions of students and families are reinforced when they misread the data that their limited contacts with parents provide. Our interviews with Tina's teachers revealed the following basic assumptions about Tina, her family, and her educational experiences:

Tina shows little interest in learning.

Tina probably had limited early literacy experiences at home.

There is little or no support of school learning in Tina's home.

Tina's mother is illiterate and therefore cannot help Tina with literacy-related activities at home

Tina and her family don't value learning.

But as we talked with Jan ourselves, and as we observed the involvement of Jan and her children in the family learning centre, we saw a different picture.

Rebutting the Assumptions

Assumption 1: Tina shows little interest in learning.

In class, Tina achieves very little. She is slow to begin working and often doesn't even attempt set tasks. She fails to copy assignments from the chalkboard and rarely hands in projects or other work required to be done at home.

Out of school, the picture is quite different. Three afternoons each week, Tina walks one kilometre from her school to the family learning centre. Once there, she spends an hour engaged in a variety of literacy and learning activities. She reads, writes, practises spelling, and completes maths and reading comprehension worksheets. Sometimes, she reads to the younger children, or listens to them read. When she has a project to complete for school, she visits the public library across the road from the learning centre. She uses the computer catalogue to find the books she needs, then returns to the centre where one of the tutors helps her read the books and complete her project.

Tina's engagement with literacy in her out-of-school experiences belies any assumption that she lacks interest in learning. While she often complains about the tasks set for her by the tutor at the learning centre, her mother explains, "She has a little whine, but she doesn't really mind it. And they know her now, so they don't take any notice of her whining—they just go along with her." This view is reinforced by the following observation of Tina working with her tutor, Margaret. Margaret and Tina are sitting side by side at a large table. Margaret takes out a set of six pictures.

M: Have a look at these pictures.
T: Not this again!
Margaret offers mock sympathy, then asks Tina to arrange the pictures in order.
T: Do you know what order they should be?
M: Yes, I do.
Tina arranges the pictures; then, at Margaret's request, she explains what is happening in each picture. Together, they discuss possible alternatives.
M: Now I want you to write a story. One sentence for each picture.
Tina begins to moan and asks if she can do the task at home. Margaret insists that she do it now, and cajoles her to begin.
M: Remember to write complete sentences.
T: For all of them?
M: That's only 1, 2, 3, 4, 5, 6 sentences. You can do that!
Tina does so in the next ten minutes.

Although the task set by Margaret might be considered a typical school literacy task, the manner in which she interacts with Tina is quite different from the interactions between Tina and her classroom teacher. At school, little attention is given to Tina's failure to complete work, and few efforts are made to structure tasks in ways that would enable her to work independently. During one whole day's observation at school, Tina wrote nothing; at the family learning centre, she produced a paragraph in ten minutes.

Assumption 2: Tina probably had limited early literacy experiences at home.

At school, Tina struggles with reading. When asked to read aloud, she lowers her head and stumbles over words until her teacher prompts her to "sound it out." Her classmates sometimes laugh or simply stop listening.

At home, Tina likes to read by herself. Her favourite books are the Baby Sitters Club and Goosebumps series. When she was young, Tina read story-books with her mother. In Tina's home there are constant interactions and rich experiences based on strong relationships of love and trust. What Tina's teachers would probably find surprising is the extent to which Jan supports her children's school learning:

> Well, we sit down in the afternoon, and if they've got homework I always sit there and try to help them, but it's frustrating 'cause I don't know. Or we go out together. We might go to the movies, I take them swimming. . . . We do things together. We sit down for a meal together.

While Jan doesn't read much, there are magazines and some books in the home, and they are read. Basic written tasks include writing checks, filling in forms, and writing notes.

Much literacy is also associated with the family learning centre. Tina began attending weekly lessons at the centre when she was six. Jan regularly attended sessions with her and learned "how to go through the work with the kids at home, and what to do with them." Jan was then able to support the children: "We used to sit at the table with the kids on each side of me, and I'd help them." As the children grew older, the practice of sitting together to complete homework continued, even though it became increasingly difficult for Jan to offer any real help. While Tina's teachers believed that she had limited literacy experiences, at home she engaged in a variety of rich literacy practices that matched her everyday needs.

Assumption 3: There is little or no support of school learning in Tina's home.

Tina's teacher believes that lack of parental support contributes to a student's educational disadvantage:

> The children who have no support at home for one reason or another, they have no idea of what they have to actually do to succeed in the future. Their expectations are so much lower of what they have to do. They don't take responsibility—you set them an assignment and they don't do it. Mum and Dad don't care, whereas the children whose parents are more supportive at home tend to do it, and that's the big difference.

Jan tries to monitor her children's homework, but it isn't always easy to do. Jan assumes that if the children are not completing their work, the school will contact her. She also assumes that merit certificates will not be awarded to Josh if he does not complete his work. Yet, both of these assumptions may be false. Josh was consistently failing to complete his homework, but his school made no attempt to contact Jan about the problem. It was only when one of the tutors from the family learning centre requested an interview with one of Josh's teachers that the situation became apparent. Jan explained:

> We had a meeting with one of the teachers up at the school and she told me that he gets homework, but it's [difficult] getting Joshua to do it. . . . Well, I've heard nothing about it. They haven't told me anything really. We wouldn't have known anything except that we went and saw one of the teachers up there, and she just told us. . . . But he must be doing all right because he brought a couple of merit certificates home, one for maths and something else the other day. So he must be doing his homework somewhere along the line.

Jan sees monitoring homework as a two-way process between home and school. If the school gives no indication that there is a problem, and in fact, by awarding merit certificates to Josh, reinforces Jan's belief that no problem exists, then it is difficult to argue that Jan's stance in the matter of homework constitutes lack of support. Yet, that is how it is perceived by the school.

What was obvious from our work was that Jan gave her children enormous support. While this support may not have been in the form that Tina's teacher imagined was ideal, it involved many hours each week and up to five afternoon sessions each week at the family learning centre.

Assumption 4: Tina's mother is illiterate and therefore cannot help Tina with literacy-related activities at home.

Jan Robinson sees herself as lacking basic literacy skills. Contrary to her perception of herself and that of others, Jan engages in a wide range of literacy practices. She is responsible for record keeping associated with the homework centre for Aboriginal and Torres Strait Islander children, where she is the coordinator, and she also assists these children with their homework when needed. She reads popular magazines, fills in forms (with some assistance), and often helps children at the family learning centre by reading to them and hearing them read.

When we first met the Robinson family, Jan had decided to try to obtain a driver's licence. She had arranged for an adult literacy tutor to help her once a week for six weeks. By the end of the first session, Jan had telephoned the Motor Registry to find out what she needed to do, had gone to the Registry to complete the appropriate forms and collect the *Road Rule Handbook*, and had taken a "trial run" of the necessary computer-based knowledge test.

Tina was at the family learning centre when her mother arrived with the newly acquired *Road Rule Handbook*. Both Tina and Josh were enthusiastic about the possibility of Jan's obtaining a driver's licence, even though the family did not own a car. Jan and Tina set to work together to find the answers to the sample questions provided by the Motor Registry. Jan read aloud each question as Tina searched for the appropriate page in the handbook. By suggesting possible headings, and guiding Tina's use of the index, Jan supported Tina's efforts to locate the required information. Tina then read aloud from the handbook and together they considered alternative answers to each question. When Tina hesitated at unknown words, Jan waited patiently, only intervening when Tina asked for help. At times, several alternative answers seemed plausible, so together they reread the questions and the handbook until they had agreed on a solution. This interaction was a powerful example of the ways that mother and daughter supported each other's attempts to use written language for personally meaningful purposes.

Assumption 5: Tina and her family don't value learning.

While Tina's teacher may have formed the impression that her family did not value learning, this was inaccurate. Far from failing to recognise the importance of learning, Jan's own difficulties with literacy have prompted her to value learning highly. When asked about her reaction to the initial suggestion that her children needed extra help to develop their literacy skills, Jan replied:

> I just said, "Well, if they need help, I'll do it." So I went to the centre because I know what it's like not to, you know, do anything, not to read. So I agreed [to take them].

The value Jan places on learning, and literacy in particular, is also reflected in her commitment to her own literacy education. Despite economic hardship and serious health difficulties, Jan has succeeded in completing two basic literacy courses provide by the family learning centre over the past two years. She is also committed to continuing to provide additional literacy support for the children and tries to encourage the children to share her enthusiasm for learning.

> I've told them that next year I can get an Aboriginal tutor, you know, someone to tutor them at home. I'm going to try to get them for two days a week. Josh said, "I don't want to do it!" but I said, "The only way you're gonna learn is to get someone in." I've already spoken to the Aboriginal Field Officer and he said I can get one in for them. . . . [Josh] isn't very happy about it—he says he's doing okay at school now—but I said it couldn't hurt to have someone to help and he said, "Okay, if you want it, we'll do it."

Jan's educational aspirations for her children are influenced by what she sees as their academic potential. In her eyes, educational success is determined to a large extent by the child's innate ability to learn, something that she believes cannot be predetermined or changed. "I hope that they get a good education, but it's just in them. I can't push them yet, 'cause I don't know how they're going to turn out." Jan believes that her job now is to "try to get them through school, try to get them a good education."

What the Inaccuracy of These Assumptions Tells Us

Given the broader view of Tina's educational experiences, it would be easy to blame the school for her lack of school success. Yet, it's not as simple as that. The school Tina attends has made significant efforts over the past few years to develop closer ties between families and the school. Tina's mother reports that she has a good relationship with Tina's teacher, whom she finds approachable and helpful. The school uses a number of avenues for keeping parents informed about school issues, including a weekly newsletter, parent committees, and notice boards strategically placed around the school. A meet-the-teacher session at the beginning of the school year is used as a forum for providing parents with advice on supporting their child's learning at home. Two written reports and one parent-teacher interview each year are intended to keep parents informed about their child's educational progress. A large number of parents help in the classroom in the early grades, but this involvement decreases in the upper grades, leaving teachers thinking that parents aren't, or don't want to be, involved in their children's learning. But the continuing desire of parents to be involved in their children's learning and to help them with schoolwork at home was clear in their response to a parent education program: when the school offered the *Talk to a Literacy Learner* (Cairney and Munsie 1992) program, the response was so enthusiastic the program was run twice.

It is clear that the teachers at Tina's school see the importance of families to students' success at school. Tina's grade-six teacher believes that success in literacy is crucial to academic success:

> If a child is not literate to the extent of being able to comprehend—not just reading, to me reading is just one of the by-products of literacy—if they can't communicate things orally or in writing then they're gone. . . . They still have to do other things and numeracy is still extremely important, but I think nothing functions if the child is not literate.

But like many other teachers, he believes that children who come from backgrounds that do not reflect middle-class culture and values are somehow deficient and that this assumed deficit causes their educational disadvantage:

It's getting more frequent that we are getting the children of parents who didn't enjoy school, didn't succeed at school, and have no real parenting skills. There is no reading at home, the parents don't read. There is no expectation of routine. There is no expectation of responsibility. I'm not [criticising] them—it's because that is what they grew up with. You get parents who come up saying, "I hated school," and that is what they are thinking, and so you get a lot of parents here who really put the teachers down. [They say,] "You don't have to do what he says!" and things like that. . . . So I really think that culture of appreciating what you get out of school and the institution that school represents and what it can do for you, that is just being eroded.

This case study shows that there are multiple perspectives possible regarding Jan and her children's experiences with schooling and the steps that are necessary to help Tina succeed in school. On the one hand, the school recognises the importance of parents and sees that some children find school difficult because of differences in family cultural practices—differences they see as being potentially removed by offering parents new skills and strategies. On the other hand, Jan as a parent sees that there are things that she needs to know and do to help her children. She isn't sure where to gain this knowledge, but she wants to obtain it.

The family learning centre offers a means to build more effective links between home and school and to work against narrow definitions of parent involvement. The staff members support parents and families in a variety of ways. The programs they offer do not seek simply to change parents but to offer families support as they take control of their own worlds.

A recurring theme in the recent literature is that parents must be viewed as equal partners, and that there must be a reciprocal relationship. It has been argued that we need to go beyond token involvement and recognise the vital role that parents play in education (Cairney and Munsie 1995a; 1995b). Parental involvement in literacy learning has much greater value than simply as an aid to what teachers do. Harry (1992) argues that parent initiatives must forge collaborative relationships that create mutual understanding between parents and teachers—a "posture of reciprocity"—and that are associated with a shift from the school to parents and the community. This requires agreeing on activities, their goals, and plans for reaching these goals. It may also require deliberately shifting the site for many of these initiatives from the school to the community. The experiences of Jan and her family indicate the potential that nonschool-based initiatives have for supporting families. At the same time, if teachers' attitudes toward parents are to change, school-based initiatives will be needed. Parents, teachers, and educators recognise that school-based initiatives offer access to specific literacy practices that help students and parents cope with school literacy and learning and that at the same time can offer the potential for new partnerships to develop.

Obviously, bringing parents and teachers together in any initiative has the potential to develop new understanding by each party of the other's specific cultural practices. Such mutual understanding offers the potential for schooling to be adjusted to meet the needs of families. As well, it offers parents the opportunity to observe and understand the literacy of schooling, a literacy that ultimately empowers individuals to take their place in society.

The great strength of the work of the family learning centre that Jan and her children attend is that the staff attempts to recognise and build on families' strengths. They create opportunities for families to use their skills for meaningful purposes and encourage greater emphasis on literacy in the home. They support, encourage, cajole when necessary, and hold families accountable for their own learning.

The family learning centre has had an enormous impact on Jan and her family. Jan believes that without the centre, her children's educational difficulties would be even greater: "If I wasn't going to [the centre], the kids wouldn't have got anywhere with anything. They would've grown up without learning." The support provided by the centre and the attitudes of staff members are crucial elements in Jan's continued efforts to help and support her children. During Tina's grade-six year, when the *Talk to a Literacy Learner* program was offered to parents at Tina's school, Jan didn't attend. Despite her commitment to doing all she could to help the children, she explained, "I can't get mobile to get to the school. It's the people around, I think, and who you've got to mix with up there. . . . They sort of look down on you up at the school. I don't know why. I just don't feel comfortable there." When the same course was offered at the family learning centre soon after, Jan had no hesitation in taking part, even though the centre was much farther from her home than the school was and participating meant increasing the number of times each week that she made the long walk to and from the centre. She found the course very beneficial and regretted that it had not been available when her children were younger.

The centre's influence on Jan herself was indirect at first, but gradually became more direct. She recounted her early experiences at the centre, and what she has gained:

It's only been in the last four years that I've really been out and about. . . . I wouldn't move, I just stayed home. I'd just [take the children to school] and pick them up, and that was it. I just used to stand way back in a corner and wait for them. I wasn't a contact person. Even when [the staff at the family learning centre] first had meetings and things going, I used to stand right back in a corner and I wouldn't sit in a group or anything. . . . They've done a lot for me. I can understand things better now, and I can read better than what I could. I still have trouble with their schoolwork, but that's about it. For day-to-day, I can get by. Even when I don't want to do things, they ring me up and remind me. [The coordinator at the centre] pushes sometimes, but it's good to have someone on your back. We had a run-in a few months ago: I didn't like the way she said something to me, and I told her so. She said, "I'm glad you told me—the old Jan wouldn't have said anything."

One of the most difficult tasks Jan faces is balancing her need for help against the embarrassment caused by needing to seek help. Contemplating future pursuit of literacy education, Jan remarked:

> I want to learn more, but I'm too frightened to go to [a technical college]. I can't stand crowds, groups. It scares me in a group. I can't talk in a group. I could take the work down to [the centre] to get help, but after a while you start to feel a bit funny about always having to ask for help.

The Robinson family is now at the crossroads. In one sense, the help and support that the staff at the family learning centre have given to Tina and Jan are now in danger of holding back the family's progress toward independence and educational success. The long hours of after-school tutoring sessions have taken their toll on the children and, in some ways, prevented them from participating in the social worlds of their friends. Both of the children still need additional literacy support, but this must be balanced against their need to have a measure of control over their time and to join in their friends' activities.

While they all recognise the enormous benefit they have gained from their involvement at the family learning centre, they also recognise that the time has come to be independent—to seek assistance in their own way and on their own terms. At the same time, they don't want to offend the very people who have guided and supported them over a long period of time. What they have perhaps not recognised is that having the skills and the confidence to move on, to seek their own way, is what the learning centre has given them. By building on the family's strengths, rather than dwelling on their perceived weaknesses, the centre has empowered Jan to take control of her family's educational experiences. This type of collaborative approach that is based on significant and close relationships between families and educators is what is needed in the name of family literacy. Schools have a special responsibility to move beyond tokenistic approaches to parent involvement toward partnerships with families that acknowledge and build on the richness of culture and language evident in our communities.

References

Au, K. and A. Kawakami. 1984. "Vygotskian Perspectives on Discussion Processes in Small-Group Reading Lessons." In P. Peterson & L. C. Wilkinson (Eds), *The Social Context of Instruction*, pp. 209–25. Portsmouth, NH: Heinemann.

Auerbach, E. 1989. "Toward a Social-Contextual Approach to Family Literacy." *Harvard Educational Review* 59:16–81.

Bourdieu, P. 1977. "Cultural Reproduction and Social Reproduction." In J. Karabel and A. H. Halsey (Eds), *Power and Ideology in Education*. New York: Oxford University Press.

Cairney, T. H., and L. Munsie. 1992. *Talk to a Literacy Learner*. Sydney: UWS Nepean Press.

Cairney, T. H., and L. Munsie. 1995a. *Beyond Tokenism: Parents as Partners in Literacy*. Portsmouth, NH: Heinemann. (First published in a slightly different form by the Australian Reading Association in 1992.)

Cairney, T. H., and L. Munsie. 1995b. "Parent Participation in Literacy Learning." *The Reading Teacher* 48(5):392–403.

Cairney, T. H., J. Ruge, J. Buchanan, K. Lowe, and L. Munsie. 1995. *Developing Partnerships: The Home, School and Community Interface*, Vols 1–3. Canberra, Australia: DEET.

Cazden, C. 1988. *Classroom Discourse: The Language of Teaching and Learning*. Portsmouth, NH: Heinemann.

Delgado-Gaitan, C. 1992. "School Matters in the Mexican American Home: Socialising Children to Education." *American Educational Research Journal* 29:495–516.

Gee, J. 1990. *Social Linguistics and Literacies: Ideology in Discourses*. London: Falmer Press.

Harry, B. 1992. "An Ethnographic Study of Cross-Cultural Communication with Puerto Rican American Families in the Special Education System." *American Educational Research Journal* 29:471–94.

Heath, S. B. 1983. *Ways with Words: Language, Life and Work in Communities and Classrooms*. Cambridge, UK: Cambridge University Press.

Moll, L. 1988. "Some Key Issues in Teaching Latino Students." *Language Arts* 65:465–72.

Scribner, S., and M. Cole. 1981. *The Psychology of Literacy*. Cambridge, MA: Harvard University Press.

pedagogical principles about families and literacy programs

No single, narrow definition of family literacy can do justice to the richness and complexity of families and literacy.

❑ Underlying the rhetoric of many deficit-driven family literacy programs is the belief that the poor have to be saved from themselves.

❑ The process of defining family literacy cannot be left in the hands of those outside the families and communities that are affected by the decision-making process.

❑ The culture of the community and the experiences of the families who live in the community must be the foundation of all family literacy programs.

❑ Literacy cannot be taught in isolation from the functions it serves in the lives of the families who participate in family literacy programs.

Educators should recognize the expertise of families and view all family members as knowledgeable, capable learners.

❑ When working with families, the educator is the novice and the family members participating in the program are the experts of their own experience.

❑ Narrow definitions of families and literacy that lead to the establishment of professional "experts" in family literacy should be rejected.

❑ Family literacy should receive increased attention by educators but educators should seriously question the establishment of family literacy as a separate discipline.

At the core of any locally developed literacy program is the reciprocal practices that are established between family members and educators.

❑ *Confianza* is the word often used to describe reciprocal relationships that are built on mutual trust.

❑ Locally developed literacy programs that are based on mutual trust—*confianza*—recognize that parents should be active in the decision-making process.

❑ Preestablished, prepackaged, or "nationally developed" programs by definition fail to meet local requirements of community development.

❑ Every member of the community, including caregivers in social agencies and teachers in schools, can play a key role in supporting families in the continuing process of literacy development.

❑ Educators understand that life changes are a personal decision. Teachers should be supported in their efforts to view education as an emancipatory process that provides opportunities for all families—especially parents and children—to work to change their life circumstances in ways that make sense to them.

❑ In school situations and in nationally and privately funded family literacy programs, family members and teachers should be equal participants in the development of the curriculum.

Literacy programs should support families in ways that make sense to both parents and children.

❑ All language and literacy experiences should be based on knowledge about and respect for the diverse language and literacy resources of students and their families.

❑ Literacy programs should support the everyday lives of families. They should recognize the important relationships that parents and children have with their communities and schools.

❑ It is essential that educators supporting the literacies of parents and children work with families, household members, and communities to identify literacy practices which are meaningful to them, and then use these descriptions to determine how programs could be designed to best meet their needs, concerns, and interests.

❑ Family literacy programs should move beyond cultural tokenism. For example, a Native American prayer wheel is a sacred artifact and not an object for children's play as some family literacy educators have suggested.

❑ As literacy educators find out more about the cultural and language resources of families that are available for learning and teaching, parents themselves can participate in this endeavor and have the opportunity to consider the many ways in which their own funds of knowledge and ways of knowing are worthy of pedagogical notice.

❑ Literacy practices in educational settings should broaden the opportunities for family members, including parents and children, to experience other types of literacy uses based on their personal and shared needs.

We must honor, validate, and use the languages of the parents and children who are enrolled in our schools and who participate in family literacy programs.

❑ English should not be taught at the cost of the home language. If the home language is not supported, cultural groups will be systematically destroyed.

❑ Speaking and being literate in more than one language creates social and intellectual resources that are antithetical to the concept of compensatory education.

❑ It seems that it is only in English-speaking cultures that fluency in more than one language is viewed as a deficit.

❑ ❑ ❑ ❑ ❑

Family Literacy Programmes and Home Literacy Practices
David Barton

A fuller version of this paper appears in D. Baker, J. Clay, and C. Fox (Eds.), Challenging Ways of Knowing in English, Maths and Science *(London: Falmer Press, 1995).*

The words *family* and *literacy* have the wholesome glow of something we all approve of: we are all in favour of families, however we define them, and we all believe in literacy, however we define it. The difficulty is that *family* and *literacy* mean different things to different people. The two words have been put together to make *family literacy,* an idea that has become prominent in contemporary discussion of literacy education, linking adult literacy and child literacy. In Britain and in North America family literacy is on the public agenda. I want to examine the reading and writing people do in their everyday lives, drawing primarily on data from the Literacy in the Community project, part of which has been concerned with the ways in which people use literacy in their home lives.

In order to relate this to current notions of family literacy, I begin with a media image of family literacy, taken from the June 1994 *British Times Educational Supplement.* The image is a photograph (a sketch of it is reproduced here) illustrating an article on a government initiative to develop

Figure 2: A questionable image of family literacy

family literacy. The picture is of a white woman in her early twenties and two children, a girl around four years of age and a boy of about five. They are all sitting close together, looking at a large book the woman is holding. Behind them on the wall are the words "story corner." It is an intimate picture, and I interpret it as a mother with her two children sitting in a school. The large heading next to the picture is "Tool Kit to Fix Family Illiteracy" and the sub-heading refers to "pioneering work to stop children repeating their parents' underachievement." Although this is in many ways a positive image of literacy, I want to challenge it if it is the *only* image thought relevant to family literacy. I want to question each aspect of this image of family literacy, to move it beyond young mums, beyond four- and five-year-olds, beyond books, and beyond schools.

The Literacy in the Community study was a detailed four-year study of the role of reading and writing in people's day-to-day lives in Lancaster, England. The study included intensive interviews with adults attending basic education classes, a door-to-door survey, a detailed study of fourteen households in one neighbourhood, and interviews with managers of bookshops, the library, advice centres, and other access points for literacy in the city.

The fourteen households in the neighbourhood study were contacted mainly through the door-to-door survey. One member of each household who agreed to take part in the study was interviewed extensively about everyday literacy practices; the interviews covered a wide range of activities at home and in the local area. There were regular household visits for follow-up interviews and observations. Our contact with each household developed in different directions, depending on the household members' literacy activities. Often other household members were interviewed and people were accompanied on trips to the library and to community associations. Some people kept literacy diaries for us, and others collected documents such as letters from school or junk mail. After a space of more than a year we returned to some of the people who had been interviewed and asked them to reflect on interview transcripts and on our analysis of their literacy practices. (For details of other aspects of the study, see Barton & Padmore 1991; Barton & Hamilton 1992a, 1992b.)

Households or Families?

We refer to several overlapping domains in our study, including family, household, neighbourhood, and community. (For more details on the domains and other framing concepts used here, such as different literacies and networks of support, see Barton 1994.) Obviously, contemporary families and households come in many forms: sometimes the two terms refer to the same entity, often they do not. There are households of one person, several people, related people, and unrelated people, and households can be structured in various ways. Families are diverse, too: they can be with or without children; they can be single-parent; they can be many forms of extended or complex families; there may be links with other generations, or there may be none. What was important for our study of literacy practices was whether or not these categories—household, family, neighbourhood, community—were useful in describing people's literacy activities. The validity of the terms became an empirical question.

We found that all four of these terms were useful, they all had a role in describing some aspects of people's literacy. We knocked on the doors of *households*; households were the groups of people who shared living space and, usually, ate together in a home. Some aspects of literacy had to do with household management and communication. *Families* were important when people talked about their informal literacy learning and some networks of support; often people referred to relatives, who in some cases lived nearby, on the same street or around the corner, and in other cases lived elsewhere in Lancaster or in nearby towns. The physical *neighbourhood* had some salience, where people relied on neighbours for support and where common local issues, such as traffic problems and street lighting, were addressed. The notion of *community* is more amorphous, but people nevertheless identified with particular communities of interest, such as allotment associations or as parents of children attending particular schools; literacy often had significant roles in these communities.

Both families and households are important in terms of support for literacy. People used a broad notion of family. We asked adults to recall who were the significant people in their childhoods in terms of education; it was not just their mothers they referred to and not just their parents. Often people remembered a particular person who had been important to them, in many cases a more distant relative or family friend. We referred to such people as *guiding lights*, a term that one informant used (examples are given in Padmore 1994).

The Diversity of Home Practices

We were struck by the wide diversity of literacy that goes on in the home. There are many different literacies beyond book reading. Literacy at home is tied in with daily activities. Often it combines many sorts of reading and writing and draws as well on spoken language, numeracy, and much more. People deal with shopping lists, TV schedules, and junk mail. They write and receive personal letters and cards; some keep diaries, some write poems; they deal with official letters, bills, and forms; they have notice boards, calendars, scrapbooks, recipe books, address books; they read local newspapers, catalogues, and advertisements; people keep records of their lives, and read and write to make sense of this complex world; they belong to community organisations and pursue leisure interests bound by a web of newsletters, magazines, notices, minutes, and messages; there are instructions that accompany every consumer good and service, from a bicycle helmet to a gas bill; people are even told by written instructions how, when, and where to put out the rubbish. It is this range of practices that children are exposed to and participate in.

At first we imagined we would encounter a distinct home literacy that could be contrasted with work literacy or school literacy. To some extent this is true; there is a distinctiveness to many home literacy practices, but what is more striking is the range of different literacies that are carried out in the home, including work and school literacies that are brought home. We came to see the home domain as "the centre from which individuals venture out into other domains" (Klassen 1991, p. 43). Within the home there are many patterns of how literacy is distributed as people participate in different relationships with each other and assert different identities. One form of patterning is through gender, and many home literacy practices are gendered; in relation to issues of family literacy, women's literacy lives were complex and certainly could not be defined solely in terms of their relationships with their children's education.

It is important to emphasise that everyone participates in literacy activities. Parents may have problems reading and writing; nevertheless, they engage in a wide range of literacy activities. In our data we have many examples of adults with difficulties who keep diaries, maintain household accounts, write poetry, take phone messages, send letters. They are not empty people living in barren homes waiting to be saved and filled up by literacy, as is sometimes implied in the media. For the most part, adults who identify problems with reading or writing are ordinary people leading ordinary lives, and if they have children, like everyone else, they are concerned about their children's education.

Home Is Distinct from School

Home life is very different from the formal school life of the classroom. There are several ways in which differences between home life and school life have implications for literacy. In school, literacy is focused on as an object of study in that it is explicitly talked about and taught; literacy is central to many classroom activities. At home, literacy is brought into many activities, but it is often incidental to the main purpose of the activity, which may be shopping, paying the bills, or finding out local news. Literacy is used to get other things done. Connected with these differing purposes there are different ways at home and at school of evaluating whether or not it is successful. School reading and writing is usually evaluated in some way, sometimes formally, and often in terms of correctness and accuracy. Tasks are often carried out in a way that makes them explicit and open to evaluation. Home literacy is not usually explicitly evaluated; it is successful if it serves its purposes.

There are other aspects of home life that affect how literacy is carried out. Home and school have different notions of public and private and different rights regarding personal space. In our research we are beginning to describe these differences; we would emphasise that it is important to find out what actually goes on in particular homes, rather than make assumptions about one universal way of using literacy common to home and school. Parents are experts on their own experiences. Rather than intervening in families, teachers and others need to investigate together the existing literacies in homes and communities. Our overriding impression was that, whatever their levels of literacy, all the parents we interviewed were concerned about their children's education. They were looking for further ways of supporting their children, and there are many existing practices in homes that can be identified and built on in that regard.

Lifelong Learning

Participating in and learning about literacy is not only important at the age of five. Many of the literacies we observed people using they had learned as adults, and when people recalled where they had learned particular aspects of literacy they talked of learning at work or learning informally as adults from friends and relatives. Households are significant places for learning, from infancy right up through the school years. The teen years are of special significance, and in our study parents were involved in the homework projects of their teenage children, as well as in providing support for younger children learning to read. Issues of teenage literacies are no less important than those concerning very young children.

Adults of different ages participate in quite different literacy practices, so the literacy demands on twenty-year-olds, thirty-year-olds and forty-year-olds can be quite different. We were also struck by the fact that those with the fewest resources in society often had the greatest literacy demands imposed on them, so that claiming benefit, for example, demands a complex configuration of reading, numeracy, form filling, and background knowledge of the benefit system. Life changes such as leaving home, starting a family, getting a job, losing a job, retiring, all bring different literacy demands, and people encounter new literacies at all points of their lives. Older adults in their sixties and seventies take on new literacies, sometimes embarking on major new literacy projects such as researching their family tree or writing their memoirs.

Related to the notion of differing demands on people is the notion that support for literacy takes many forms; people take on different roles in the home and support is not just in one direction. Children help their parents and may take on some of the literacy chores of the home: programming the video recorder, making sense of the letters sent home from school, reading maps on car journeys, and taking charge of the new home computer. It was when trying to help their children with schoolwork that some adults confronted their own difficulties in reading or writing and sometimes sought help. More generally, several adults talked of learning from their children's or grandchildren's school activities, including homework.

Family Literacy Programmes

Through ALBSU, the Adult Literacy and Basic Skills Unit (renamed the Basic Skills Agency in 1995), the British government has set up a series of family literacy programmes in England and Wales. (It was this initiative in June 1994 that sparked the article that included the image of family literacy with which I began.) The aim of the initiative is to set up projects that teach both parents and children. Projects include speakers of English as a first or second language (although ALBSU defines literacy as being only in English, or Welsh in Wales). Projects are located in a variety of settings, including libraries, schools, colleges, and family centres, and many projects involve partnerships between two or more providers. Initially, four demonstration programmes were funded for two years, and more than two hundred small grants have been awarded to individual projects. A wide variety of activities takes place in these projects. ALBSU encourages fixed-length courses with assessment of both children's and adults' progress. There are also other family literacy programmes in Britain unconnected with ALBSU, including ones in Scotland, ones funded by European Community money, and ones funded locally.

In the actual practice of these diverse projects, there are various views of family literacy, and in many ways these are exciting developments, offering many possibilities to rethink some fundamental aspects of education. Such initiatives give the opportunity to reassess home-school links and to rethink the role of community in education. Schools get the opportunity to involve parents; adult literacy programmes get the opportunity to act on the need some adult learners feel to help their children learn. Family literacy provides the possibility of educational innovation that need not be constrained by traditions of formal education.

However, for this to be a productive exchange it is essential to examine the concepts of family literacy most critically and not to accept unchallenged narrow versions of what is possible. The battle between home literacy and school literacy is not equal. School literacy is a dominant literacy, supported by powerful institutions and infiltrating other domains. Some versions of family literacy turn out to be an invasion of the home by school and its practices (see Street and Street 1991). While there is more than a decade of research evidence on the significance of events such as the bedtime story (for example, articles in Goelman, Oberg, and Smith 1984), our research and the research of others suggests that it is important to look beyond book reading at home. Children are observing and participating in a wide range of activities, and a general positive attitude toward literacy and children's participation in ongoing literacy activities is important (as in Clark 1975). For parents to take on the role of teacher, especially with preschool children, is probably misguided. Attempting to replicate in the home what children do in school is probably a mistake: it may not be effective, it leads to an impoverished notion of literacy, and it will alienate some parents and children.

The common media image, and the one often represented in government propaganda, of a mother helping her young children learn to read is one such narrow, politically charged concept of family literacy. It is important to deconstruct the rhetoric of blame surrounding the term. There is the rhetoric of falling standards that blames teachers. At the same time, there is often a rhetorical strand that blames families for children's lack of progress in school (rather than blaming the government for the lack of funding to support children who find learning to read difficult in increasingly overcrowded classes). Often the term *family literacy* is part of a deficit model that concentrates on what children and families lack, rather than examining their strengths. The newspaper headline "Tool Kit to Fix Family Illiteracy" is part of this deficit image of families—the switch from *literacy* to *illiteracy*, in the phrase *family illiteracy*, is proof that talking of literacy in fact so often really means illiteracy (see Barton 1994, p. 219).

Conclusion

The contribution that studies like the Literacy in the Community project can make to the debate is to provide a view of what actually goes on in the home in terms of literacy. As I hope I have shown, the home is a distinct domain of life, distinct from school; home is a place where literacy means different things, where the purposes, the values, the roles people take, are all different from formal schooling. Studying the home reveals a richer view of literacy than that portrayed in the media image we started with. Family literacy needs to move beyond the stereotypes and beyond school literacy. If there is real concern about particular families' underachievement, a detailed examination of family life might reveal hidden strength and resilience in those families. It may be found that literacy is not the root of people's social problems, and that families survive despite odds of extreme poverty and deprivation (see Taylor and Dorsey-Gaines 1988). Family literacy could draw upon existing strengths, upon vernacular forms of learning and, as Moll (1994) terms, "families' funds of knowledge."

Each aspect of the image we started with—a mother with young children reading a book in school—can be challenged. Family literacy needs to move beyond the young mum, to include, obviously, fathers, other siblings, and the range of relations and family friends that people cite as important in their literacy lives. Focusing exclusively on parent-child relations excludes important social relations and community resources. It needs to move beyond five-year-olds and recognise that homes are significant from infancy right up through the teens, and to accept that parents learn from children too. Notions of family literacy need to move beyond the book and take account of children's participation in a wide variety of home activities. Finally, images of family literacy need to move beyond the school as a site of activity; rather than seeing homes as needing to replicate what schools do, family literacy should look to supporting the things people do in their lives already.

References

BARTON, D. 1994. *Literacy: An Introduction to the Ecology of Written Language.* Oxford, UK: Blackwell.

BARTON, D., and S. PADMORE. 1991. "Roles, Networks and Values in Everyday Writing." In D. Barton and R. Ivanic (Eds.), *Writing in the Community*, pp. 58–77. Newbury Park, CA: Sage.

BARTON D., and M. HAMILTON. 1992a. Literacy in the Community. Final Report to ESRC. Unpublished.

BARTON D., and M. HAMILTON. 1992b. Collaborative Ethnography. Final Report to ESRC. Unpublished.

CLARK, M. M. 1975. *Young Fluent Readers.* Oxford, UK: Heinemann.

GOELMAN, H., A. OBERG, and F. SMITH. (Eds.). 1984. *Awakening to Literacy.* Portsmouth, NH: Heinemann.

KLASSEN, C. 1991. "Bilingual Written Language Use by Low-Education Latin American Newcomers." In D. Barton and R. Ivanic (Eds.), *Writing in the Community*. Newbury Park, CA: Sage.

MOLL, L. 1994. Presentation at International Forum on Family Literacy, Tucson, Arizona.

STREET, J., and B. STREET. 1991. "The Schooling of Literacy." In D. Barton and R. Ivanic (Eds.), *Writing in the Community*. Newbury Park, CA: Sage.

TAYLOR, D., and C. DORSEY-GAINES. 1988. *Growing Up Literate*. Portsmouth, NH: Heinemann.

Intergenerational literacy and learning approaches are appropriate to South African contexts in that they already exist in the homes and communities of the caregivers who participated in this study. Regardless of their own educational background, caregivers value and support their children's learning in a variety of ways. These include the investment of money, long hours of work, sending children away to live close to good schools, and migrating to find work. Other strategies include reading and helping with homework, and being creative in circumventing shortcomings in English literacy to make sure their children get the help they need. Caregivers also make attempts to upgrade their own education and participate in discussion groups to "learn more about our babies" and use children's books and school correspondence as resources for their own literacy development. Thus, while caregivers already do a lot to support their children's education, creating ways for them to be involved in informal and nonformal activities at the learning centre helped to support them in these efforts and build their confidence.

—S. Smythe

Soweto, South Africa: A Parent Involvement Model

LETTA MATSIEPE MASHISHI

Soweto is a creation of apartheid. The welfare of the residents was not the main concern of the people who created the sprawling African township in the southwestern part of Johannesburg, South Africa. Their major concern was to make available cheap labour to the whites while at the same time situating those who provide such labour as far away from the white towns and cities as possible. Areas like Soweto have very few resources. They tend to have very high unemployment and crime rates. This should not make us overlook the fact that in spite of these things the majority of the people living in such places are continually battling to lead normal lives under very trying conditions. They are prepared to make sacrifices to enable their children to get a better education. Those who intend to work with such parents should also be prepared to make sacrifices, not only in terms of resources, but also in terms of being prepared to work at very inconvenient times.

A parental involvement model for a place like Soweto would therefore involve the following:

1. *Negotiated timing of workshops.* The times when workshops should be held should always be negotiated with parents. The most convenient times for workshops seem to be Saturday mornings, Saturday afternoons, and Sunday mornings.

2. A *multidisciplinary and holistic approach.* Because of the range of issues that impact the education of children in such areas, people involved in parental initiatives need to work very closely with child welfare, social welfare, community health services, and similar departments.

3. *Parent educator training based on progressive adult education principles.* Volunteer parent educators in these areas tend to be younger people who have had some education. It is important that they be made aware that adults come into the learning/teaching context with a lot of knowledge and skills acquired over the years. Such knowledge and skills should be fully exploited in the workshops. Secondly, adults seem to prefer more participatory approaches to teaching and learning in which educators act more as facilitators than teachers. Two important attributes that parent educators should have are sensitivity and flexibility.

4. *Parent involvement in the design of the curriculum.* Parents do not only bring a wealth of experience to the workshops but also suggest issues of immediate interest and concern to them that could serve as a basis for developing workshop materials. For example, some parents living in informal settlements expressed concern about children in their neighborhood drinking poisonous liquids (e.g., paraffin) by mistake. This often happens because parents in such areas use soft-drink bottles to store such liquids. Concern was also expressed by some parents that urban children were ignorant of certain aspects of their own culture. To correct this, parents suggested that topics such as poisons in the home, family histories, family totems, family praise poems, African dishes, and folk tales be incorporated into the curriculum.

5. *Meaningful workshop materials and activities.* The materials that seem to work are those that are based on group approaches and involve a lot of participation. Favourite topics are those that relate to the home (e.g., poisons in the home), or experiential learning (e.g., getting parents and children to determine average sunrise and sunset times by actually recording over several days and averaging these out). Activities used to inculcate the reading habit in children tend to be very popular (vocabulary games, interpreting pictures, use of prediction, story dramatization, etc.) Also very popular are the stories, rhymes, and folk tales that the parents contribute themselves.

6. *Parent involvement in the administration of the programme.* In most instances, parents come to the workshops with a wealth of administrative experience developed through their involvement in community organisations. Such parents often volunteer their services and when this happens, the parent body takes possession of the programme and makes it its own.

7. *Action research.* Practitioners need to engage themselves in ongoing research to be able to determine needs, find out what participants can contribute, and assess what is likely to work in a particular context. Such research will be necessary if the sociocultural context of the participants is to be taken into consideration

8. *Avoidance of instant solutions.* There are very expensive educational packages or toys being marketed by firms in the United Kingdom and the United States that, it is claimed, can solve the educational problems that parents are confronted with. We know that in education there are no instant solutions.

❑ ❑ ❑ ❑ ❑

Deficit perceptions lead many educators to propound a highly structured and rigid environment for poor children, with respect not only to cognitive and verbal abilities but to socialization skills as well. Teaching the children of poverty confronts many teachers with a world they would rather not confront, for such children reveal the inequities and injustice that shape their young lives in the other America. Their poverty is frequently condemned as the fault of their parents' immorality, irresponsibility, drug habits, or dependence on social services. When children are poor and of color, they are doubly disadvantaged. Blaming the victim has not disappeared; the discourse has changed, and the labels have turned, but at-risk children are still seldom seen as children of promise.

—Valerie Polakow

□ □ □ □ □

Navajo Family Literacy

JENNIE DEGROAT

At the International Forum on Family Literacy in Tucson, Arizona, Jennie DeGroat, who was sitting in the audience, was asked if she would like to speak. Jennie was in her first semester of graduate school and working on a paper addressing Navajo family literacy. Without hesitation Jennie joined the presenters at the front of the auditorium. Shirley Thornton galvanized the audience with the power of her oratory, and Klaudia Rivera, Elsa Auerback, and Luis Moll were equally compelling. Then Jennie spoke. Quietly, she calmed us with the cadence of her voice while we held on to every word. Jennie's presentation was an important contribution to the development of the Declaration of Principles but in the year that followed she moved several times and we lost contact with her. All we had was a faint audio recording of her speech, which we used to construct the article that follows. Then, just as we were about to send the manuscript to the publisher, we found Jennie. She read the draft of this article and added the postscript.

Let me begin by describing an experience I had at a local meeting of parents concerned with Indian education. They had been listening to a speaker give an overview of the services provided by the Indian Education Program when a mother stood up:

> Your programs all sound good, but what have they done to help children? My own children are suffering right now. One needs a tutor. Yes, you *do* provide tutoring, but I have to find my way to your tutoring place, and I don't have a ride. My middle child [is] dropping out. He's joined a gang and he has lost all his self-esteem. . . .

This mother was so frustrated she cried. Just for that moment, I and the other Native American people at the meeting could see ourselves in this mother's situation. We had dealt with similar insensitivities before, and knew we would continue to deal with these issues in the future. We also knew that the programs being discussed were not designed to address the personal kinds of concerns that this mother was describing.

Although as a teacher I have had much experience with Navajo education, my attempts to share stories such as the one above in the academic community are greeted with responses such as, Where is your research? or How do you document what you're saying? [*Jennie smiled as she reflected on her reaction to these responses.*] It is unfortunate that my life and the stories I have lived are not treated as valid data. I am documentation. This morning I come to you with my experiences. That is all I have.

Many of the educational programs that are set up for Native Americans do not help children because they are not designed around the lives that Native American people live. To illustrate, let me describe various aspects of a program for families and children in which I previously worked.

The program was funded by the government and designed to focus on family literacy. The goals of the program were to help parents become better parents, to break an alleged "cycle of illiteracy," and to break a longtime cycle of poverty. The program was designed to put the parent and the child together so they could interact, and they were *supposed* to learn through these interactions. The program was *supposedly* based on the whole language philosophy, in which education is learner centered, but the program participants' success was measured with standardized tests. [In whole language programs, test-taking skills are neither taught nor rehearsed; academic knowledge is developed as learners engage in meaningful, real-life experiences.] The preschool educators involved in this program were *supposed* to "train" children for school. The idea was that Native American children were not "organized" and needed to be. This would allow them to succeed in life, become literate, and thereby break their cycle of poverty.

I objected to this program on the grounds that it was a conditioning program to train Navajos. Children were being "trained" into an unfamiliar way of life in order to ensure their success at school. The program was designed to meet the "deficit needs" of Native Americans. The parents were being taught school terminology, such as "circle time," "nap time," and "preschool time." It was assumed that when the time for school came, the children would know what was expected of them at those "times."

Those who were directly involved with running the program decided to rethink what they were doing and to let the program sit for a while. Meanwhile, they did what they thought would help people learn in the "real Navajo world." Recognizing the need for the participants to develop trust in the program and a sense that those who were implementing it really cared about the parents and their children, the organizers attempted to involve the parents directly and encouraged them to take ownership of the activities.

Rather than exercising control and thereby instilling the feeling that the leaders were thinking only from an "educated person's" view, they encouraged parents to develop their own learning centers for children. They told the parents, "This is your program. This is for you."

The parents did not understand this unfamiliar philosophy of education; when they were in school they had not been given choices and had never been shown what it meant to own something in the world of education. Our schooling led us to believe that learning only happens off the reservation. The Navajos also fit the standard qualifications for illiteracy—we have low economic status and we are second language learners. This leads many people to believe that Navajos are illiterate and that what we do know is not of value. Furthermore, the Navajo people equate literacy only with knowing the English language; we have been taught not to see literacy as something beyond knowing English.

Many Navajos do not view learning and education as the same thing.

Although we are learning as we live our lives and although there are a great many skilled activities going on in the home—sewing, silversmithing, weaving, macramé—we do not equate these highly specialized skills, which are deeply embedded in Navajo culture, with literacy. The multitude of knowledge in the home is not viewed as something that makes one literate in the greater society.

Family and community knowledge is not acknowledged by many literacy programs. These programs do not fairly address the culture and the language of the people they serve. Their purpose is to teach the culture and the language of the people they serve, but it is people from faraway places who tell the organizers how they should be teaching culture and language.

Culture cannot be packaged and taught as if it is something that is not lived. Language is something we live. Culture is something we live. We can't just put it in the classroom and say, I'm going to teach culture today. Hopefully we walk out and learn how to live in a Navajo way.

Evaluators came to my school and recommended ways to "better" the program. One recommendation was to incorporate a "culture area," a place for the students to sit in a corner and experience culture. Another recommendation was for the students to role-play in a fabricated *hooghan*; another was to put cradle boards in the play area.

Some Navajos still live in the *hooghan*; they do not play in the *hooghan*. A *hooghan* is a place to live, not a place to role-play. A cradle board is a secure place where young children are protected during the first year of their lives. Cradle boards involve rituals; only certain people can make cradle boards. It is not right for children to carry around cradle boards as if they were toys.

The recommendations given by the evaluators were based on *their* understanding of the kinds of objects that should be on display in a preschool; the Navajos see these objects in a different way. This program would have been a good one if it had been given to the community and if the organizers had said, Here's the money. These are the things we would like. Do it your way. Because our ways are very unique and different.

These are the things that I see. These are my experiences. Unfortunately, right now, they're not valid. People are always trying to change us to make us "better." Better at what? That's all I have to say.

Postscript

I would like to add my reasons for my critical analysis of foreign programs that continue to be imposed on the Diné Nation from the outside without prior consideration of the people.

A number of family education programs have recently been brought to the Navajo Nation to help Navajo families meet the standards developed by the National Center for Family Literacy. These types of programs use models that are developed from a monocultural perspective and do not address conditions on the Navajo reservation.

It is true that schools and communities throughout the Navajo Nation are experiencing the same national issues—gang activities, high dropout rates, unemployment. However, the models of family literacy still being implemented today are not culturally based and therefore are not effective for the problems on the Navajo Nation. Navajos are dealing with two cultural childrearing practices, traditional and the Western. The Navajo people are never asked for their perspective on how to solve their problems or how they could meet national standards or whether the standards are relevant to them.

Instead of meeting standards, educators should be concerned with helping families construct knowledge and share in the learning process. With assisting individuals in understanding their history, in understanding why things are the way they are today. With giving them the responsibility to question the conflicts in their lives and, as Freire says, "to read the world." This is what is needed in the Navajo Nation. They have enough programs to tell them what to do for another century or so.

An effort has to be made to reclaim traditional childrearing practices through dialogue with and stories by local people, especially the elders who are sitting in nursing homes throughout the Navajo Nation. This attempt, if presented within a holistic pedagogy, would begin a healing process, would bring back a state of *hohzo*, which means to be in harmony and balance.

Through this literacy experience, the Navajo families can help themselves and their children. Therefore, it is imperative to understand the root of the underlying principles that have affected Navajo and other Native American lives and education in the past and why it continues to affect them today.

Today many Navajo families blame schools for the failures of their children. They see school as a place in which to become someone else. It's a place to learn English or to get ahead in this society. Education is only for those who are in school. Schools are alienated from their lives. They depend on schools to teach the native language and sometimes the culture. The Navajos will continue to depend and depend as long as foreign standards, curricula, and programs are implemented in schools and communities. They will never become independent, able to grow in a positive way with their language and their culture, if they continue to legitimize themselves through the lens of someone else.

Although the concerns in schools and families in the larger society are mirrored on the Navajo Nation, the people arrived at this stage from a different direction. They need to unlearn and reeducate themselves from their own perspective, to reconceptualize the knowledge of traditional childrearing practices. This is the challenge most difficult to meet. The process can begin with talking about the traditional ways. If we present literacy from a holistic perspective, we might help educators, parents, and policymakers come together and develop community-based learning with Navajo pedagogy in mind. It's time to give our Navajo way a chance to help Navajo people.

□ □ □ □ □

My own perspective is that family literacy programs have to be community based, run by people who are from the learners' communities and who have deep ties in those communities, but I think that people will start coming when the programs are run by the communities. And I think that this is particularly threatening because what it entails is letting go of traditional notions of expertise and the ways that we privilege ourselves as academics, those of us who are academics.

—Elsa Auerbach

□ □ □ □ □

Local Knowledge, Families, and Literacy in a Navajo Bilingual School

GALENA SELLS DICK AND TERESA L. McCARTY

"I thought only the Anglos wrote books," an elder recently told us on being presented with a storybook written entirely in her native Navajo. Statements such as these are not uncommon, even in the Navajo community of Rough Rock, Arizona, where our work with a K–3 bilingual program uses local knowledge to cultivate intergenerational literacy—in Navajo as well as English.

Families and literacy have always been important at Rough Rock. An indigenous response to civil rights reforms of the 1960s, Rough Rock School was the first to elect a community-based, all-Navajo governing board and the first to insist on education in and through Navajo. Yet the union of community knowledge, schooling, and literacy has not been easily forged. Convinced by a brutally punishing English-only experience in federal boarding schools that "our language is second best," many parents resolved that their children would learn English, even at the expense of the heritage language and culture.

Why focus schooling around local knowledge? And what does this entail for families and literacy in indigenous settings? We begin with a premise: at its heart, schooling "is all about the telling of people's stories" (McLaughlin 1993). The key questions for us then become, Whose stories will be told? By whom? Who benefits from the telling of particular stories?

The answers to these questions—and the transformative power of the stories constituting Rough Rock children's educations today—can only be understood by examining the stories of the past. Here we share one such story text, that of Galena Dick. This personal narrative illustrates how current conceptions of family literacy, especially those purporting to "assist" parents and children who have been societally marginalized, must acknowledge, critique, and respond to the historical conditions that shape the here and now. Simultaneously, we hope to show how those conditions and the stories growing out of them can make a positive difference for Navajo and other American Indian children and families today.

Galena Dick's Literacy Journey

I grew up in Rough Rock, in a home where only Navajo was spoken. I lived in a one-room dirt-floor *hooghan* (an earth and log dwelling), with no modern facilities. I spoke my native language and learned to greet people by kinship.

My "formal" education began at age seven in a boarding school thirty-five miles from home. School was a totally different environment. I had to change my eating habits, clothing, values, religion, and other expected ways of doing things. But the most important change was the language. We were forced and pressured to learn English. We had to struggle. It was confusing and difficult. If we were caught speaking Navajo, teachers made us scrub the floors and slapped our hands with rulers. Some students had their mouths "washed" with yellow bar soap.

My first English literacy experience was with the *Dick and Jane* basal readers. Looking at the books, I wondered where this fantasy place was. I used to think, Will I ever get to see this place someday? I learned how to read by remembering the formation of words and how they looked on the page, the curves and shapes they had. If you remembered all the words, the teacher gave you privileges.

When I went to school my parents weren't involved in my formal education, because the native language and culture were not accepted by the school. My parents and grandparents wanted me to succeed, but they had no control over my schooling.

Formal education in English schools did change my behavior and attitudes. At the same time, I maintained a strong belief in my language and culture. Looking back, I believe this led me to pursue the work we are now doing in our school.

When the Rough Rock Demonstration School began in 1966, there was a great need for bilingual teachers and literacy materials. As I worked on my teaching degree and in my own classroom, I began to learn to read and write my language. I was learning along with my students. I had to pick up where I stopped when I entered boarding school, because my language and culture had been taken away from me.

Now that there are more Navajo teachers at the school, we are becoming the producers of school knowledge. We are not simply receiving someone else's literacy "fantasy." As I see it, we are actually reversing the type of schooling we went through.

The Power of Community Knowledge

The changes Galena Dick's narrative suggests would not be possible without a core of local bilingual teachers. All teachers in the present bilingual program have their roots in the Rough Rock community; all endured schooling experiences similar to those Galena Dick describes here. The impact of these teachers cannot be underestimated: their presence as community members and their commitment to transforming the circumstances of their own schooling have opened up new possibilities for an education genuinely rooted in the stories and social realities of the community.

Creating such possibilities has required letting go of the cultural artifacts typically associated with schools—basal readers, workbooks, and the commercial programs that legitimate them—with bilingual teachers instead relying on their own knowledge and stories and those of their students and their families. Rough Rock bilingual teachers thus have become the writers of children's storybooks in Navajo. From their life accounts and those passed down from parents and elders, teachers are generating authentic Navajo literature that now anchors theme studies in Rough Rock classrooms. Parents and grandparents provide complementary cultural lessons in the classroom and in natural settings within the community (Dick, Estell, and McCarty 1994; McCarty 1993).

What difference does this all of this make? Through their writing, their talk, and their performance in multiple learning contexts, Rough Rock students show us the myriad affirming ways in which they make connections between texts and their lives. Their work provides constant evidence of the joy they find in reading and writing. These outcomes in turn are catalyzing community consciousness about Navajo language and culture as academic resources, in effect reversing the English-only brainwashing attempted in federal boarding schools. Parents and grandparents now have tangible demonstrations of texts produced by local people in their own language; from the stories of their lives, parents and grandparents have become the authors of such texts.

In short, as bilingual teachers and family members create curriculum together, they are transforming community values and the understanding of literacy. Literacy is not something received, imposed, or held by a few; it is not, as the boarding schools taught, words on a page. It is instead a constructive social and personal process that grows out of local knowledge—the stories and histories of a language community. By bringing the texts of their everyday lives directly into the social transaction that is education, Rough Rock parents, teachers, and children are validating the multiple literacies that constitute the complex dynamics of their community. In the process, they are negotiating a new culture of schooling. We hope and expect this process will lead to more widespread changes in curriculum and pedagogy for indigenous students.

As teachers and parents transform their literacy histories, they simultaneously transform the future possibilities for children. Galena Dick sums this up when she observes, "When we went to school, all we learned about was Western culture. We were never told the stories that Rough Rock children now are told and write themselves. We're telling those stories now. We see both sides of it—and we're helping children make connections through literature to their own lives."

References

DICK, G. S., D. ESTELL, and T. L. MCCARTY. 1994. "Saad Naakih Bee'enootí í lji Na'alkaa: Restructuring the Teaching of Language and Literacy in a Navajo Community School." *Journal of American Indian Education* 33(3):31–46.

MCLAUGHLIN, D. 1993. "Personal Narratives for School Change in Navajo Settings." In D. McLaughlin and W. G. Tierney (Eds.), *Naming Silenced Lives*, pp. 95–117. New York and London: Routledge.

MCCARTY, T. L. 1993. "Language, Literacy and the Image of the Child in American Indian Classrooms." *Language Arts* 70(3):182–92.

❏ ❏ ❏ ❏ ❏

Parent/Child Interaction Through Play Indicators:

(a) *Each parent's attention is focused on his/her child and their play together.*
    1   2   3   4   5   6   7

(b) *Teachers model techniques that encourage children's language, imagination, and choices.*
    1   2   3   4   5   6   7

(c) *Through smiles, laughter, and physical affection, parents and children show that they are enjoying their time together.*
    1   2   3   4   5   6   7

—Family Literacy Program Rating Scales, National Center for Family Literacy

❏ ❏ ❏ ❏ ❏

That's Not Who We Are

STEVEN BIALOSTOK

Eight men dressed in jeans and long-sleeve shirts sit in a circle around a large ceremonial drum. A large, thick stick with burning thyme leaves at its tip is passed from one man to the next; each one inhales it as if the smoke provided a hallucinogenic effect. The burning ember is then extinguished and put aside. An aged woman joins them, her skin brown and rough, like cow leather. She stands outside the circle, arms folded. Her solemn appearance, wrinkled skin, purple satin dress, and ostentatious jewelry convey matriarchy.

One man slowly raises another stick and begins beating the drum. He quickly adds an ancient chant. The other men begin to join him, so that eventually they are all working together, beating and chanting. The sound crescendos to a feverish pitch that captures the attention of everyone in the crowd, including the young children, who had ignored the long ceremonial speeches. Infants now sit up in their strollers watching the men who are beating the drum loudly in complete synchronization with voices that periodically rise to a falsetto and then yelp like a wild animal. The chanters' long black hair, braided and tied in the back, twists and turns as their heads bounce in frantic rhythm. The woman, standing with her eyes closed, finds a voice that rises above the rest. The music is infectious, primal. Then it comes to a sudden halt.

There is silence. Everyone stops moving.

So does the red ribbon on the shirt of each man.

The one that reads "Just say no."

It is Say No to Drugs Week on an Arizona reservation.

A disk jockey approaches the stage where the men had been sitting. A large portable amplifier is placed on the stage, obscuring the view of the ceremonial drum. Over the loudspeaker, someone sings, "Hey, Joe, que paso." If I walk past the sweat lodge and make a right where the tribal council meets I can get a free hot dog and soda and a ride on the fire truck.

The White Knight

He is a white knight driving a dirty gray Ford Explorer to save the Indians. There are no street lights. The dark night, the light rain hitting the windshield, and the realization that he is driving on a street named after a spiritual mentor make the mission that much more altruistic and noble.

Except for the chain-link fence and unattended weeds, the house is indistinguishable from any other. Closer examination reveals that it is a garden overtaking the house. He feels anxious approaching the door, his arms filled with the same binder, papers, and books that he brings to these kind of presentations. But tonight is different. Tonight is for the Indians.

The room is a combination office and living room. One side of the room has a desk, copy machine, and clutter. The other side has an old vinyl plastic sofa, a television, and chairs set up in a circle. One tall young man with brown skin sits awkwardly with nothing to do. His legs are extended and crossed at the ankles. They switch to a different position and then switch back again.

The white knight offers a sort of smile, unsure of how it will be taken, hesitant about being too friendly or not friendly enough. Mostly he ignores the brown man sitting nervously on the black couch. The room slowly fills with other men. The white knight notices that they are all much younger than his forty years. White knights in 1995 are significantly older than in the old days when they saved damsels in distress.

The brown men all sit on the chairs and sofa, acknowledging neither one another nor the white knight. Pizza Hut delivers. The tension is broken for everyone except the white knight, who sits anxiously in his seat, sipping a soda and wondering how to start, what to say, what should be different.

Stomachs are full. The men sit down. Silence. Then introductions. The white knight is noticeably passed over as each man states his name, the number of children he has, and his marital status. The white knight is introduced as someone who will talk about reading.

There is a liberating speech to be spoken, a well-known, well-rehearsed speech, inside the head of the white knight. He has given this speech so often that he knows just the right way to pause for a joke, the amount of time to reserve for questions, the correct way to reassure anxious parents. He is there is save the Indians.

But he looks at their faces. Eight men. Staring silently. The chiseled face of a young hunk with five daughters. The long braided hair of a man with a two-year-old whom he raises alone. The tattooed man with a shortly cropped moustache who announced that his wife made him attend. The heavy man who had earlier appeared confused about filling out a form.

What did they want to hear? How could the white knight save them?

The hunk with five children is not hesitant. "The easy part was fathering my kids. The hard part is being a dad. There are so many things about being a dad that I don't understand. There are so many things about little kids I don't understand."

Says the tattooed man: "My daughter has homework and she needs to spell 'hat.' I spell it for her over and over and then she still spells it wrong. I don't understand. And then I get frustrated and just have to walk away."

An hour later the white knight takes out his car keys, saddles his Ford Explorer, and returns home to his own son. He does not notice the darkness, the rain, or the famous street. He thinks about the evening. He thinks about how several of the men came up afterward and thanked him, finding the talk informative. But mostly he thinks about how, toward the end, the hunk stood up and said, "Now you're sounding like a poster."

And the white knight felt ashamed and embarrassed. He had saved no one. He had been full of information and simple answers. He might just as well have handed out ribbons that read, "Just say no."

The Story

John Tyler is a kindergarten and first- and second-grade school located less than a half a mile from an Arizona Native American reservation, just north of a road named after the man who worked so hard to gain tribal recognition.

Sixty-eight percent of the children at the school are from the reservation. It is a modern, spacious building with a large, complete library, contemporary offices, a computer lab, and a parent's room. For several months, a small group of mostly young mothers from the reservation have brought their preschool children to participate in a forum that is part child education and parent education. It is sponsored by a nonprofit organization called Family Ties.

My initial contact with this organization was not part of any research project but rather as a participant. When I first moved to Arizona during the hot summer of 1994, I had no friends in the city. Without even distant contacts, trying to establish myself—a single father of a two-year-old—in a new environment was difficult, particularly in 116-degree heat. I searched for anything that catered to children.

One day while driving I spotted a large white sign that read "Family Ties." Feeling that the name expressed my very current needs—to be connected with other parents—I quickly swerved my car into their parking lot and entered a small, busy building. I was thrilled to discover an (air-conditioned!) organization with unstructured play groups, classes in parenting, single-parent support groups, child CPR classes, music and art classes for children, and a host of other special events—and that the cost of these services was based on one's ability to pay (music to a doctoral student's ears).

Since Family Ties was reasonably close to my house, I brought my son there once a week in the evening. Eventually, I began chatting with two employees, Ruth and Terry, about my doctoral work and interest in family literacy. Ruth had recently received a grant to work in conjunction with the local reservation's Even Start program to develop "a family support and education program for severely stressed, low-income neighborhoods." I expressed an interest in Even Start and in observing the reservation's program. Ruth and Terry got me in touch with those in charge, but at the same time suggested that I might like to talk with the mothers in their series of parenting classes being held at John Tyler.

I contacted the reservation Even Start program and met Robert, Even Start's Community Education Specialist. He had heard of me from Ruth, had read my book about reading, and asked that I speak about the subject to a fathers group that met monthly.

Meanwhile, I observed Family Ties' parenting classes in preparation for my own presentation. But my casual observations shifted to taking formal field notes as I began noticing a program philosophy that in very subtle ways perceived these families as functioning without an adequate understanding of childrearing. I kindly opted out of the reading presentation (the same presentation I would give to the Even Start fathers) and instead spent several months looking at the structure and content of each parenting class.

Each session was divided into two segments: the first hour focused on the children, providing activities that were standard preschool circle-time fare. Either Ruth or Terry sang several songs, read a book, and sometimes directed dramatic play. Circle time was always followed by an art activity, usually related to the book just read. One day, for example, the children made play dough from flour, water, and salt, and with the help of their mothers, formed the dough into the various characters from the story that Ruth had read. Mothers altered between talking with their children and with one another across the table. Of the four children—two boys and two girls—the two girls spoke only Spanish. One was assisted by her mother, who was bilingual; the other, whose mother was monolingual in Spanish, was assisted by the two Spanish-speaking aides. The children's interest and involvement for both the circle and activity time was typical for preschool age. During the forty-five minutes, they faded in and out while the moms encouraged their attention. The children then had a snack and went outside to the playground with the two aides.

The mothers then sat ready at tables for the parent education portion of the program. Each session focused on some parenting skill, and most of the information was presented as a lecture. The first session was on "effective and ineffective communication skill." Even though Ruth tried to solicit parents' comments, the responses were few. Ruth and Terry also demonstrated "effective communication skills" by role-playing those skills with each other. Finally, Ruth summarized her presentation:

> It is important for people to communicate effectively. Issues like getting lost while traveling can sometimes result from poor communication. It is easy for children to misunderstand exactly what a parent means. Parents use expressions such as, Be a good boy or good girl, which may be confusing to children because words like *good* and *bad* aren't easily understood. When we tell children to behave, *behave* is an ambiguous word. I can never assume that my daughter will follow my train of thought. I told her to take her skates off on the front porch, but there's lots of ambiguity in that statement. It's half-communication.

Attendance remained consistent during the first series of classes. The atmosphere was always relaxed and friendly. What changed from meeting to meeting was the topic, each topic representing a parenting philosophy that reflected the beliefs and values of Ruth, Terry, and a host of well-known parenting experts.

When Ruth and Terry decided to hold the second series of classes on a different day of the week, attendance became sporadic and irregular. Sometimes I would show up and no one but Ruth and Terry were there. Sometimes there was only one other person. No matter how few were in attendance, the "show went on." Once, when only one parent and myself came, Terry lectured about "different parenting styles" (authoritative, permissive, etc.) using a chalkboard as if we were in a university lecture hall with two hundred eager note takers. The art activity with one child went on as scheduled.

Ruth and Terry offered several possible explanations for the low attendance—the school's intersession break, Easter vacation, and a conflicting Even Start field trip. During my final observation, no families were in attendance. Instead, Ruth, Terry, and the community liaison, Sarah, planned an "attendance solution." They would change the day to Wednesday and provide families with lunch. The families would receive a telephone reminder two days prior to the meeting. I returned the following week to see how many families would attend. There were three.

Ruth felt that the lack of participation had nothing to do with satisfaction. The evaluations by participating parents at the end of the first series of classes indicated a high degree of satisfaction. Those same attitudes were reflected in interviews with two participating parents. It was my general observation that the mothers very much enjoyed coming. I wonder, however, if just getting together regularly and talking with other women at a similar stage of life might be the overriding reason for their satisfaction. Speaking as someone who participates in a play group, whatever my son may gain in this weekly social situation is far surpassed by his father's satisfaction at being around other adults who are in similar life circumstances. All of these women are full-time stay-at-home mothers of at least one young child, a stressful and demanding situation even under the best of circumstances. Having opportunities to get together with others in the same boat seems like a useful activity, whatever the actual long-term goal of the project. As a friend of mine with grown children has assured me, "The friends you have at this stage of life are the most important friends you'll ever have."

Family Ties presents its classes to diverse groups of parents all over the city. According to Ruth, the content of each presentation is the same, regardless of the population. This one-size-fits-all approach was evident as I observed Ruth and Terry's complete lack of concern for how this group of women might perceive and understand the world. In fact, during my interview with her, Ruth did not know and had not even considered a specific way that members of this tribe of Native Americans might communicate with a husband or parent their children. When I questioned Terry about this, she adamantly shook her head and very definitely maintained that the communication skills being presented transcended cultures. "People are people are people, and you see it with all the cultures."

Behind one insensitive use of language (the children were once told by Terry to sit "Indian style" on the carpet) was a greater tragedy, best expressed by Maria, a Native American woman in her late fifties who works for Even Start and sat in on the initial classes: "I don't think [Ruth] knows anything about [being Native American.] The ways she carries on, the way she prances around. That's not who we are."

Ruth's response when I mentioned Maria's comment was quite revealing: "Well, for her that would be her reality. I know that with the younger [mothers] that has not been our feedback."

So often we associate culture with observable phenomena such as daily dress (head covering), dietary laws, or regular rituals. Had Family Ties presented before a group of Orthodox Jewish, Amish, or Palestinian mothers, whose culture and traditions are easily identifiable, the parenting classes might have differed. The facilitators might have begun by asking, What are the ways in which your people/culture/tradition suggests that you parent? then built from an established base. But during my observations of the parenting workshops, there was not one instance of building on the strengths these women already had as parents or as a family. Without building on their strengths, without helping parents become aware of their own internal and external resources, offering parenting advice is like teaching an isolated reading skill. Focusing on some specific detail, the advise is at the most only short term.

Is there a unique way in which culture is reflected by the way women "communicate" with their children? Ochs and Schieffelin (1984) point out how caregivers and children speak and act toward one another is linked to cultural patterns "that extend and have consequences beyond the specific interactions observed. . . . How caregivers speak to their children may be linked to other institutional adaptations to young children. These adaptations, in turn, may be linked to how members of a given society view children more generally (their 'nature,' their social status and expected comportment) and to how members think children develop" (p. 284).

Are there ways in which all parents should treat children—ways that transcend culture? White middle-class parents share similarities in such areas as mother-infant gazing, turn-taking styles, and elicitation of stories from small children, but there is not necessarily homogeneity in discipline styles. Just ask a random group of ten white middle-class parents their perspective on such issues as spanking or "time-out."

The subtle tendency to "know what's best" for a group of people, particularly a group already marginalized, is common. Ruth told me how parents had responded to their survey by requesting to learn about "discipline" strategies. Their requested topic was ignored (or at least bypassed) by Ruth and Terry, who believed the real issue (communication) would ultimately help parents with discipline. The information presented may have been useful, caringly provided, and happily received by the women. But Ruth and Terry's "strategy" also created a power relationship that placed the mothers in a subordinate position to the "facilitators." The organization of the class certainly structured that hierarchy, but the language of the grant application itself—which suggested that the parenting program might prevent future antisocial behavior by these current three-year-olds—created the climate for that structure. One of the grant's purposes is to "save" these people from themselves, and the two instructors were the saviors. Revoicing the subject matter from "discipline" to "communication" is the perfect example of a rescue. In other words, "We know better than you what your real issues are."

Prevention programs around the country reflect these identical "benevolent" attitudes. Literacy "salvation programs" can also share their subtle, deficit-driven framework. On the one hand, what could be considered more altruistic in this society than an organization wanting someone to read? On the other hand, like the Family Ties grant, the language in the documents of many family literacy programs sends implicit messages as they seek to connect so-called illiteracy with unemployment, crime, and poverty.

Children from educated families are exposed to print at an early age. Their parents read to them, encourage their early "reading" and "scribble writing," develop their language skills through conversation and their thinking skills through questioning. Through their own reading and attention to their children's school activities, these parents demonstrate that they value learning. All this happens naturally in many homes. But "at risk" children most often come from disadvantaged, undereducated homes, and they do not acquire the preliteracy skills developed by more fortunate children. As a result, they begin their schooling behind, and may never catch up (Darling 1992, p.1).

Without the funding, the agency can't exist. Without the agency, illiteracy rates will increase. An illiterate society is the end of civilization as we know it. In other words: fund our agency!

Family Ties finds itself in the same dilemma that many organizations that depend on grants for their existence. "The tendency to emphasize deficits rather than strengths may be exacerbated by the fact that funds for these projects are typically 'compensatory,' a category that traditionally connotes a set of problems that need to be remediated" (Department of Education 1993, p. 36). It's tough, if not impossible, to receive grants to work with people who don't appear to have significant problems. Ruth told me that she didn't even believe in some of the language she used when writing the grant application, but claimed that without it, the project wouldn't have been funded. The language of the grant application suggests that gangs are lurking to recruit children of this particular Native American tribe, that loving homes and happy memories will prevent it, and that the Family Ties parenting classes will contribute to those positive environments. Beside the stereotypes being perpetuated simply to receive a grant, the oversimplifications are beyond description. There are many factors that lead to violence, gang membership, and other anathemas of our society. Isolating "parenting skills" (or literacy) dismisses numerous other larger social factors. The reality is that the way Ruth conducted the sessions indicated that she *did* believe the language of her grant application. But that belief manifested itself in such subtle and compassionate ways that one must look deeply at the entire system to recognize it.

Neither Ruth nor Terry is an ogre. Each is, in fact, a warm and compassionate woman of whom I, quite frankly, grew enormously fond. Ruth is bubbly and charismatic with an endless supply of energy. Terry is quiet and compassionate with soulful, direct eyes. The two complement each other well, and they like each other and the families with whom they work. The program time devoted to the children shares qualities of some nationally known and popular play groups such as Gymboree. In fact, had it not interfered with his nap time, I considered bringing my son. My concerns do not reflect the quality of the presentations to either the children or parents. How often have I presented the same "well-received" lecture on how kids learn to read? It has become too easy for me to go on a four-city speaking tour and change only the geographical references, never considering who these people are and what their needs are. Is it possible to move beyond a polished speech? How many experts make a living off the same speech?

I said at the beginning that the parenting classes were a small project with larger implications. The circle time for the children—appearing so much like conventional school—remains a metaphor for how Family Ties reflects our larger system, whether it be the teaching of parenting skills, reading, or even psychotherapy. Whenever we look at "marginal" parents—and in America today we consider them to be people who are from any ethnic, racial, or linguistic minority group—we assume they know less than they actually do. The school's job, in that view, "is to motivate those children by placing them on the bottom rung of a ladder of skills and having them practice simple skills" (Hiebert 1991, p. ix). But families themselves must define how and what literacy (or parenting) is in their everyday lives. Ways of knowing, behaving, and communicating are embedded within the culture of each family and community. Outside organizations—schools, family literacy programs, or parent education groups like Family Ties—cannot possibly define for a culture or family what it shall do or learn. Facilitators in organizations such as Family Ties need to be aware of this and avoid riding in on a horse dressed as a white knight.

References

DEPARTMENT OF EDUCATION. 1993. *Model Strategies in Bilingual Education: Family Literacy and Parent Involvement*. Washington, DC: U.S. Department of Education.

DARLING, S. 1992. *Family Literacy: The Need and the Promise*. Louisville. KY: National Center for Family Literacy.

HIEBERT, E. 1991. *Literacy for a Diverse Society*. New York: Teachers College Press.

OCHS, E., and B. SCHIEFFELIN. 1984. "Language Acquisition and Socialization: Three Developmental Stories and Their Implications." In R. Shweder and R. LeVine (Eds.), *Culture Theory: Essays on Mind, Self and Emotion*. Cambridge, UK: Cambridge University Press.

❏ ❏ ❏ ❏ ❏

Many of the programs designed to sensitize parents to their role as teachers of reading and writing provide them with specific suggestions on the "how to" of reading instruction, yet there is nothing in the literature to suggest that children who successfully learn to read and write are specifically taught by their parents. . . . Literacy is deeply embedded in the social processes of family life and is not some specific list of activities added to the family agenda to explicitly teach reading. The thin literate veneer of present programming cannot substitute for such learning opportunities and may not necessarily be desirable, for it may unwittingly undermine the natural and exploratory educational initiatives of the child as well as the initiatives that the parents and children have evolved together.

—Denny Taylor

❑ ❑ ❑ ❑ ❑

Often, when people are literate in their own language, but do not know English, they are placed in literacy classes in English. The message is that literacy in another language doesn't count. . . . Our challenge is to open forums for participants to be the authors and actors of their own lives and to conduct their own research, to struggle against the backlash against immigrants and other minorities, to keep literacy and education in languages other than English as a real option for children and adults. Our challenge is also to educate the public about the resources that non-English-speaking families bring to this country and to the classroom. We must not lose sight of what is important: the participants' stories, the wealth of their knowledge, their experience as parents and workers, their personal and community knowledge, their dreams and aspirations.

—Klaudia Rivera

❑ ❑ ❑ ❑ ❑

El Barrio Popular Education Program
KLAUDIA RIVERA

El Barrio Popular Education Program is a community-based native-language organization located in New York City in one of the oldest and most vibrant Puerto Rican communities in the United States. It began in 1985 as a research project of the Language Policy Task Force of the Center for Puerto Rican Studies at the City University of New York, and has grown from two literacy classes to a comprehensive project that includes community and economic development activities. The current student population consists primarily of women, the majority of whom are immigrants from Puerto Rico and the Dominican Republic.

The premise of the program is:

- To create a forum for teaching and learning in which the participants have a voice and can exercise their rights—including the right to learn to read in their native language using curriculum and materials that are rooted in their experiences.
- To provide the means for the participants' voices to reach new audiences through the documentation and publication of their stories and the production of videos filmed and edited by the participants about the issues that they research and identify as important in their lives.
- To implement an educational program that starts from the known, the already experienced, the lived.
- To engage in projects that bring school and community together, to inform others about what is important to the community, and to work with other Latino organizations.
- To provide the space necessary for economic development projects that validate the participants' working stories, provide them with additional income, and open the possibilities for a meaningful employment—employment that meets their needs as parents and allows them to continue their economic traditions.
- To involve participants in running the program as teachers, administrators, and members of the board of directors.

Educational Goals

The overall educational goal of the project is for students to develop their reading, writing, speaking, and listening abilities in Spanish first, and then to apply these abilities to learning English as a second language. The curriculum is community based and student generated. It is aimed at validating the linguistic and literary practices of the community and uses materials that are generated by the participants' life stories and struggles. Students are encouraged to write about their families, their countries of origin, their experiences as women and as immigrants, and other life experiences. The writings are published on an ongoing basis. This process contributes to the overall documentation of community life, allows individuals to examine their experiences in the larger context of community history, and shows how reality is collectively constructed.

Another major goal for the organization is that it be managed and run by students and former students. Currently, 50 percent of the paid staff are women who have graduated from the program; half of the board of directors are either graduates or current students.

A final major goal for the organization is to contribute to the self-sufficiency of the participants and to the overall economic development of the

Tema: _Mi hijo y yo_

Cuando mi hijo fué por primera
vez a la escuela pasé mucho
trabajo con mi hijo por que yo no
sabia leer ni escribir, no podia
ayudar lo con las asignaciones que
le daban en la escuela. Tuve que
buscar ayuda y pagar para que le
ayudaran a mi hijo hacer las
asignaciones y ahora el me ayuda a mi
con mis asignaciones que me dan
a mi en la escuela. Hace ocho
meses que estoy estudiando.
Y quiero progresar.

Lucia Vega

40

My Son and I

When my son went to school for the first time, it was hard for me because I didn't know how to read or write—I couldn't help him with the assignments they gave him in school. I had to pay someone to help my son with his homework. Now my son helps me with my school work! I've been studying for eight months and I want to learn more.

Figure 3: Lucia Vega, El Barrio Popular Education Program

community. At the group level, the goal is to work toward creating a community able to sustain its own educational institutions; at the individual level, the goal is to help women develop the tools necessary to obtain financial independence. To this end, students have initiated and are running two cooperatives (food/catering and computer). All of the educational activities at the program reinforce the self-sufficiency and economic development goals by critically analyzing the role that women play in the economy and by devising strategies to address their economic situation. The program also offers High School Equivalency classes, leadership development, economic development and health education workshops, and computer and video instruction.

Educational Philosophy

The organization's educational philosophy is that it is important for students to learn and develop literacy in their native language; Spanish is viewed as a prerequisite to English as a second language. This allows the program to integrate the linguistic resources and strengths that the students

Aprendo Todos los Dias

Cuando empecé a estudiar mi esposo me decia—¿Cómo puede ser que ahora despues de vieja tu vayas a aprender?, los mudos despues de viejos no pueden hablar". Yo le contestaba esta es mi oportunidad y la voy a aprovenchar".

Pasaban meses y volvia otra vez con lo mismo. Hasta me ofrecia consequirme trabajo. Yo le contestaba "no me enamore que mi meta es ir a la Universidad." Ahora que él ve los videos que hacemos en el Programa ye me ve aprendiendo ye desenvolviéndome en el Inglés me dice—"te felicito ya estás progresando. No dejes el estudio, sigue, que es bueno aprender".

Mis hijos están orgullosos de verme estudiando y me dicen "siga que nosotros le ayudamos con las tareas, pero queremos que siga, que no se de por vencida, como nos decia usted a nosotros". Ellos me preguntan todos los dias cómo me va. Tambien compartimos el trabajo de la casa y las tareas todos los dias. yo me siento muy bien con mis estudios.

I Am Learning Every Day

When I started school my husband used to say to me, "How could it be that you will learn anything at your age? Mutes don't learn to speak once they are grown." I would answer, "This is my chance, and I am going to take advantage of it."

Months went by and he came back at me with the same thing. He even offered to find me a job. I said to him, "Don't distract me, my goal is to go to college." Now that he sees the videos we make in the Program, and sees me learning and getting by in English, he says, "Congratulations. You're really making progress. Don't stop studying, keep going. It's good to learn."

My children are proud to see me studying and tell me, "Keep going. We'll help you with your homework, just keep going and don't give up, like you used to tell us." They ask me every day how I'm doing. We share housework and homework every day. I feel very happy with my studies.

Figure 4: Antonia Tapia, El Barrio Popular Education Program

already have to help them develop the reading and writing skills they need for the future.

The organization is also committed to integrating technology with native language literacy. Computers are available to the students so that they may develop the computer literacy necessary for full participation in society.

Leadership development is another essential. Women's issues (e.g., welfare problems, day-care availability, health issues) are interwoven into the curriculum. Formal workshops are held on topics important to women's everyday lives (domestic violence, substance abuse, AIDS, individual rights). The goal is to help women work toward their own empowerment, to help them develop their ability to take control of their lives, to become aware of their rights, to become more assertive, and to advocate for themselves and their children.

The program helps students analyze critically and respond concretely to the issues they confront. The pedagogy is holistic, in that all four skills—reading, writing, speaking, and listening—are taught in an integrated way; one reinforces the other through meaningful activities that students help develop. Options include getting involved in one of the cooperatives (food or computer), taking a specialized tutorial in math or reading, working in the computer lab, participating in art workshops, making a video, and/or suggesting a new project. All of the projects currently offered at El Barrio Popular Education Program have been developed as a result of requests and suggestions by students.

Collaborative Planning and Arrangements

In order to provide comprehensive services to students, the organization has established a network of collaborative relationships with a number of other organizations both in the community and citywide. After a student is referred to a cooperating agency and services are secured, the counselor provides ongoing follow-up with both the student and the agency, maintaining appropriate records throughout the process.

The collaborating organizations provide support and/or training in areas such as domestic violence, breast and cervical cancer prevention, citizen rights, therapeutic and psychological evaluation and services, medical screening and services, AIDS education workshops, welfare and food stamps, transportation money, alcohol and drug rehabilitation, family therapy, housing rehabilitation, and senior citizen services.

Evaluation

The program is evaluated in accordance with the participatory philosophy of empowerment. Students are not only involved in conceptualizing new projects but also in evaluating them. Personnel policies and staff evaluations are also participatory: students provide input and feedback. Participants also assess their own progress on an ongoing basis.

Summary

The goals and curriculum of El Barrio Popular Education Program are based on the cultural and language resources of its participants. The project is aimed at validating the linguistic and literary practices of the community and at working toward individual, community, and economic development. The equal balance of power between the participants and staff allows for a curricular emphasis on meeting the needs of the participants. Students and staff work together toward empowerment.

❑ ❑ ❑ ❑ ❑

We must be able to speak to the principals, to the overwhelmed elementary teachers, to the Head Start workers inundated with NCFL ideology who have never encountered the notion that poor, culturally diverse families bring with them rich and varied "funds of knowledge" that are valuable, that count, that are the strong foundations for these families, and that these resources can be the starting points for practitioners—together with parents and children—to create curriculum.
—Kim Gerould

❑ ❑ ❑ ❑ ❑

What changes have I undergone? Fundamentally, I have redefined my conception of the term home visit. I was trained during my first years of teaching (some fifteen years ago) that my goal during a home visit was to teach the parent. I had an agenda to cover. I was in control. Now I go to learn. I have some questions I want to explore. I might want to learn about some particular home activities like what the family does for recreation. However, these questions are open-ended. I start an interview and follow the conversation to wherever it might lead. I am an active listener. I am a listener who returns to pick up the conversation from the last visit.
—Anna Rivera

❑ ❑ ❑ ❑ ❑

From Untapped Potential to Creative Realization: Empowering Parents
MARLA HENSLEY

This article first appeared in Practicing Anthropology *17(3)(Summer 1995):13–16.*

Parents in the neighborhood where I teach in Tucson, Arizona, are sometimes viewed as lacking—lacking in parenting skills, lacking in education, lacking in knowledge. In reality, it is the people who hold this view who are lacking—lacking in knowledge of the parents and the community. They have failed to take the time to get to know the parents, to delve into their world and to discover their true "funds of knowledge."

In the Funds of Knowledge for Teaching Project, the teacher becomes a researcher, an observer, and a learner in the parents' world. The primary focus of the project is to discover funds of knowledge in students' homes and to incorporate those funds into the classroom curriculum. As a result, the educational model is changed. The experiences and skills of the child and other family members become vehicles for classroom innovations, and teaching becomes student centered.

Those of us who agreed to participate in the project in the fall of 1992, when it was expanded to encompass African American as well as Hispanic and Native American homes, still had doubts about its value. What is the purpose, we wondered, of spending hours of time in your students' homes gathering all this information? Is it worthwhile? And what do you do with all this knowledge?

According to Dr. Amy Powell Wheatley, in a presentation at the Early Childhood Conference held in Tucson, Arizona, on August 6, 1993, entitled "Building an *Active* School Community," there are five factors that motivate people to learn and to grow: enjoyment, control, interest, success, and self-worth. As I relate events that took place during my involvement in the Funds of Knowledge for Teaching Project, the role of these five factors will show why this project has been so successful.

Creating a Musical

I chose Amanda's family for my first interview. I was having some difficulties with Amanda in terms of behavior, and I thought working with the family would help. I had gone on home visits many times over the previous ten years, but the focus was always a teacher agenda: what could the parents and I do to help the child?

Contrast this with an *ethnographic* visit. The teacher goes into the home as a learner. There is a questionnaire that focuses on family background, relatives, previous residences, job history, hobbies, philosophy of childrearing, educational attitudes, religious views, and opinions on various other topics. The teacher asks questions about things seen in the home and shows genuine interest in the family. What develops is a format for conversation that weaves in and out of the specific questionnaire agendas. The whole atmosphere changes as the parents do the talking. A rapport develops that puts everyone at ease.

Prior to my home visit, Joseph Jarman, Amanda's father, had brought their pet rabbit to school during our study of pets. When I found out he cared for plants in his job as groundskeeper, I was excited: I had wanted some expert advice in starting a garden with my kindergarten class. Within the next few weeks Mr. Jarman helped us prepare and plant a vegetable and flower garden.

Now, as far as I was concerned I had tapped into a fund of knowledge, and my project was a success. If I had not continued my home visits I would have thought that gardening was the most important fund of knowledge that Mr. Jarman had to offer.

By the end of the second interview, however, I had discovered that Mr. Jarman had impressive communication skills. He would ponder each question and respond in an articulate, eloquent fashion. Noticing a guitar propped against a closet, I learned that Mr. Jarman played guitar and keyboard and wrote songs and poetry. Clearly his oral and musical communication skills were another fund of knowledge.

If I had sent home a survey to parents I may have discovered Mr. Jarman's musical talents, but at most I would have asked him to come in to play for us. Instead, I had an incredible thought. What if he would write children's songs and create a musical based on a familiar children's story? *The Little Red Hen* would be perfect! It would tie in the music and the gardening.

When Mr. Jarman came to class with his first two songs written, it was amazing. The children loved the words and tunes; they were so catchy. Mr. Jarman used his guitar and his keyboard, and we began to put the play together and practice on the stage. By the end of the year the children had learned seven songs for the play.

Wanda Wright, the head of a second family (her own son and many foster children) I was interviewing that year, had a background in dance, so I asked her to help choreograph our play. Although Ms. Wright worked full-time, she was able to come to school on her days off and help us. We organized costume-making workshops, and many other parents participated.

The musical was an incredible experience for students, parents, and teachers. We performed it five times for the parents and for other classes in the school.

Impact on Children and Parents
The musical and the instruments that Mr. Jarman brought sparked a whole thematic unit on music and sound. The children designed and made their own instruments and created a musical workshop. They investigated sound through many science experiments. They brainstormed ways that their bodies make sounds and created a language web of the ideas. They were fascinated with all the sound rhythms they could invent just with their hands.

Two of the songs Mr. Jarman wrote led to spin-off projects. The first song describes the process of making tortillas. My teaching assistant's *nana* and *tia* (101 and 102 years old!) came to school and made tortillas with the children. The children sang the tortilla song over and over. We also made fry bread guided by a Navajo parent. I would not have thought to have these bread-making experts come in had it not been for the Funds of Knowledge for Teaching Project.

The second song explains the process of making yarn from wool. We read multicultural legends and factual text relating to this process and focused on

Native American literature and culture. The children visited a farm and observed the shearing of sheep. In class, the children created weavings and viewed artifacts shared by our Navajo parent.

Performing in the musical, the children grew dramatically. When they first went on stage some were shy and wouldn't sing, but by the end we had a class full of soloists and performers. They gained a tremendous amount of self-esteem. The parents saw the growth in their children as a result of this performance, and many of them were moved to tears.

In a community where parent participation is often considered to be poor, we had all but one family at the performance. Many parents participated by making costumes and serving as stagehands and makeup experts. Some created unique designs, which built up their self-esteem and confidence. The designs were not imposed by the teacher! Both children and parents benefited. They could see that parents are valued and that their talents can be utilized.

Amanda, especially, was proud of her father, and that made her proud of herself. She adjusted better to school, as we had a special relationship. She knew me as a person rather than just a teacher.

The play gave the class a special bonding that they will remember for the rest of their lives. The children from this class still talk about the musical and have asked to perform it again. They seem to share a closer rapport with one another even though they are now in different classes. These students are more open with me than are students from previous years.

Impact on Mr. Jarman

The talents that Mr. Jarman shared with us in creating the musical were great, but what happened later far surpassed the musical itself. Mr. Jarman realized he loved working with children and coming to the school. He experienced *enjoyment*. He had *control*. He was *interested*. He felt *success*. His *self-worth* increased as he saw that his skills were needed. No one judged him by the way he looked, the clothes he wore, the amount of education he had. He could see how the children reacted to his songs, and he was valued for what he had to offer.

All five factors that motivate people to learn and grow were present. Mr. Jarman realized that his musical talents could be shifted to children and to writing children's songs. He saw that he had hidden talents and untapped resources. Next, Mr. Jarman wrote a musical for his son's fifth-grade class with the children's help. This play focused on the issues of drugs, violence, and gang pressures.

Mr. Jarman's work with the musicals was only the beginning. After becoming involved in the school in this way, he developed an interest in the Parent Teacher Association. In the past he had been totally uninvolved, but now he wanted to make some changes. He ran for president and was elected.

Mr. Jarman has conducted the PTA meetings with sensitivity, and he leads the organization in a positive direction. This year an issue came up concerning the right of our students to attend their neighborhood middle school instead of being bused across town. Mr. Jarman rallied the parents around this cause. He spoke to the school board about the injustice of the busing program, and his speech was featured on the evening news on all three local channels. Currently the issue is being brought before a federal judge.

Mr. Jarman's involvement in school issues has been a catalyst for others and has helped to empower students and parents. He has inspired much greater attendance at PTA meetings, and this has resulted in a more balanced ethnic representation than in the past. Parents who never attended meetings before are suddenly not only coming to the meetings but speaking out, asking questions, demanding answers, and addressing officials brought to the school to listen to their concerns.

Mr. Jarman was obviously an untapped gold mine of funds of knowledge. He had knowledge of gardening. He had musical talents. He had the ability to relate to children and adults. He had a desire to make a difference in people's lives. His ability to express himself and at the same time listen to others and empower them has made him a great leader.

Impact on Teacher-Parent-Child Relationships

Through in-depth case studies of families, the teacher ethnographer discovers a wide range of resources he or she previously did not realize were available. The enthusiasm the teacher exudes in discovering these talents is critical in motivating the parent and child. If the teacher places value on this knowledge, then the parents feel valued. This alone can dramatically change the climate of the teacher-parent relationship. The barrier between the "professional" and the home caregiver is broken. Friendship develops and the relationship becomes ongoing and permanent.

Back in the classroom, the teacher shares the discoveries with the children. A child hears the teacher "bragging" about all the skills and knowledge her parents have, and that child's perception of her own parents is improved as well as the child's perception of herself. This often creates a special bond between the child and the teacher that helps them cope better when there are conflicts.

When the teacher has seen the child in her home setting, he or she views this child differently. The teacher is able to relate classroom experiences to situations that the child has experienced. The teacher listens more attentively and is more enthusiastic and sensitive. The teacher understands the whole child.

Once a teacher has spent time in one child's home, he or she can have a better feel for the home lives of all the students. Homes are different, and it is beneficial to visit each family as time permits, but once you have "connected" with one family you are forever more acutely aware of the parents as people — people with successes and struggles, people with goals and dreams, people with skills to offer. The teacher takes more interest when children discuss happenings in the home. He or she asks more questions and wants more information. This can lead to the discovery of additional funds of knowledge.

For example, a child came to school wearing a T-shirt with a hand-painted cactus. Prior to being involved in this project, my response might have been simply, "Isn't that a cute shirt!" Instead, I wanted to know where he got it and who made it. When he told me his grandmother painted it, I knew I had found another fund of knowledge that I might tap into. Eventually more than half the parents became involved in the project, raising money to buy shirts and helping the children paint them.

Later, when I was interviewing another family, I discovered that the father was exceptionally artistic. (Without a home visit I would only have known that he was a school custodian.) When I told the class that Crystal's dad was an artist, Crystal beamed with pride. That night I took the T-shirts to Crystal's house, and the family did decorative lettering and designs on the backs of all the T-shirts. Normally I would not have had any contact with this family, as both parents work full-time. This project allowed them to participate in the class outside school hours. In addition, Crystal, who was intensely sensitive at the beginning of the year, has adjusted better to school.

This spring we were studying quilts as part of a math investigation. A child mentioned that his grandmother makes quilts. Previously I would have just said, "Wow, that's great!" This year I saw his comment as a clue to another fund of knowledge and another potential project. Why not have every child make a family quilt? Each family drew pictures of family members and special events on the quilt squares and intermingled them with scrap material. Parents who didn't have time or knowledge were helped by the parents who did. Many parents had made quilts, so this project tapped into the talents of many families.

Almost any fund of knowledge can be used as a class theme. In selecting which fund of knowledge to use, many factors must be considered. Is the topic one that will motivate the children? Can the topic be linked to curricular goals? Can learning by doing be incorporated? Can parents become involved? Does the teacher understand the topic well enough to make the project succeed? Deciding whether to tap a fund of knowledge for classroom use is a professional judgment each teacher must make.

In Conclusion

Teachers who take the time to go into a child's home in order to learn about the family and about household knowledge will gain a new perspective on the children in their classes and develop increased sensitivity. The typical teacher-parent connection is transcended, and a friend-to-friend interchange and sense of common purpose are fostered. If the funds of knowledge discovered in the process are used in developing the curriculum, an even stronger bond is forged between home and school. Children are more motivated to learn, enjoy school more, and feel more self-esteem and more highly valued. The children and parents feel more ownership of their school.

The five characteristics that motivate children's learning and family involvement are all in evidence in this project. The families that participated *enjoyed* being involved. The participants were given *control*; they were empowered to use their skills and talents. The parents and children were *interested* because the ideas were theirs. There was no doubt that the parents and children felt *success* with their efforts. They made a contribution and a difference. Finally, they felt *self-worth*. They felt pride in themselves and their accomplishments and felt valued.

If teachers include parents and families in their plans for educating children and seriously listen to and value their funds of knowledge, we will turn the key that unlocks the door to a bright future for children, parent, and schools.

❏ ❏ ❏ ❏ ❏

If change agents (teachers and parents) were willing and involved, knowledge about language use could proceed along a two-way path, from the school to the community, and from the community to the school. Traditionally, education research has emphasized the need to train parents of children who are not successful in school achievement to conform to school practices. Knowledge had proceeded along a one-way path from school to "culturally different" communities. In this research the movement of ideas along that path was made two-way, so that a we-they dichotomy did not develop. In the past decade, research has identified standard English structures and patterns of discourse as "school talk" and nonstandard English as "at-home" talk. Prescriptions derived from this dichotomy have found their way into parent education programs, encouraging early home initiation of children to "school talk" and school tasks and ways of thinking. There has been a decided we-they dichotomy, emphasizing how "we" of the school can enrich the background of the "they" of culturally different communities.
—Shirley Brice Heath

❏ ❏ ❏ ❏ ❏

Home-school partnerships can have a positive impact on literacy and learning if families and schools together develop ways of communicating, and build meaningful curriculum that extends the insular classroom community. The key elements of reciprocity and respect must be jointly constructed and locally interpreted.
—Betty Shockley, Barbara Michalove, and JoBeth Allen

❏ ❏ ❏ ❏ ❏

principles for the assessment of family literacy programs

Assessment should be informative about the program and not a value judgment about the family members who are participating in the program.

❑ Emphasis should be placed on ensuring that the program meets the needs of the participants.

❑ Assessment should reflect the values and beliefs of the families participating in the program.

❑ Formal assessments—such as general certificates of education and general education diplomas—have a place within this framework when the goal of the family member is to study for the exam. The question then becomes: how successful is the family literacy educator in supporting the program participant in this endeavor?

Educators should resist large-scale assessments of family literacy programs. Standardized assessment measures should not be used in family literacy programs.

❑ Standardized assessment measures—which are falsely considered objective and neutral—create an imbalance in the power relationships between educators and family members participating in family literacy programs.

❑ School literacies dominate and family literacies are denied.

❑ There are no known standardized assessment measures that represent either family literacy or family literacy programs. Therefore the use of such "tests" is invalid.

❑ The use of standardized assessment measures can have adverse consequences for both family literacy educators and, more important, for the families who participate in family literacy programs.

❑ When funding is dependent on the performance of family members— usually economically disadvantaged mothers and their young children—educators will narrow instruction to preparation for "the test."

- Opportunities for family literacy educators to work collaboratively with family members on curriculum development is greatly reduced—or is simply not an option.

- Family members participating in the program are disadvantaged when family funds of knowledge are not valued and literacy opportunities are lost.

- The inherent cultural bias of all tests is particularly toxic to program participants from racial and ethnic groups who were not considered when the particular test was "normed."

- Program participants whose home language is different from the language of the test are also disadvantaged.

Family members should have the opportunity to work with educators to develop informative assessments of the family literacy program in which they are participating.

- If the purpose of assessment is to improve the quality of programming and the personal opportunities of family members to develop their many literacies, then the participants must be included in the development and implementation of the assessment procedures.

- When conversations about assessment take place, educators and program participants learn from one another and the observations of family members become important.

- The documentation of the strengths of a family literacy program by the program participants becomes the focus of discussion. Problems with the program are explored, tensions acknowledged, and solutions sought.

- Family members reflect on their own learning and make judgments about their own literacy development.

❑ ❑ ❑ ❑ ❑

Standardized Tests in Family Literacy Programs
PETER JOHNSTON

Assessment is a matter of representing people and their learning and includes the conversations that revolve around these representations. In different schools children and their learning are represented by numbers, by letters, and by words:

- "Dennis is an A student, yet he often gets B's in his writing."
- "Molly's reading is at the 20th percentile, much worse than Lamar's."
- "Anthony is consistently choosing books that are challenging for him to read, like the *Polk Street Kids* books by Patricia Reilly Giff. Even though they are still a little difficult for him, he persists for up to twenty minutes at a time. His favorite author is still Roald Dahl (though Dahl's books are beyond his current range), and he mimics Dahl's style often when he writes. His invented spelling shows that he can represent all speech sounds, though his representations are not always conventional yet. For example he writes *wot* (*what*) and *lbne* (*Albany*)."

These different ways of representing students' literacy are not merely interchangeable. They have profoundly different implications. It is from these representations and what we say about them that learners ultimately build their understandings of themselves and their literate relationships to others.

The questions we must ask about assessment, then, have to do with the conversations that take place in the process. But conversations are not simply made up of words and numbers. The glue of conversations is the relationship that underlies them. Consequently, we must also ask questions about how assessment practices affect people's understandings, their practices, and their relationships with others. Who chooses the nature of the assessment is obviously important. If learners have no say in the assessment of their own learning, then they are being subjected to a controlling relationship that becomes part of what they learn about literacy. To insist that standardized tests be used as part of assessments of family literacy programs is not a trivial matter.

To begin with, it is not necessary to have such tests to show that programs have had an impact. These instruments measure only a limited aspect of literacy and they do it in a way that is completely at odds with the ways in which family literacy programs tend to operate. They do not contribute valuable information beyond what can be made available through other means. But it is not just that they are unnecessary that makes them a bad idea. They represent a particular kind of intrusion on both families and the family literacy programs they serve. We have learned about the effects of these intrusions in school settings, where they are normally taken for granted. But we should not take them for granted in either setting. The guidelines for application to the National Family Literacy Project include a requirement that "for each of the measures used [in a proposed program], you should discuss validity and reliability of the instrument. . . . For nonstandardized measures, discuss these issues in detail." To make such a distinction is unfortunate. Standardized measures should be subjected to just as rigorous an examination.

Validity

The past few years has seen a shift toward increasing interest in the validity of assessment. At the same time, people have been changing what they think *validity* means: it is now examined within a framework of *construct validity* and *consequential validity*. Construct validity refers to the value of the constructs through which people make sense of what is being assessed, and consequential validity is the value we place on the consequences of using a particular assessment procedure. A physical education instructor, for example, might assess students in terms of the number of push-ups completed and the number of minutes taken to run a mile. Although these will be fairly reliable measures, if these instruments represent the program's values, such an assessment points to a rather narrow notion of physical education. By contrast, a physical education instructor whose efforts emphasize children's learning to manage their own physical well-being would not choose these measures. In the first place the data they provide would not be relevant to an assessment of his program. The measures would have no construct validity—they would not represent the valued features of instruction.

But there is a second reason why he would not choose these measures: having every child engage in such an assessment would do violence to his instructional efforts. The students would be encouraged to make simplistic interpersonal comparisons, to simplify their notion of what it means to be physically healthy, and to give control of such decisions back to the person controlling the tests. This is what consequential validity is about. Using such tests would minimize the value of social, collaborative arrangements in maintaining physical health and would alter the relationship between the teacher and the students. Furthermore, the greater the stakes attached to the assessment, the more serious the effects.

I hope you see the parallel to the field of family literacy. There are two reasons why using a standardized test would be an unfortunate part of a family literacy program. First, such tests do not represent the nature of either family literacy or family literacy programs, rendering the tests invalid by virtue of their inadequate constructs. Second, they are invalid by virtue of the consequences of their use. We have learned about such consequences in studies of testing in schools. These consequences are most destructive within programs that emphasize a notion of accountability and that have stakes attached.

Consequences for Providers

The impact of standardized testing on providers is the source of much of the consequences for participants. First, the standardized test scores affect not only initial funding but also continuing funding of programs. This means that providers' jobs are on the line—high stakes. The higher the stakes the more teachers' attention narrows to test preparation, an effect that increases over time.[1] This in turn reduces teachers' experimentation with new and innovative ways of going about instruction and the extent to which they collaborate with one another.[2] The greater the accountability pressure felt by teachers through tests, the lower their self-regard and job satisfaction and the higher the probability that they will experience burnout.[3]

Accountability based on standardized tests also changes the way teachers describe their students.[4] The more teachers' work is governed by standardized test accountability, the more their descriptions of students' literacy development will be brief, impersonal, and nonspecific, the more they will focus on what students cannot do rather than what they can do, and the less they will include reference to students' personal literate interests. Such descriptions, incidentally, also distinguish teachers who refer a lot of students to special education from those who refer few students.[5] The depersonalization produced by standardized testing practices has been found particularly alienating with minority families in the context of special education.[6] Furthermore, the more teachers are held accountable for their students' test scores, the more coercive they become in their relationship with the students,[7] a pattern also seen with parents and their children.[8]

Consequences for Program Participants

The narrowing of the learning that takes place in the context of standardized testing has been particularly well documented.[9] Testing also takes up valuable learning time while simultaneously increasing students' tension and anxiety, a consequence that is likely to be exaggerated in family literacy programs, where the adults involved have had unsatisfactory experiences with standardized tests in the past.

In schools, accountability pressure through standardized tests has caused teachers to shunt out of the classroom students who are different and who are not learning as well as others.[10] It is possible that the family literacy equivalent would be for those proposing programs to find ways to exclude participants who appear unlikely to present quick gains on tests. This problem is compounded by the cultural nature of literacy and the impossibility of producing unbiased literacy tests,[11] a point conceded by test makers. For example, the makers of the California Achievement Tests point out that "no test designed to be used nationally can be completely unbiased. The best one can do is minimize the role of the extraneous elements, thereby increasing the number of students for whom the test is appropriate."[12] But since reading, for example, draws heavily on personal knowledge, and since family literacy programs often involve people living at the margins of the mainstream, people whose language patterns and experience are not favored by the tests, bias remains a serious problem. Standardized testing programs also have unequal effects on student motivation as students explain to themselves the nature of their performance on the tests.[13]

Considering Alternatives

There are dangers, then, in merely enforcing the use of standardized assessment measures as they are commonly understood. On the other hand, not all standardized assessments are necessarily as problematic. For example, procedural standardization can be productive. As an example, we might think of an assessment instrument like The Primary Language Record,[14] developed by the Inner London Language Authority. This instrument is standardized in the sense that it requires the collection of a particular range of examples of language and literacy use. These examples are representatives of a quite complex notion of literacy development (construct validity). Examples are not merely checked off but are recorded in concrete detail, with attachments as necessary. This means that efforts to reduce the complexity of literate development to more general indicators cannot lose track of the concrete example. It also makes problem solving a much more concrete affair.

The instrument is standardized in another sense too. It's use requires those involved in observing and judging development (teachers, parents, and in some instances students) to meet regularly to establish the reliability of their assessments. These sessions are called "moderating" sessions and they begin at the local level but extend to include those not associated with the program but involved with similar programs, thus achieving some of the "distance" necessary to help those more closely involved avoid the blindnesses of local communities.

Besides establishing reliability (about 80 percent among beginning observers and 95 percent among experienced observers) and a common language for analysis of literacy development, the moderating procedure engages the participants in learning. When people disagree, they must return to the concrete data and discuss the evaluative issues involved. Such conversations cannot produce learning when the data available are from standardized tests. If assessment is intended to improve the quality of the program, then only conversations about concrete detailed observations will be of benefit. Indeed, the more program staff are able to describe specific changes in literate learning, the more effective they become in providing support. Such approaches offer the reliability desired for examinations of progress while keeping learning conversations and relationships open and focused. These outcomes are thwarted by standardized testing practices, which only produce unspecific abstractions and closed, adversarial conversations.

Principled Process

We have ample evidence that standardized testing produces unproductive learning relationships as well as data that cannot lead to productive programmatic change. No funding source interested in developing family literacy should support such practices. There are better alternatives. When the data we collect are concrete observations of participants' literate actions, we will have grounds for conversations that lead to productive programmatic development. When the involvement of students and family members is a routine and central part of the assessment process, we have the possibility of literate engagement along with productive literate relationships. Let's look toward assessments that have built into their use the means of community learning and involvement—the building blocks of democracy.

Endnotes

1. J. Herman and S. Golan, *Effects of Standardized Testing on Teachers and Learning—Another Look*, CSE Technical Report #334 (Los Angeles: Center for the Study of Evaluation, 1991).

2. M. L. Smith, "Put to the Test: The Effects of External Testing on Teachers," *Educational Researcher* 20(5):8–11 (1991); S. Stodolsky, *The Subject Matters: Classroom Activity in Math and Social Studies* (Chicago: University of Chicago Press, 1998).

3. I. Friedman, "High- and Low-Burnout Schools: School Culture Aspects of Teacher Burnout," *Journal of Educational Research* 84(6): 325–33 (1991); J. Herman and S. Golan, *Effects of Standardized Testing*.

4. P. Johnston, P. Afflerbach, and P. Weiss, "Teachers' Evaluation of the Teaching and Learning of Literacy and Literature," *Educational Assessment* 1(2):91–117 (1993); P. Johnston, S. Guice, K. Baker, J. Malone, and N. Michaelson, "Assessment of Teaching and Learning in 'Literature Based' Classrooms." *Teaching and Teacher Education* 11(4):359–71 (1995).

5. K. Broikou, "Understanding Primary Grade Classroom Teachers' Special Education Referral Practices," Ph.D. dissertation, State University of New York at Albany, 1992.

6. B. Harry, "An Ethnographic Study of Cross-Cultural Communication with Puerto Rican American Families in the Special Education System," *American Educational Research Journal* 29(3):471–94 (1992).

7. E. Deci, N. Spiegel, R. Ryan, R. Koestner, and M. Kauffman, "The Effects of Performance Standards on Controlling Teachers," *Journal of Educational Psychology* 74:852–59 (1982).

8. P. D. Renshaw and R. Gardner, "Parental Goals and Strategies in Teaching Contexts: An Exploration of 'Activity Theory' with Mothers and Fathers of Preschool Children," paper presented at the meeting of the Society for Research in Child Development, Baltimore, MD, 1987.

9. H. Corbett and B. Wilson, *Raising the Stakes in Statewide Mandatory Minimum Competency Testing* (Philadelphia: Research for Better Schools, 1989); G. F. Madaus and P. W. Airasian, "Issues in Evaluating Student Outcomes in Competency-Based Graduation Programs," *Journal of Research and Development in*

Education 10(3):79–91 (1977); M. L. Smith, C. Edelsky, K. Draper, C. Rottenberg and M. Cherland, *The Role of Testing in Elementary Schools*, CSE Technical Report #321 (Los Angeles: Center for the Study of Evaluation, 1991).

10. R. Allington and A. McGill-Franzen, "Does High Stakes Testing Improve School Effectiveness?" *Spectrum: Journal of School Research and Information* 10(2):3–12.

11. P. Johnston, *Constructive Evaluation of Literate Activity* (White Plains, NY: Longman, 1992); C. Marvin, "Attributes of Authority: Literacy Tests and the Logic of Strategic Conduct," *Communication* 11:63–82 (1988).

12. CAT/5 [California Achievement Tests (5th ed.)] Technical Bulletin 1, p. 25 (Monterey, CA: CTB Macmillan/McGraw-Hill, 1992).

13. J. Nicholls. *The Competitive Ethos and Democratic Education* (Cambridge, MA: Harvard University Press, 1989).

14. M. Barrs, S. Ellis, H. Hester, and A.Thomas, *The Primary Language Record: Handbook for Teachers* (Portsmouth, NH: Heinemann, 1988).

❏ ❏ ❏ ❏ ❏

The assumption that literacy cannot be assessed and measured in an absolute manner must be clear. As it is not feasible to "discover" a definitive and unequivocal definition of literacy, or the one best way of defining it, any literacy assessment or measurement will be relative, depending upon what (which reading and/or writing skills and/or literacy social practices) is being assessed or measured, why (for what purposes), when (at which time) and where (in which socioeconomic and cultural context) it is being assessed or measured, and how (by which criterion) it is assessed or measured.

What is then possible and necessary for carrying out any literacy assessment or measurement is to define the phenomenon being assessed or measured on an ad hoc basis, then establishing a precise interpretive framework to serve particular purposes in a specific context. Because a common universal definition is not feasible, a deliberately operational definition, even if it is arbitrary, is both possible and extremely necessary to meet the practical requirements of assessment and measurement procedures. In this way, we can anticipate as many operational approaches to measuring literacy as literacy assessment or measurement programmes. In other words, recognition of the multiple meanings of literacy argues for a diversity of operational definitions, each one meeting the requirements of a specific assessment or measurement programme.

—*Magda Becker Soares*

❏ ❏ ❏ ❏ ❏

Who's Reading Whose Reading?
The National Center for Family Literacy Evaluation Process

SHARON MURPHY

In education, we often either look on assessment as an act of benevolence toward the "assessees" or treat it as benign, something neutral and objective, something that cannot be influenced. But new perspectives from the testing community ask us to examine the consequences of assessment and place assessment within a larger social landscape (Messick 1988; Moss 1994). Whenever I see a battery of literacy assessment tools, I now ask about the relative positions of the assessors and the assessed. I ask what is missing and what is so powerfully assumed that mention is forgone. I ask whose interests are served by the assessment. In essence I ask, Who's reading whose reading? When I took a look at the rating scales/processes of the National Center for Family Literacy (NCFL), they raised serious questions for me about their widescale use as an evaluation measure for family literacy initiatives.

Whose knowledge is valued? I found that the NCFL wasted no time in asserting that families are responsible for their literacy situation. Its stated objective is "to break the intergenerational cycle of undereducation and poverty, one family at a time, by changing the messages communicated in the home" (NCFL 1994a, p. 3). This immediately places families in the position of being inadequate, seemingly unfit places for childrearing. It also denies that literacy experiences occur within homes that participate in family literacy programs.

When I looked through the NCFL rating scale (NCFL 1994b), I discovered that the assumption of family inadequacy stated in the objective pervades the items. For instance, one of the things that the NCFL scales evaluate is the "parent group" component of family literacy programs. To do this, it has items clustered around two themes: item set 15, Balanced Parent Group Content, and item set 16, Supportive, Empowering Parent Group Environment. The users of the scale must rate each item on a scale of 1 to 7. Item 15a states, "Topics for Parent Group are identified through parent interest inventories, observation of families, or group discussions" (p. 9). This item seems odd to me especially given the rhetoric of empowerment in item set 16. The wording of item 15a implies that someone other than parents controls topic choices. This, in turn, suggests that parents are inadequate to make such decisions and bypasses parental empowerment.

Item 16a does more or less the same thing. It states, "Policies (group rules) are established for Parent Group discussions to protect individual privacy and ensure respect for differing opinions and feelings" (p. 9). This item seems to be based on an expectation that parents will be uncooperative or unsociable. What's worse, it seems to imply that providing rules solves group tensions. This controlling stance is far from empowering and fails to recognize that group behavior is complex. Tensions are more likely to be solved by the creation of a culture within the parent group that sustains tolerance, sociability, and community.

These examples show that family knowledge is not valued, despite superficial rhetoric to the contrary. The NCFL focuses on transferring skills to the home (see NCFL 1994b, items 27a through e, pp. 15–16) rather than building on the literacy engagements of the home (see, for example, Goelman, Oberg, and Smith 1984). The knowledge that is valued seems to operate on the simple principle that some forms of literacy and literate behavior can be imposed.

What is missing and what dominates? I found the most explicit statement about what form of literacy really counts in the guidelines for application to the NCFL (NCFL 1994c). In these guidelines, users of NCFL instruments are directed to provide, for both children and adults, "at least, entry and exit test score data as evidence of academic or developmental gains" (p. 5).

When I examined the NCFL scales for assessing adult learning, an emphasis on standardized tests in preference to "informal" measures was apparent (five of eight items are on standardized tests). However, none of the items for the Appropriate Assessment of Young Children (items 23a through 23f, pp. 13–14) mention standardized testing. This seems puzzling. I am not advocating standardized testing here. Instead, I want to suggest an explanation for this paradoxical presence and absence of standardized testing. The NCFL scales seem to reflect a desire to give lip service to the critique of early-childhood testing (see, for example, Perrone 1991) even though, ultimately, standardized tests are demanded as evidence of achievement. The prominence of standardized testing within the adult assessment component seems to suggest that the NCFL has risked using measures that are more "traditional" and archaic (see, for example, Chittenden 1987) despite the ever-growing consensus that standardized tests as a whole are biased toward white middle-class views of the world (see Murphy, under review).

Even though the NCFL lets itself off the hook by admonishing standardized test users to establish the appropriateness of tests for clients (NCFL 1994c, p. 5), test users often uncritically accept the general statements on test appropriateness presented in test manuals. Given the NCFL's statements on the likelihood of the poverty of family literacy clients, it seems that the expectation that standardized test instruments be used is a bias against the very clients the NCFL's family literacy projects are intended to serve.

Whose interests are served by the assessment? Ultimately, the procedures and scales used by the NCFL maintain the status quo. This may seem odd given the astounding level of services the NCFL's scales suggest a family literacy program should have. There seems to be a benevolence in providing literacy programs not only for children but for their illiterate parents! But this seeming act of benevolence is also an act of forgetting—forgetting that, as

Taylor (1993) points out, unless larger societal questions of equality and equity are addressed, these acts further convince society's ghettoized that they bear the responsibilities for their failures to succeed. Without broadscale redress of these issues and without initiatives that recognize the richness and dignity of the lives of participants engaged in family literacy programs, assessment practices such as those of the NCFL will continue to find out what everyone knows—some folks are better off than others. In the meanwhile, I'd suggest that people should be wary of those who are put in positions of "reading" and assigning value to the reading practices of marginalized groups.

References

CHITTENDEN, E. A. 1987. "Styles, Reading Strategies and Test Performance: A Follow-Up Study of Beginning Readers." In R. O. Freedle and R. P. Duran (Eds.), *Cognitive and Linguistic Analyses of Test Performance*, pp. 369–90. Norwood, NJ: Ablex.

GOELMAN, H., A. OBERG, and F. SMITH, Eds. 1984. *Awakening to Literacy.* Portsmouth, NH: Heinemann.

MESSICK, S. 1988. "The Once and Future Issues of Validity: Assessing the Meaning and Consequences of Measurement." In H. Wainer and H. I. Braun (Eds.), *Test Validity*, pp. 33–45. Hillsdale, NJ: Lawrence Erlbaum.

MOSS, P. A. 1994. "Can There Be Validity Without Reliability?" *Educational Researcher* 23(2):5–12.

MURPHY, S. Under review. "Literacy Assessment and the Politics of Identities." *Reading and Writing Quarterly.*

PERRONE, V. 1991. "On Standardized Testing." *Childhood Education* 67:132–42.

NCFL. 1994a. *Family Literacy Program Quality Self-Study.* Louisville, KY: National Center for Family Literacy.

NCFL. 1994b. *Family Literacy Program Rating Scales.* Louisville, KY: National Center for Family Literacy.

NCFL. 1994c (November). *Welcome to the National Family Literacy Project.* Louisville, KY: National Center for Family Literacy.

TAYLOR, D. 1993. "Family Literacy: Resisting Deficit Models." *TESOL Quarterly* 27(3):550–53.

❑ ❑ ❑ ❑ ❑

🚫 *Existing assessment procedures and documents provide meaningful, objective measures of learning and development, which can be summarized for program stakeholders.*

—Family Literacy Program Quality Self-Study

❑ ❑ ❑ ❑ ❑

Well-Designed New Member Induction Activities Indicators:

(a) Environment for initial testing is distraction-free and relatively private.

　1　2　3　4　5　6　7

(b) Counseling sessions are held to establish initial goals and learning plans.

　1　2　3　4　5　6　7

(c) The program provides for a formal expression of commitment to the group, in the form of an event, activity, ceremony, etc.

　1　2　3　4　5　6　7

—Family Literacy Program Rating Scales

❏　❏　❏　❏　❏

Program Evaluation: A Practitioner's Perspective

LUCILLE FANDELL

The organization I work with received a federally funded grant that included conditions I feel disabled me. So much was required by the grant that preparation for and reflection on teaching got short shrift! We as teachers need to understand how the conditions of the state and society bear down on the conditions of our teaching. We need to recover our voices, even as we work to encourage learners to recover theirs. We need to separate our stories from the federal version.

For example, we were obliged by federal Even Start requirements to pay a prescribed portion of the budget to engage an outside "evaluator" and to use certain standardized tests for the adults (the choices were the TABE or the CASAS tests). These requirements represent a mindset that wants to be able to measure learners' progress by a few standardized yardsticks that are not sociolinguistically appropriate to the wide variety of adult learners represented by a program such as ours. In fact, our director managed, with the help of the evaluator (and an act of God when the program was flooded out of its quarters and lost a lot of materials, records, etc.) to get our program released from the federal requirement for standardized testing. The requirement is there, however, as part of the federal mindset. Apart from this, we still had to spend time and money "translating," with the help of the evaluator, our assessment findings into language the federal funders could deal with.

This mandated approach to assessment is problematic for us in that such standardized testing has no place in our curriculum. Assessment within the program, starting from the initial interview, involves parents discussing their various literacies—at home, in the community, at work, etc.

Parents are regularly involved in setting learning goals (through learning contracts) and in reviewing and assessing progress toward those goals. Adult learners have their own portfolios, take part in selecting what goes into them, and discuss their choices. This kind of participatory assessment makes it possible to recognize important strengths and knowledge that adults bring to their learning situation and to incorporate it into their instruction. It also fosters power sharing between students and teachers. How we teach is what we teach!

Individual children's portfolios have also been maintained by the early-childhood teachers. We have also worked with parents to begin family portfolios, which we call "memory books," in which they are encouraged to collect memorabilia from all the family. The program has a wonderful record of individual parents and children playing and learning together. However, when the evaluator produced the official "program evaluation" so much had been lost, so little of the families was to been seen!

From what I have heard, some representatives of programs such as ours tried to address issues such as these in national meetings in Washington, D.C., but failed to alter the federal requirements. I now realize that I was mistaken to think that we could take the federal funds and do the kind of program we wanted. I am inclined to believe at this point in the political history of the United States that programs wanting to do critical education need to find their own funding so that they will be free to operate as they want.

❏ ❏ ❏ ❏ ❏

When Will the National Family Literacy Program Discussion Take Place? An Evaluator's Concerns

THEODORA NIEMEIJER

In our roles as funders, policy makers, practitioners, evaluators, researchers, and advocates, we view models, standards, and evaluations as necessary tools to develop programs that support families in their quest for expanded literacy. Sometimes, blinded by our earnest efforts to best serve families, we fail to see the shortcomings of the tools we choose to use. When prescriptive models and the standards developed to evaluate them are perceived as the definers of family literacy nationally, we risk losing the main focus of family literacy programs to respectfully support all families.

Models and Standards: Frameworks or Prescriptions?

An important characteristic of human beings is our search for patterns or structures in order to make sense of and to exercise some control over our world. One of the outcomes of our search is the development of sets of beliefs, which sometimes become theories or models. According to the *American Heritage Dictionary*, a model is "(1) a preliminary pattern representing an item not yet constructed and serving as the plan from which the finished work, usually larger, will be produced or (2) a tentative ideational structure used as a testing device."

As frameworks for guiding action, models can be valuable tools. The problem with a model occurs when it is too narrowly defined, particularly when the definition of the model does little more than offer service-delivery parameters. As a model becomes more and more prescriptive, it becomes a limiting structure rather than one enabling inventiveness, adaptability, and expansion.

Many factors cause this evolution from a "tentative ideational structure" to a narrower definition. When a model is general, a quality that enhances its adaptability, it does not readily lend itself to a claim of distinctive identity, which is necessary for purposes of copyright ownership and intellectual property rights protection. Models often become defined by their least consequential aspects, resulting in a prescription that renders adherence to a model paramount to meeting the needs of those served by the model's implementation. In the case of many program models, including family literacy programs, service-delivery characteristics (e.g., hours of required attendance, required procedures, or specified client outcomes such as obtaining a GED) define the model and limit local program adaptations.

The need to replicate the model faithfully is another factor in the model's evolution from a framework to a prescription. Program operators often feel compelled to focus on precise replication, especially in the initial stages of implementation, and lose sight of whether the model "fits" within the local context. The tension between faithful replication and local needs and concerns presents an ongoing dilemma.

Another factor that narrows the definition of a model is the need for evaluation. Evaluation designs based on past research and paradigms tend to concentrate on the prescriptive elements of the model (e.g., hours of service delivery offered, attendance), which are the most readily quantified but perhaps not the most important aspects of the program. One result is that the evaluation centers on the model and how it fits with or serves the needs of different populations. The recent focus on client-centered needs calls for an evaluation design centered on the needs of different populations and how the model or services have adjusted to meet those needs.

Evaluation can narrow the definition of a model in yet another way: by imposing "standards" as prescriptions for adequate performance (e.g., participants will gain one grade level on a standardized achievement test per twenty hours of instruction). This use of the term *standards* in the traditional psychometric point of view is increasingly confused with the national focus on "standards" as frameworks or principles for guiding—not determining—local program design, implementation, and evaluation (Research and Training Inc. 1994).

When the interaction of these factors renders a model for educational or social services prescriptive, services based on the model are less able to serve populations, which exist in dynamic, evolving systems. We must be wary when in our search for answers, a model is seen as the panacea for the solution of our social problems.

We Need a National Discussion About Family Literacy

As they are currently defined, many family literacy programs are characterized by the above limitations. They employ models defined by required program components and prescriptions for service delivery and client participation. They are evaluated by precise "standards" of performance that may be irrelevant to the populations they serve.

Consistent with the national focus on establishing standards as frameworks for local decision making, a national discussion about family literacy standards would help promote the importance of family literacy on the national agenda. Among the important questions that need to be discussed are: (1) Do family literacy programs address the rich complexity of literacy within individual families and within the different community contexts nationwide? (2) Do we operate from a strengths rather than a deficit perspective? (3) Is literacy a corollary or cause of poverty? (4) How are family education programs different from family literacy programs?

Reference

RESEARCH AND TRAINING INC. 1994. *Standards Test: Conclusion from the Literature on Standards.* Overland Park, KS: Research and Training Inc.

❑ ❑ ❑ ❑ ❑

Developing a Framework for Program-Based Family Literacy Evaluation
ADELE THOMAS AND BRAM FISHER

Adele Thomas and Bram Fisher worked with four practitioners in Ontario, Canada, to explore the ways in which family literacy programs could be evaluated effectively and appropriately. The synopsis below has been adapted by Gretchen Owocki from an interim version of their comprehensive report, Assessment and Evaluation Strategies in Family Literacy Program Development *(Ottawa: Bonanza, 1996).*

In start-up years, family literacy programs in Ontario developed ongoing program procedures and specific literacy goals that reflected the diverse needs of individual communities. Practitioners and participants have recently turned their attention to issues of program accountability. Because the field of family literacy is developing at a time when alternative perspectives on program evaluation are receiving increasing prominence, there is little consensus on the characteristics of effective evaluation practices for family literacy.

The present project sought to establish a process and a framework for family literacy evaluation among diverse programs. Researchers and practitioners explored processes by which effective, feasible evaluation strategies could be adopted across a range of program types. A major goal was to ensure that evaluation would be viewed as an informative asset to program development and to communication with learners. The initial project objectives were to:

- Review methodologies for family literacy evaluation.
- Investigate current practices related to program evaluation.
- Design appropriate evaluation instruments.
- Develop alternative approaches to program evaluation.

A major goal was to institute a family literacy evaluation framework that would enable practitioners (1) to clarify program strengths and weaknesses in light of learner perspectives and (2) to obtain information that would document progress. A critical component in developing this new framework was a commitment to shared reflection on evaluation and to open discussion of how evaluation activities were working.

In early phases of the project, practitioners were asked what kinds of evaluation strategies would provide evidence of the long-term effects of family literacy programs. Project participants (all of whom were program coordinators or key teachers in the four programs) reflected on their current evaluation activities and presented their views on what was needed in their individual programs.

At the outset of the project, there were differences among the programs' literacy goals, frequency of contact with families, and extent to which parent and child interacted. While each program had adopted routines for monitoring activity, none of the practitioners considered their current evaluation procedures adequate for documenting learner progress. An organizing scheme that laid out an array of available evaluation options helped the practitioners select procedures that would best fit the needs of an individual program.

Reflection on a core set of family literacy standards helped practitioners clarify specific components of family literacy, target areas for evaluation, and set goals for future program initiatives. The practitioners reviewed program characteristics considered important by the Family Literacy Commission of the International Reading Association (IRA) and by the Ontario Training and Adjustment Board (OTAB). They discussed which of the standards were relevant to their individual programs, and rated themselves as to how well they thought their programs were meeting the various objectives and guidelines. They also discussed challenges in evaluation, set goals for future evaluation activities, and developed routines for conducting evaluation tailored to their individual needs. The practitioners were successful in developing a range of evaluation strategies that reflected individual program objectives. The extent of evaluation activity was related to the specific family literacy programs adopted.

Over the course of the project, all of the programs were fine-tuned based on trials with program participants. In all, the evaluation process was effective in providing feedback on conditions that facilitated or hindered the accomplishment of family literacy objectives.

Successful and informative evaluation can occur when programs develop their own evaluation schemes. Organizing schemes and preset standards are also useful when selected and revised in response to the individual goals of individual programs.

❑ ❑ ❑ ❑ ❑

Family Literacies:
What Can We Learn from Talking with Parents?
HELEN JAMES

First published in the United Kingdom in Language Matters, CLPE, 1993/94, No. 3, *pp. 25–28.*

At Bangabandhu School [in Tower Hamlets, London] we are very aware of the importance of parents as partners in the education of their children. Our parents have a lot to offer their children and a lot to offer us as a school. We want parents to feel confident to value their own role in their children's learning and to share their expertise about their children with us. We also know that we will learn very little from parents unless the atmosphere in the school is one that welcomes and values parents. If parents feel excluded and undervalued, they will not share their knowledge about their children with the school. We know that we still have a long way to go and that the things we have put in place so far have constantly to be followed up by a willingness to take seriously the issues of class, racism, and the status of bilingualism

বঙ্গবন্ধু প্রাইমারী স্কুল

Bangabandhu Primary School

আপনার সন্তানের সাথে বই পড়া

Reading with your child

Figure 5

within our community and the wider society, which so affect the relationships between parents and schools. We also have to commit time, effort, and
money to continue home-school links.

Bangabandhu is a new school that is still expanding. Eighty-six percent
of the children are Bangladeshi, and a wide range of other languages are also
represented. Eight percent of the students are monolingual in English. Since
many parents are bilingual and some of them are not familiar with the English education system, part of our job is to make the school accessible and
understandable to parents and to involve parents as much as possible in the
life and work of the school. We cannot assume that parents' reluctance to get
involved in school means that they are not interested. It is up to us to explain
the culture of school to them and to make them part of it. At Bangabandhu
we have tried to involve parents in our school in a variety of formal and informal ways. They are not all directly connected with literacy, but they all work
toward providing a context in which the cultures and language of our parents
and children are valued.

As a staff we make the effort to find out about the languages and literacies of the community we are working with. Two staff meetings have been
led by Bangladeshi members (both connected with the Section 11 projects,
which are currently under threat from government cuts); they talked about
the history of Bangladesh, the Bangladeshi education system, and the history
of the language and literacy of our Sylheti community. As with so many language issues, there is a lot of disagreement about the significance of the language history and about the status of the Sylheti dialect of Bengali that the
majority of the students speak. Some of the non-Sylheti staff members began

to learn Sylheti from our year-6 children during lunchtime. The children enjoyed seeing us make mistakes and they enjoyed seeing us squirm when we forgot something they had just taught us. Being put in the position of a language learner was an important reminder of what most of our children experience at school. The lessons taught us a lot more than the very useful words and phrases!

We also run a parent and toddler group and toy library every Tuesday morning. This is an important way of talking with parents informally. It provides opportunities for parents to talk with each other and with staff members about the school and about their children. From these sessions it has become clear that we have to work especially hard to encourage our Bangladeshi parents to join the group, although they are in the majority in the school. Ways to do this are to involve the whole school in talking with parents about coming to the group and to offer the kinds of activities that parents consider helpful. The opportunity to come and talk while the children play with some toys is not automatically seen as valuable. A programme of talks from health professionals and some practical workshops on sewing and keeping fit have been tried so far, and we intend to offer more directly literary-based workshops as well, such as book making and bilingual storytelling.

Some of our parents are now participating in a course on how to set up a toy library. This is another way of developing women's confidence and giving them skills. When we had a Bangladesh Festival, to show some of the work that the infants had been doing in their work on Bangladesh, some of the women from the toddlers' group arranged for food to be sold throughout the day. The day was a big and enjoyable success and an important event in making the Bangladeshi parents feel a valued part of the school.

Informal contacts with parents seem to be a very important way of creating the right context for sharing knowledge about children. Our new building makes this easy for us, since all the classes have an outside door where parents come to collect the children. During our Friday morning assemblies, a different class each week shows some of the work they have been doing. These children's families are invited to the assemblies and to the staff room afterward for a cup of coffee and a chat.

We also hold talks about reading for parents and give out our home-school reading booklet. Currently we talk to parents with children in the nursery [three- and four-year-olds] and in the reception class [four- and five-year-olds], and also hold a general meeting for parents of children in any class and those who are new to school who may have missed the original talks. We are now planning parents' meetings to look at extending reading in the junior [elementary] classes. We always have an interpreter at these meetings to make them as accessible as possible, and they do provide useful starting points for discussions with parents about reading. Parents have started to volunteer to work in classrooms, too.

As the range of languages used by children in school increases we need to use parents more in order to provide our school with texts and artifacts that reflect this. Part of our focus for home-school liaison is encouraging parents to help us make signs, labels, tapes, and books in a variety of languages. This helps provide a context in which children can feel confident about and proud of their home language. Since this work requires that parents feel confident enough to share their languages with us, we spend a lot of time and effort talking with parents. (I was asked to write a welcome label in German, which I studied at university. I instantly became paranoid about spellings and mistakes, taking days to write a few words. All the times I had said to reluctant parents, Don't worry, it doesn't matter if it's not absolutely right, came back to haunt me!)

One formal way we talk with parents about literacy is to discuss their child's Primary Learning Record with them during the autumn and summer terms. All the informal ways of involving parents in the life of the school mean that when we discuss the Primary Learning Record, a lot of the underlying principles about the way we approach literacy and the way we want to involve parents in that process are already understood. Some teachers have been concerned that parents would only say what they thought we wanted to hear. However, when parents know we are genuinely interested in their knowledge about their children, we are far more likely to have a more genuine dialogue. The longer parents are involved in the process, the more informed they will be about what is going on in the school and the more confident they will feel about telling us what their children do at home. The same is of course true for children. We can learn so much from children about what they know, about how they learn best, if the classroom and school are set up to encourage them to reflect and to talk honestly about what they know about their own learning.

Let me use an example from my own reception class. F. had spent several weeks crying a lot, walking around the classroom, never getting involved in any of the activities. In whole-class sessions on the carpet he looked distressed and didn't seem to be a part of the class at all. During my discussion with his mother—with Aysha, the primary helper in the class, as interpreter—she said: "At home he sings songs from school and teaches me and his dad "Hickory Dickory Dock" and other songs. He loves school. He's worried about going to the toilet on his own and wants to take his sister with him. He's nervous with non-Bengali people, but he's getting a bit better. He's very nervous with strangers at home or when people fight." Not only did we find out that F. was understanding what was going on in the class and indeed had enough confidence to teach his mum and dad, but also that he had a fear of non-Bengali people that we needed to address. When we sang nursery rhymes together in class, I said that F. knew these well. (Several children looked a bit bemused, never having seen him join in.) I tried to speak to F. whenever possible in the few Bengali phrases I know in order to build up more trust. We also tried to offer him more time with the Bengali helper. Using what his mother had told us, we found ways to tap into what he knew and

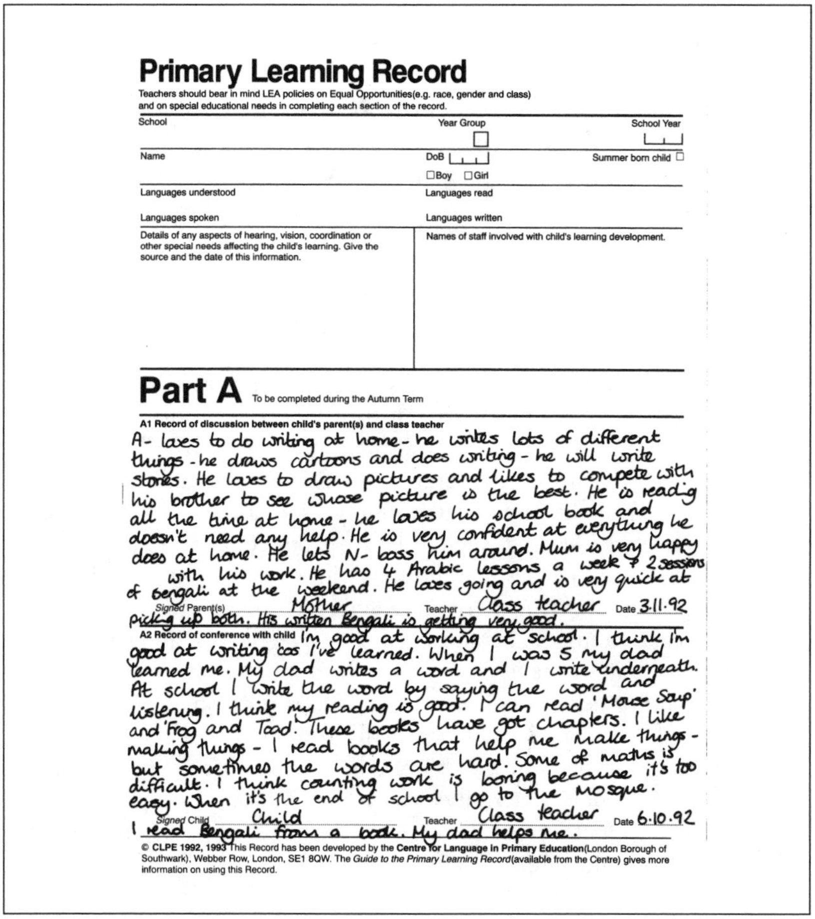

Primary Learning Record

Teachers should bear in mind LEA policies on Equal Opportunities(e.g. race, gender and class) and on special educational needs in completing each section of the record.

School | Year Group | School Year

Name | DoB | Summer born child

☐Boy ☐Girl

Languages understood | Languages read

Languages spoken | Languages written

Details of any aspects of hearing, vision, coordination or other special needs affecting the child's learning. Give the source and the date of this information.

Names of staff involved with child's learning development.

Part A

To be completed during the Autumn Term

A1 Record of discussion between child's parent(s) and class teacher

A- loves to do writing at home - he writes lots of different things - he draws cartoons and does writing - he will write stories. He loves to draw pictures and likes to compete with his brother to see whose picture is the best. He is reading all the time at home - he loves his school book and doesn't need any help. He is very confident at everything he does at home. He lets N- boss him around. Mum is very happy with his work. He has 4 Arabic lessons a week & 2 sessions of Bengali at the weekend. He loves going and is very quick at picking up both. His written Bengali is getting very good.

Signed Parent(s) Mother Teacher Class teacher Date 3.11.92

A2 Record of conference with child

I'm good at working at school. I think I'm good at writing 'cos I've learned. When I was 5 my dad learned me. My dad writes a word and I write underneath. At school I write the word by saying the word and listening. I think my reading is good. I can read 'Mouse Soup' and 'Frog and Toad'. These books have got chapters. I like making things - I read books that help me make things - but sometimes the words are hard. Some of maths is difficult. I think counting work is boring because it's too easy. When it's the end of school I go to the mosque. I read Bengali from a book. My dad helps me.

Signed Child Child Teacher Class teacher Date 6.10.92

Figure 6: A page from a Primacy Learning Record

felt confident at, and we found ways to minimise his fears about school. Neither of these things would have been possible without a culture in the class and school that encouraged the use of children's home languages.

In order to learn more about our children's knowledge of language and literacy, and in order to encourage parents to have more confidence in their role in their children's language and literacy development, we need to continue talking with parents. We need to listen to what they have to tell us about their children and to share with them what we know about their children's learning. As teachers we need to know what messages parents are getting from the things we do in school. This is not a straightforward process, and we have to work hard as a school in order to maintain and improve these contexts for discussion with parents.

❏ ❏ ❏ ❏ ❏

Standardized Tests:
What Family Literacy Programs
Can Learn from Schools
MARY BENTON

Some gates are so locked up they couldn't be doorways.
—Arnie, Grade 4

Mention the word *assessment* and most people immediately think *test*. And, indeed, a test is a form of assessment. But in most schools in the United States tests are the *only* form of assessment used or valued. This obsession with testing began early in this century when educators tried to replicate the factory-like model of the industrial economy. Our naïveté about how tests are constructed, the misleading way results are reported, and the impact of the scores they generate has resulted in their widespread acceptance, with little or no attention given to the detrimental effect they have wrought.

For decades testing companies, educators, legislators, and families have allowed invalid and unreliable tests to have drastic effects on teaching and learning, harming generations of students. First, the complex nature of learning is ignored by using tests that target only those areas that can be easily and cheaply scored. Second, the scores from these tests either define students' capabilities in terms of predetermined categories or dismiss their potential in favor of ranking them from highest to lowest within a preestablished, unyielding distribution curve.

1990

In 1990, armed with enthusiasm and optimism, I prepared an analysis of the test-taking and -reporting processes that were then mandated by the state for use in my school as well as in all other public schools in New Hampshire. Here is the gist of that report:

Over the past several years, schools in New Hampshire and in many other states have made tremendous progress in establishing developmentally appropriate curricula that address the complex literacy demands students need to exist in our ever-changing world. These curricula focus on creating students who value learning and are able to think, problem solve, and synthesize information.

Along with the knowledge of how important it is for schools to develop this type of curriculum, we have also come to understand the need for assessment practices that measure the many things we are teaching. Some of these presently in use include portfolio assessments, individual profiles of students' observable learning behavior, and in-depth evaluation of student performances and products. Alternative assessment is presently a major focal point for education researchers. They, like the classroom teachers, have learned that schools must use and value assessment practices that are congruent with the learning and knowledge reflected by the developmentally appropriate curricula that are being implemented.

But a serious problem exists. As educators we have known for years that tests that rely on comparative scores have provided misleading and inaccurate information about our students and schools. Unfortunately, standardized testing has gained a stranglehold on the educational system. Just as educators and researchers are realizing the positive benefits of alternative assessments, we are faced with parents, community members, and legislators who have been led to believe that psychometric test scores are the only way to measure school and student achievement. Because so many people believe standardized tests are crucial to assessment and because many of us, for the time being, are still shackled to their use, it is imperative that we become knowledgeable and articulate about all that is wrong with both the tests and their overuse.

Reliability

Test developers fill their manuals with scores of intimidating graphs and charts that they contend support the reliability of the test. In actuality, they misuse these charts to purport inaccurate information. For example, the reliability of a test can be determined by consistency over time or by what is referred to as *internal consistency* (after a single administration of the test a formula is used to establish a reliability estimate). Although internal consistency is considered a lot less reliable, it is the only type inherent to standardized tests. According to the test developers, even under the best conditions, a student's "true score" on any given subtest could be much higher or lower than what was reported, especially if the score is "near the floor or the ceiling." In other words, low scores could in fact be much higher and high scores could be much lower!

Distorted Use

Because of the weight the scores of these tests carry, the need to achieve "high scores" often encourages schools to spend hours preparing and practicing for the test. Skills are often taught in test format rather than as they would be used in real life. For example, instead of having students practice language mechanics by editing connected pieces of text, they fill in worksheets. Worse yet, researchers have found that testing shapes classroom instruction and negatively impacts educational goals and curricula. Studies show that many schools forsake instruction that encourages thinking, solving problems, and synthesizing information, in order to promote memorization of isolated facts that can be regurgitated within the confines of the multiple-choice format of standardized tests.

It is up to us to become informed about the issues. It is also up to us to help others make connections between these issues and what happens in classrooms. Many of us must still administer standardized tests and share the results with parents. Instead of just passing out the tests to our students we need to take the time to look at the administration and technical manuals. We need to find out how these tests were developed and how various factors influence the reporting of scores. Next, we need to take a careful look at the specific items of each subtest. When we share the results with parents, we should take the opportunity to use our knowledge of teaching, learning, and child development to point out some of the contradictions between what the developers are claiming to test and what is actually being tested.

Multiple-Choice Format

The multiple-choice format of standardized tests constrains content and prevents students from demonstrating their procedures or explaining their answers. It also inhibits them from changing answers even when they realize they have marked the wrong choice. One reason standardized tests are widely used is that they can be optically scanned. This saves time and money for the testing companies, but our students waste hours making sure that there are no stray marks on their answer sheets, that they have filled in the circles and boxes completely and made their marks heavy and dark, and that when they want to change an answer they erase the mark (which they have been instructed to make heavy and dark!) and make a new mark. From the students' viewpoint it is often not worth the trouble.

Testing Conditions

A student's frame of mind during the test has more to do with actual performance than how much he or she knows about the question asked. The California Achievement Tests (CATs) examiner's manual cautions teachers to:

- —Test on Tuesday, Wednesday, or Thursday.
- —Avoid days just before or after vacations or important school functions.
- —Avoid testing just after students have had strenuous physical activity.
- —Be sensitive to the fatigue level and attention span of the children.
- —Eliminate distractions.

Additional instructions tell teachers, "The test was standardized under carefully controlled conditions (another of the factors which contributes to the reliability), and to obtain the most valid results, it is important to simulate the standardization conditions as closely as possible." Despite these warnings to establish the best possible conditions, the State Board of Education mandates a specific time frame for the test to be administered, thus making the cautions worthless.

Validity

The tests are constructed by test developers who often have an inaccurate understanding of areas the tests claim to measure. Examples from CATs subtests administered to fourth graders illustrate this point.

Most people would assume that a subtest entitled Word Analysis would measure a child's ability to decode unknown words by analyzing their elements. However, the directions instruct the child to "choose the word that does not contain the same sound as the underlined part." The child looks at the stimulus word and its underlined part—exp<u>er</u>t, for example—then chooses the correct response:

furnace	terrify	mermaid	hurricane
A	B	C	D

In order to respond correctly, the child must be able to read each of the words. Knowledge of phonetic principles by which to analyze these words are of little help, and regional dialects can seriously affect anyone's ability to find the word that does not match the stimulus.

The Reading Comprehension section—the major subtest in the entire battery—is set up to contradict everything we know about determining how well a child can read. The untitled passages are short and unrelated. Children are penalized for having background information. Unfamiliar proper nouns are used in every passage. Passages are chosen without students' interest in mind. Instead, they reflect the kinds of reading and topics found in the basals that are often published by the very same companies that develop the tests.

After five of the eight stories in this subtest, students are asked, "Which sentence tells something that could not really have happened?" For example:

Which sentence tells something that could not really have happened?
A The banana bread overflowed the pan.
B The banana bread cried out, "I'm done!"
C The banana bread recipe won a prize.
D The banana bread was the best the boys had ever eaten.

According to the answer sheet B is the correct answer, but I wonder. Should children whose favorite story is *The Gingerbread Man* be penalized for thinking inanimate objects often talk in stories? What about the child who chooses D because banana bread is something he would never consider eating? The lack of clarification in the directions and the obvious disregard for what children bring to every reading experience is astonishing. Students could easily give "incorrect" responses throughout the comprehension section simply because they thought differently from or knew more than the person who developed the question.

Perhaps so little thought has gone into the construction of this part of the test because developers consider the passages irrelevant. The technical manual states "passage dependency (the degree to which it is necessary to read a stimulus passage in order to answer the test questions based upon the passage) should not be used as a criterion for item selection." This means that instead of being concerned about whether or not our students are able to read, understand, interpret, and make meaning from a variety of materials, the developers measure comprehension by developing questions that can be answered without reading any text.

The Spelling section of the test is constructed with this same lack of understanding about what spelling really is. We know that spelling is a cognitive process, not rote memorization. Children acquire spelling concepts by learning about phonetic and structural elements and morphemes. In addition, we know that spelling is connected to our personal use of words and to the frequency with which those words are used. Choosing the correct word from several other similar choices has been found to be ineffective in assessing the ability to spell. In fact, a study published by the *Journal of Educational Psychology* found that mixing the correctly spelled word with incorrect variations *interferes* with the ability to spell the word. When we ask fourth graders to choose the correct, often unfamiliar, word from a group of four close approximations, we are not judging their ability to spell. Even more discouraging, we are learning nothing about the concepts they may or may not know.

Language Mechanics appears to be the test developers' way to judge how dexterous children can be with visual tasks before they become totally frustrated and overwhelmed. As with all the other subtests, they are required to move back and forth between the test booklet and the answer sheet. If this isn't tedious enough, students are also asked to follow directions and sort through confusing formats that are constantly changing. Students who are just completing the first month of fourth grade are given an array of tasks that have nothing to do with their ability to use or proofread written language. The following is an example from a section that directs students to "decide which punctuation mark, if any, is needed in the sentence."

Yes I did ask you to set the table for dinner.
F .   G :   H ?   J ,   K None

Do you think the test developer has F or J in mind as the correct response? Would you want your ability to use written language to be measured by this and similar items?

Distorted Scores

Concern about the construction and scoring of items in all the subtests of the total battery is compounded by the way scores are reported. The CATs, like all other standardized tests, continue to include grade-equivalent scores as one measure of achievement. This is the most misleading score, yet unfortunately the one most people view as understandable.

I don't want to belabor the technical information inherent to the use of grade-equivalent scores, but it is important to understand the faulty assumptions behind them, the primary one being that the knowledge of a fourth grader with a grade-equivalent score of 7.0 is the same as that of an eighth grader with a grade-equivalent score of 7.0. It is also important to know that because of the differences in the grade-equivalent distributions for various subject matters, a fourth grader might have a 5.3 in reading comprehension and 4.6 in mathematics and yet have a higher fourth-grade percentile rank in mathematics.

Even when stanines and percentiles are used to report scores, accurate pictures of performance are distorted because raw scores have to be distributed along normal distribution curves. For example, because the size of percentile units are not constant in terms of raw score units, the raw score difference between the 80th and 90th percentile is much greater than the raw score difference between the 40th and 50th percentile. This means students functioning in the 40–50th percentile range are allowed fewer errors than those functioning in the 80–90th percentile range. Even if the tests were testing the skills they say they are, the present system of reporting scores would still be an inaccurate portrayal of a student's achievement.

Misrepresentations of Test Results

Presently parents, community members, and legislators rely on testing companies, not educators, to provide them with information about how well our students and schools are doing. This information usually comes in newspaper accounts. These articles rarely do little more than echo the recommendations or points made by the testing company. Journalists never point out that if these scores are true reflections of how well schools are doing, there should be more consistency across grades when the schools with the "best scores" are listed. When the *Manchester Union Leader* recently listed the ten best New Hampshire schools, they had to make separate lists for fourth, eighth, and tenth grades. Only two schools appeared in each of the three lists. Why didn't the reporters question why schools performed well at one grade level but not another? Readers were not alerted to the implications that can be drawn from the fact that four out of the ten "best" fourth grades had fewer than thirty students. No indication was made in these reports whether schools included special education students in the group of students tested. Questions were not asked about what is achieved by comparing student A to student B, Manchester to Groveland, New Hampshire to Texas.

Our goal is not to malign the present tests in hopes that they will be replaced by ones that may or may not be more reliable or better constructed. Our goal is to ensure students the best possible educational future. Definitions of learning and education have changed drastically. These definitions demand that students learn far more actively than ever before. We can no longer use a testing system that is in total opposition to this kind of learning. We must use assessments that reflect our students' abilities to communicate effectively, to solve problems, and to learn how to learn. Parents, community members, and legislators have the right to know why psychometric testing can no longer provide them with the information they are seeking. They have the right to know that continued reliance on these tests will have a damaging effect not only on our schools but on the future of our economy.

1996

Since my original analysis of the state-mandated testing practices, students in New Hampshire are no longer being subjected to the California Achievement Tests. We, like many other states, now have a statewide Educational Improvement and Assessment Program (NHEIAP). The NHEIAP is a result of a 1992 state law that requires New Hampshire public schools to use an assessment program based on "what students should know and be able to do." On the surface this legislation appears to be an excellent opportunity to implement assessment practices that more accurately reflect the needs of our rapidly changing society.

Instead of making a real difference for New Hampshire schools, however, this program, like the testing system it replaced, continues to be more about money and control than about implementing sound and purposeful assessment practices. Politicians and State Board of Education members could have relied on the resources and expertise within the educational and school community, but, as in the past, they have given control of the assessment aspect of the program to Advanced Systems in Measurement and Evaluation, a company that provides statewide testing programs for eight other states. This company began in 1984 with annual revenues of $300,000. Revenues for the 1994–95 school year exceeded $12 million and for the current year are expected to top $15 million. In addition to constructing and scoring the tests, they provide workshops, materials, and other services—statewide and locally—that are designed to respond to what many schools perceive as a need for "help in making kids do better on the tests." Legislators, State Board of Education members, and representatives from the State Department of Education all proudly proclaim that the NHEIAP is a result of collaboration between themselves, Advanced Systems, and educators working in schools.

When the legislation was passed, classroom teachers and administrators from all areas of the state were given the responsibility of developing statewide frameworks that reflect our current understanding of what children need to learn in language arts, mathematics, science, and social studies. Advanced Systems was given the responsibility of developing an assessment process that would reflect the goals of the frameworks. But while educators were working in earnest to develop the frameworks, the test, "designed" by Advanced Systems, was already being administered—two spring testing cycles for all third graders in New Hampshire were finished prior to the completion and adoption of the language arts framework.

Despite the Commissioner of Education's admonition that "it is inappropriate to use the results alone to compare one school district or school to another," local newspapers continue to use test results to rank schools. While the new test has abandoned using grade equivalents and stanines—students are instead sorted into four levels, novice, basic, proficient, and advanced—journalists still contrive ways of totaling and comparing the number in each level to arrive at statistically invalid ranking conclusions. School budget meetings, often fueled by antitaxpayer groups waving these newspaper articles, result in reduced funding both to those communities who fare well (why spend more when we already have good scores?) and those whose results are not so positive (why support a system that isn't educating our children?). Money issues aside, uninformed community members tend to believe there is validity to the rankings and worry that there is something wrong with their school's curriculum or staff for failing to have more students in the higher levels. Of course, no mention is made in the newspaper article that by design Advanced Systems expects to have only 1–5 percent of the students in the advanced level, 5–15 in the proficient level, 50 percent in the basic level, and 30 percent in the novice level. Parents and community members are not told that the expectation for the majority of students to fall in the basic level is so high that it is the only level subdivided into three—top basic, middle basic, and bottom basic.

Perhaps the most insidious aspect of the "test" is in its reporting of individual student progress. While the test was constructed to determine how well New Hampshire students in general are doing and to aid local program-improvement and resource-allocation decisions, Advanced Systems, despite warnings that they acknowledge as warranted, also generates individual student reports. With no regard for a student's self-esteem or the long-term effect being categorized as novice or basic might have on the way a nine-year-old's potential is perceived and with no accompanying documentation that explains the test thoroughly and warns of its shortcomings, families receive a state-generated form letter that reduces their child's knowledge, ability, and achievement to one word.

The warning is clear to all those who give and take tests, especially those who are presently involved in family literacy programs. Tests and test taking are not about providing information. Tests and test taking are not about designing and implementing assessment practices that document literacy development and achievement. Tests are about profit. Every year millions of dollars that should be directed to programs and participants goes to increased revenues for test makers. Tests are about power. Policy makers and funding agencies exert their control by regulating who participates and what kinds of activities—both social and academic—they are allowed to participate in. In order to obtain recognition and funding for their programs, the agencies submit family members to tests that serve no other purpose than the gate keeping. As long as money and power drive tests and test taking, assessment abuse will continue.

References

BENTON, MARY. 1990. "Standardized Testing: Informing Ourselves and Parents, Every Teacher's Responsibility." *NETWORK NEWS* 2(1)(Winter). Published by the Granite State Integrated Language Network of the International Reading Association.

BRANDT, RON. 1989. "On Misuse of Testing: A Conversation with George Madaus." *Educational Leadership* 46(April):26–29.

BROWN, REXFORD. 1989. "Testing and Thoughtfulness." *Educational Leadership* 46(April):31–33.

ELKIND, DAVID. 1989. "Developmentally Appropriate Practice: Philosophical and Practical Implications." *Kappan* 71(October):113–17.

HANEY, WALTER, and GEORGE MADAUS. 1989. "Searching for Alternatives to Standardized Tests: Whys, Whats, and Whithers." *Kappan* 70(May):683–87.

HIEBERT, ELFRIEDA H., and ROBERT C. CALFEE. 1989. "Advancing Academic Literacy Through Teachers' Assessments." *Educational Leadership* 46(April):50–54.

JERVIS, KATHE. 1989. "Daryl Takes a Test." *Educational Leadership* 46(April):10–15.

NEILL, MONTY D., and NOE J. MEDINA. 1989. "Standardized Testing: Harmful to Educational Health." *Kappan* 70(May):688–97.

PERRONE, VITO, ed. 1991. *Expanding Student Assessment*. Alexandria, VA: Association for Supervision and Curriculum Development.

SHEPARD, LORRIE A. 1989. "Why We Need Better Assessments." *Educational Leadership* 46(April):4–9.

WIGGINS, GRANT. 1989. "A True Test: Toward More Authentic and Equitable Assessment." *Kappan* 70(May):703–13.

WOLF, DENNIE P. 1989. "Portfolio Assessment: Sampling Student Work." *Educational Leadership* 46:35–39.

principles for educators and funding agencies

To speak of the rights of families to become literate implies that educators have a responsibility to provide such opportunities.

❑ Unfortunately, educators are often unable to fulfill their responsibilities to families because of competing obligations to fulfill the requirements of funding agencies.

❑ Educators are often caught between competing ideologies. For many educators, literacy is a human right, while for many funding agencies— both governmental and private—literacy is a political expedient.

❑ Many educators are deeply committed to their work as family literacy practitioners but are unable to work continuously with families because of the unrealistic, "quick fix" expectations of funding agencies.

❑ In schools, the family literacy work of teachers is often unrecognized. Schools rarely define education as a collaborative venture with families and communities.

❑ A question that some teachers ask is: How do you change your practice within an institution that resists change?

Educators should be encouraged to submit proposals that are not restrained by the requirement to meet the guidelines for a single dominant model of literacy which has no local relevance.

❑ When educators are given the opportunity to develop family literacy initiatives in a local community, generic standardized programs no longer work.

❑ When family members are included in the decision-making process, family literacy initiatives become participatory and inquiry-based. Educators work to establish partnerships so that every participant—family members and educators—have an equal voice in the development of the family literacy initiative.

❑ When educators and family members make decisions together, time frames change. Attending set classes every week for sixteen weeks is no longer the norm. Evenings and weekends become important.

Participants might want to spend extended periods exploring the literacies of their families and their communities, responding to issues that affect their everyday lives, and establishing intergenerational literacy initiatives that bring elders and children together.

❑ Educators should recognize that the development of new literacy connections might take extended periods, that for communities to establish new literacies might take years.

Educators should be given the opportunity to develop assessment procedures with the families participating in the family literacy initiative.

❑ The imposition of standardized assessment procedures critically undermines both educators and families in their initiative to work together.

❑ Assessment should be informative, undertaken to improve the responsiveness of the family literacy initiative to needs of the families who participate.

❑ At the present time in the United States there are very few evaluators who are trained in such techniques.

❑ The emphasis of the external evaluation should be on the local purposes of the family literacy initiative.

❑ Educators and family participants should have the opportunity to play an active role in any external evaluation.

❑ ❑ ❑ ❑ ❑

What Do You Talk About All Day? La Clase Magica
MARGIE GALLEGO

Where to begin? I think of a line from an old country-and-western song that chronicles a relationship in which both parties realize they no longer know the other or themselves: "but you don't know me." Culture . . . that amorphous term, difficult to define, influential in my life, both for its persistence and subtlety.

As a child I remember hastily dressing and watching *The Andy Griffith Show* before school. The show purported values not so different from those by which my home operated. My father, now recently retired, was a pipe fitter/welder for over thirty-five years—the position not to be confused with a plumber. My mother is a homemaker, a quiet woman, selective with her laughter. She is the pillar of our family, ever ready to assist us in any way possible. She was briefly employed (for three months) before marrying my father; it was her only job outside the home.

The "culture shock" of schooling changed relationships between friends and family in and out of school. I spoke Spanish until the time my older brother entered school. Our boundaries extended, the family quickly learned about "speech communities." We all attended a Catholic school (the same school my nieces attend now). The language of school, English, had a great influence in shaping our lives and on how we viewed who we were and how we continue to view ourselves. Responding to school norms necessary for success, the desire to nurture budding friendships, and the pressure to fit in, we linguistically and culturally assimilated.

There were fewer audiences, opportunities, and reasons for meaningful communication in Spanish. Eventually, speaking Spanish was a controlled activity, limited to a few scripted topics. I recall the painful silence around the lunch table during our family's weekly visits to my grandparent's home, my well-practiced Spanish phrases about the Kmart flyer in the newspaper or *Bonanza* reruns—experiences hauntingly similar to those depicted by Richard Rodriguez in *Hunger of Memory*. I wasn't aware then that my experiences were being replicated around family dinner tables across the country.

I lost the ability to speak Spanish (other than simple phrases) by my freshman year of high school. In the process of constructing a cultural identity, I was especially sensitive to appearing too ethnic; I chose to participate in the National Honor Society and Pep Squad rather than the Spanish Club. Later, in search of an easy A, I enrolled in Spanish class, taught by a middle-aged Anglo woman from the Midwest; I discovered I had an "innate" language ability.

I didn't think of bilingual education as a career option until I received a gentle nudge from my father. Always conscious of the "American dream"—job security (union men take jobs when available) and good working conditions (blue collars work outdoors for extended periods—in Arizona!)—my father urged me to consider bilingual education. He was impressed by being able to work indoors with considerate hours and predictable vacation time. (Union men don't take vacations—they finish the work, then take temporary unemployment. Our family vacations were always arranged to correspond with the duration of the "job.")

I smile when I think of the working conditions of my first job, as an English-as-a-second-language teacher. The "roach room," an old storage room containing books dating back to the year the school opened. The books cleared out and put out on the "FOR FREE" table. Once the room was sprayed for bugs and painted, I moved in to teach. Imagine "teaching" English in a ten-by-nine-foot room with no windows to five sixth-grade boys coming in from recess! Good working conditions?

As an ESL teacher my job was to teach children English, and the sooner the better. I took my job seriously, carefully planning lessons and dutifully plotting children's English language progress on their personal language charts.

But I soon began to question my work. How was denying children's native language going to help? It didn't make sense. As I began to supplement English lessons with Spanish instruction, tension rose. Most teachers favored the "more [English] is better" notion of bilingualism. I found similar resistance from many of my students' monolingual Spanish parents. Many didn't understand why one would elect to maintain a powerless language, i.e., Spanish. Fueled by my personal language experiences, I talked with parents about the possibilities fostered by bilingualism. I wondered where my intentions and their goals merged.

Ironically, the taboo area of my life, bilingualism, has been my "ticket" within academia, my credential for understanding diversity. During a recent trip "home" (Tucson) I attended a local forum on family literacy. The weekend was hectic, full of meetings, and left little time for visiting. Plans to meet family for dinner didn't materialize, and my mother and I found ourselves in the rare situation of being alone for the evening. In the kitchen we compared salsa recipes (although I use the same ingredients, her salsa is never duplicated) and chatted about the incredible rate at which the grandchildren were growing. After three days of intense discussions regarding literacy, politics, and education, I welcomed the lighthearted topics.

A lull in the conversation brought a seemingly simple question; my mother asked, "What do you talk about all day?" This was the first time she had asked me about my work. I didn't know where to begin. I told her about the inequities and biases in the system and the need for change. We talked for over three hours. She told me how she and my father spoke Spanish exclusively during their courtship, about the embarrassment she endured growing up not speaking English and her wish to save her children from that embarrassment, how school officials advised my parents to speak English "for the sake of the children." We cried, talked, and cried again. She began to understand my work and I began to understand the decisions she had made in order to support my education. I shared my insecurities and my desire to contribute. I told her about my hope to merge family and school knowledge through my work with multilingual families participating in La Clase Magica, a computer-assisted literacy project in a working class neighborhood.*

---

*La Clase Magica is a cultural adaptation of the computer-assisted literacy program known as The Fifth Dimension, founded by Dr. Michael Cole. Sites across the United States, Russia, and Mexico, serving children from Latino, African American, Asian, Caucasian, and Russian ethnic, linguistic, and cultural backgrounds, collectively make up the Distributed Literacy Consortium (DLC) funded by the Andrew Mellon Foundation (Cole 1991–1994). La Clase Magica (Midwest), described in this article, was active in Lansing, Michigan, during 1991–1994. Its counterpart, La Clase Magica (West), directed by Dr. Olga Vasquez, continues to thrive in Eden Gardens, a neighborhood in Solana Beach, California. Community members there are currently preparing to assume responsibility for the program.

Because my story lacks the sacrifice usually associated with minority education, my loss is more subtle but no less painful. I completed my undergraduate education on scholarship and received a full fellowship to complete my graduate program. Although I never paid money for my education, I've come to understand that I have sacrificed and continue to sacrifice more of myself than I first realized. My personal experiences and my work in La Clase Magica continue to inspire me to highlight the valuable resources and the contributions families make toward their children's education in and out of school.

True to my academic training I initially approached La Clase Magica as a research project, an "experiment," in how computers motivate children to participate in collaborative literacy activities. However, the project soon became a transformative personal learning experience. Unlike many research or outreach efforts, parents and community members were not coached in "school" tasks nor was I the objective recorder of everyday events. Our relationship was messier; this was research in the real world. The project provided an opportunity to learn with families. It was also a means for creating a different learning environment, not quite school, not quite home, a space unique to its participants.

This relationship has resulted in the exchange of knowledge, a blending of personal/family knowledge and academic/school knowledge. This research approach is in stark contrast to those in which rich community-based opportunities for *education* are overlooked by the exclusive quest for becoming *schooled*. While working with community members in La Clase I've learned so much about children, families, communities, education, and schooling.

First, literacy and learning is constructed through interaction, not simply transmitted from a teacher to a student or from parent to child. Children who participate in La Clase Magica are encouraged to work with their peers, siblings, parents, university students, and other adults in purposeful reading, writing, and thinking, including telecommunications with local and distant peers. Participants develop literacy, computer, and communication skills together. Children and their parents become partners in learning, creating knowledge in an unobtrusive and natural way.

Second, the project acknowledges and makes use of the educative interactions between parents and children that flourish in the absence of school intervention. Without scripted "roles and responsibilities" children, parents, and other community members who participate in La Clase Magica are confident in their position and expertise as they gain knowledge together. Parents provide leadership role models for their children by voicing opinions and suggestions regarding the development of the site. Parents need not "act" like teachers, they are quite naturally their children's first teachers. Indeed "professionals" have much to learn about educating children from their parents.

Third, La Clase Magica deliberately adapts materials and curriculum to capitalize on the unique qualities of the community. Such adaptations cultivate an environment dense with positive images of the child, the family, and their community. For instance, by emphasizing families' prior knowledge (language, culture, goals) the La Clase setting provides children with positive messages about self-worth and the value of their families. Of particular importance is the development and appreciation of biliteracy skills, fostered through genuine interactions between bilingual children and parents (Vasquez 1992). Such messages work to counter the numerous messages that negate the value of family. Some negative images are portrayed in the school curriculum (history lessons that ignore contributions made to contemporary society by nonmajority leaders, for example) or in social politics (proposals that refuse health and school benefits to undocumented children, for example).

Fourth, diversity doesn't mean exotic customs and traditions. Historically, the customs, language, and routines of particular families were thought to be deficits, detrimental to children. Indeed, children from such family backgrounds are often considered "at risk" and routinely referred to as "nonmainstream." Actually, we are all diverse, and the norms typical of school are typical *only* in school, not in families, not among children and parents. What we should question is the assumption that school knowledge and ways for interaction are better, so much so that families readily forfeit family knowledge and language in its pursuit.

We don't need to be experts in the history and traditions of each cultural group. In fact there is often just as much diversity within a cultural group as there is among groups. But we do need to focus on individual children and individual families. Making curriculum relevant to participants means asking ourselves, Does it serve their purposes and their goals, is it of interest to the child/family?

We can't afford to satisfy ourselves with "culturally relevant" curriculum—although this would be a very big step in the right direction, illustrating many "right" ways. We must assess the appropriateness or the relevance of the curriculum for all children and families. We must enlist the help of those in the best position to answer these questions—the children and their families. We all need and deserve a "personally relevant curriculum" and this requires many definitions of family literacy as determined by the families themselves.

Fifth, "missionary" approaches that offer "services" and claim to be doing it "for the families" are short-sighted, naive, and prone to elitism. We must preserve the multiple ways of family for our collective good. Programs that try to "meet the needs" of family often deliver school knowledge/skills with little concern for the needs of the family and community. Unless relationships are entered into with the assumption that both will gain from the interaction, they replicate the "expert" perspective—transmitting knowledge to those who don't know any better. Community/school relationships must be interdependent. Indeed, academic institutions may have more to gain from families than the other way around.

For instance, La Clase Magica helped university students cross both physical and philosophical boundaries. Through their participation, students entered communities they previously assumed were too dangerous, drug-infested, and generally undesirable. Their interaction with community children and parents prompted them to reconsider previous assumptions about working-class communities, bilingualism, and long-held "minority myths" (Gallego 1995).

Last, sustaining after-school sites such as La Clase Magica requires the support of the community and family, both in physical labor and in continual project planning. In this way, La Clase Magica necessarily evolves based on knowledge resources within the community in which it resides. This approach does not mandate literacy prescriptions but capitalizes on the rich family literacy practices available to and important to children on a daily basis.

References

COLE, M. 1991–1994. Capitalizing on Diversity: The Distributed Literacy Consortium. Grant funded by the Andrew Mellon Foundation, New York, NY.

COLE, M. 1994–1997. Using New Information Technologies and the Creation of Sustainable After-School Literacy Activities: From Innovation to Maximizing the Potential. Grant funded by the Andrew Mellon Foundation, New York, NY.

GALLEGO, M. A. 1995. "Community-Based School Reform: Service Learning Lessons from La Clase Magica for Teacher Education." *The Journal*, Summer Edition (September). Published by the Michigan-Ohio Association of Teacher Educators, Sylvania, OH.

RODRIGUEZ, R. 1982. *Hunger of Memory*. New York: Bantam Books.

VASQUEZ, O. A. 1992. "A Look at Language as a Resource: Lessons from La Clase Magica." In M. B. Arias and U. Casanova (Eds.), *Bilingual Education: Politics, Practices and Research*, pp. 199–224. Chicago: National Society for the Study of Education.

❑ ❑ ❑ ❑ ❑

Nudging the Door: The Light Is Brilliant on the Other Side
JO-ANNE WILSON KEENAN

When I think about my son's years in elementary school, I am reminded that although we spoke English, the dominant language in the school, and our background was similar to that of many of his teachers and classmates, I often had to coax him through the classroom door. He understood the depth of the division between the world of home and the world of school that the doorway signified. We both wished the worlds were closer.

All too often, a child's passage across the classroom threshold is the first step in the process of shutting the family out of their literacy development. When a child's family does not speak the language that is dominant within the school, however, and the school attempts to replace the child's language, the devastation is profound.

I think back on my years of teaching children from a largely low-income and linguistically and culturally diverse population. Many of my students would be considered "disadvantaged" in the traditional sense of the word. Spanish is their home language. For many years I did not elevate the status of their home languages and cultures. I did not realize the value of reading and writing with my students and their families in their language.

Then, for two and a half years, Jerri Willett and Judy Solsken (professors at the University of Massachusetts) and I conducted an ethnographic research project in my first-and-second-grade whole language classroom. With Jerri and Judy's help, I invited the families to visit the class to share information about their lives. As the classroom came alive with music that the parents played, the stories that they told, and the whir of the wheel for the hamster that they gave us, I became aware that I was the one who was "disadvantaged." The parents were able to speak easily to the children and each other in Spanish, but I could not. With the families help, I slowly began to change my own ways with words.

English was the predominant language in our classroom, but home languages included Spanish and Polish. Home cultures were Polish, Puerto Rican, Irish American, Italian American, and African American. Since many of the students were Puerto Rican, I chose to learn Spanish. The children and their parents enjoyed helping me. They encouraged me. We empowered each other to take risks. Our struggle to appreciate one another's languages became public, and language differences were no longer a barrier but a common ground for generating conversations about language and cultural differences and similarities.

Miriam Rivera's mother's visit is one example of the learning that took place. Miriam's mother attended classes at a skills center and came to our classroom when her school day was over. When she arrived, she told me that she was a little worried about speaking to the children, because she had been speaking English for only a few months. I told her that I was just beginning to learn Spanish so I understood how she felt. Within a few minutes, she and Miriam were passing around photographs and telling family stories from the time Miriam was a baby. Several of the other children chimed in with stories of their own.

Next, Mrs. Ramirez told the class that she was learning how to use computers and was planning a career as a medical secretary. The conversation went like this. "I been in school since last September, and I have six more months to finish. I already learned how to type, which I never did it before, and soon I'm gonna start, ummm, medical record, and after that I'm gonna start with computers. I have to work hard, because I don't have to speak too much English. When I start in school, I didn't speak this much. I still have some problems with, ah, how do you say, ah, the verbs and the ah . . ."

One child asked, "Verbs and nouns?"

When she finished showing us the pictures, I asked her if she would read from the Spanish book I was sharing with the class. The book, *Family Pictures*, by Carmen Lomas Garza, written in both English and Spanish, depicts family events in the life of a child growing up in Mexico. Miriam's mother read, giving the children the opportunity to appreciate the fluency and cadence of a native speaker.

When she completed the book, I asked her to listen and assist as I read one of the Spanish sections. I read, and Miriam's mother helped, encouraged, and corrected my reading. At one point we came to the word *naranja* in the text. Miriam's mother hesitated and then said that it was a mistake. After negotiating the meaning of the word, we decided that *naranja* is probably the word that people in Mexico use for *orange* and *china* is the word that people in Puerto Rico use for *orange*. We were learning together.

With the help and patience of the students' families, Jerri, and Judy, I was opening the classroom door to the richness that "advantaged" families can bring to a "disadvantaged" teacher. I am continuing to nudge the door open and to encourage other teachers to do so as well. For the light on the other side is brilliant.

❑ ❑ ❑ ❑ ❑

The Story of a Fifth-Grade Boy Born in Mexico
Tomás Enguidanos

One day a mother called me to talk about her son Rene. I had worked with Rene for about three years in my Spanish bilingual special day class (third through fifth grade). In those three years Rene had excelled in all areas but reading and writing, which I felt he resisted because he didn't believe he could do it.

Rene's mother had asked the nuns in a Catholic school to evaluate him. After doing so, they told her that he knew absolutely nothing. They suggested that because he was short he could go back to the third grade. Rene's mother told me this was not my fault; Rene was brain damaged.

These words stabbed me like a knife. I told her that I didn't agree with the nuns, in terms of either the placement or their diagnosis of Rene's problems with reading and writing. I felt that we needed to meet and work together to find a way to help Rene. Rene wasn't reading and writing, as we both wanted him to do, because we were not sure how to help him, not because he was brain damaged. We set up a meeting.

The night before our meeting I sat at home making a list of other possible employment options for myself. I wanted to quit, because despite my best efforts I wasn't seeing the kind of progress that my students needed to make. I realized that although I could quit and walk away, the parents and especially the students could not walk away.

On the one hand, saying that Rene was brain damaged was a way of quitting, a way of dealing with the very deep pain this family felt in relation to his "literacy." But I question whence this idea originated. I am quite certain that they must have heard this from teachers, psychologists, and other school professionals who were also giving up on Rene.

That night I determined that I must not quit. That I must become much better at teaching reading and writing. That I must invest time in working together with the parents in finding the answers.

Thus began my family literacy program. I decided to meet individually with each student, their parents, and a community mental health partner to review what the student knows and is doing, and to set goals for the following six weeks. This means that I dedicate about three hours per week to individual conferences with parents (each meeting lasts about one hour.)

In addition, once a month I meet with all the families together. We set the agenda for the meetings together. They have questions about my evolving teaching practices and issues of child development. The parents help each other with parenting issues, as I am not a parent; they are the experts. We work together in understanding what the children need. We do this in Spanish.

While all the parents initially viewed their children as somehow deficient (brain-damaged, stupid, or lazy) in relation to reading and writing, the work of the students has inspired a new perception. Now parents are seeing their sons and daughters, through their work, as poets, artists, readers, and writers.

❑ ❑ ❑ ❑ ❑

A mother concludes: "Since I have no need to feel ashamed of speaking Spanish, I have become strong. Now I feel I can speak with the teachers about my children's education. I can tell them I want my children to know Spanish. I have gained courage."

[A] father shares: "I have discovered my children can write. I have discovered that by reading books one can find out many things. I have discovered I can read in Spanish about the history of this country and of other countries."
—Literatura Infantil: Helping Parents and Children Learning Together

□ □ □ □ □

Types and Uses of Literacy Observed in Family Settings
Denny Taylor

All of the following types and uses of reading and writing have been observed in family settings in ethnographic studies of family literacy. When we explore the types and uses of reading and writing found in family settings, our attention shifts from superficial skills-oriented perspectives to the complexities of social processes, the ways of knowing, through which parents and children create literacy configurations that are functional in their everyday lives.

Types and Uses of Reading

Confirmational: Reading to check or confirm facts or beliefs, often from archival materials stored and retrieved only on special occasions.

Educational: Reading to fulfill the educational requirements of schooling. Reading to increase one's ability to consider and/or discuss political, social, aesthetic, or religious knowledge. Reading to educate oneself.

Environmental: Reading the print in the environment—on highways, in airports, at the supermarket, in restaurants.

Financial: Reading to consider (and sometimes make changes to) the economic circumstances of one's everyday life. Reading to fulfill practical (financial) needs of everyday life.

Historical: Reading to explore one's personal identity. Reading to explore the social, political, and economic circumstances of one's everyday life. Reading conserved writings that create a permanent record of one's family life history.

Instrumental: Reading to gain information for meeting practical needs, dealing with public agencies, and scheduling daily life.

Interactional: Reading to gain information pertinent to building and maintaining social relationships.

News Related: Reading to gain information about third parties. Reading to gain information about local, state, and national events.

Recreational: Reading during leisure time or in planning for recreational events.

Scientific: Reading to gain information about or to develop new understanding of the natural or physical sciences.

Technical: Reading to gain information using the different symbolic forms of technological communications (computer, fax, virtual reality). Reading to advance one's understanding of the functions of such technologies.

Types and Uses of Writing

Autobiographical: Writing to understand oneself. Writing to record one's life history. Writing to share life with others.

Creative: Writing as a means of self-expression.

Educational: Writing to fulfill the educational requirements of school and college courses. Writing to educate oneself.

Environmental: Writing in public places for others to read.

Financial: Writing to record numerals and to write out amounts and purposes of expenditures. Writing to consider (and sometimes make changes to) the economic circumstances of one's everyday life. Writing to fulfill practical (financial) needs of everyday life.

Instrumental: Writing to meet practical needs and to "manage"/organize everyday life. Writing to gain access to social institutions or helping agencies.

Interactional: Writing to establish, build, and maintain social relationships. Writing to negotiate family responsibilities. The writer envisions or "knows" his or her audience and writes to the addressee.

Memory Aids: Writing to serve as a memory aid for both oneself and others.

Recreational: Writing during leisure time for the enjoyment of the activity.

Scientific: Writing to develop new understanding of the natural or physical sciences.

Substitutional: Reinforcement or substitution for oral messages. Writing used when direct oral communication is not possible or when a written message is needed to create a record (for legal purposes, for example).

Technical: Writing to gain information using the different symbolic forms of technological communications (computer, fax, virtual reality). Writing to advance one's understanding of the functions of such technologies.

❑ ❑ ❑ ❑ ❑

Family Literacy Is Risky Stuff

MARYANN NUCKOLLS

Family literacy is risky stuff. You have to be willing to risk exposing your own literacies to children in order to encourage them to explore the literacies of their own family and community. You have to be willing to rethink the whole idea of what children can do with their own literacies. You have to be willing to help children and their families rethink these same issues.

I begin by sharing odd bits of print from my life. I spin a story around the bills left on the backseat of my car. We read menus, placemats, and wrappers

I bring in. We read a week's worth of litter from my front yard. Sometimes we pick a piece to write about as a group.

One day when little hands reach out for the goodies, I set the print on a nearby bookcase. "This is my print. This is my story. Get your own print."

"But we don't have any print."

"Well, can't you get some?"

"We don't have any here. We just have the old print."

The others nod in agreement.

Then someone announces, "We can bring some from home."

"Yeah, we can ask our moms and dads."

"We can get some bills and sales things and letters and stuff."

"And they'll all have a story."

"And we can write about it."

Day after day the pieces of print drift into class. We no longer have time for furry animals and key rings and ponies and trophies. We have important things to share and investigate. In searching for the story in their print, they talk to their families about what to bring and what it means. Then they tell their stories to the class.

Brooke's Story

She's been out of school for only two days, but the class really misses her. Brooke comes into the room dragging a large blue bag behind her. Piece by piece, she shares her secrets. There is a brochure about a discount mall, a sales receipt, a food wrapper. The questions pour from her confused audience.

"Brooke, what are you doing?"

"What is all this stuff?"

"Where'd you get all this?"

"How much more is there, anyhow?"

"What does this mean?"

"What you gonna do with it?"

"Are we gonna look at all of it?"

Then Brooke tells us. She and her family have taken a trip to California, and she has brought her print to share with us. Knowing Brooke's purpose sparks their enthusiasm, and the questioning changes.

"What is this?"

"Where did you get it?"

"Who was with you?"

"When did you get it—what day of the trip? What time was it?"

"Can I see it?"

"Did you find it or did they give it to you?"

"How are you going to use it?"

"They really let you take this?"

"Hey! Look at this, guys!"

A room full of unrelenting first-grade detectives are on the job and they are leaving no stone unturned.

"We can sort this!"

"Yeah, but how we gonna do it? We can put it together lots of ways."

"These are shaped the same."

"Aw, that's too easy. Look. These are shaped the same but they sure are different."

"Okay! Lets put sales things together and books together and things with maps and tickets."

"Disneyland stuff goes over here."

"Hey! These receipts are different. Why?"

"Oooh. Some of 'em are for gas. Some of 'em are for hotels. JBs. That's a restaurant! I ate there once!"

"We can do this by days of the trip!"

The room is filled with a flurry of print. Children fly around the room trading print and arguing where it should go. They negotiate for prized items that they need to fill out their part of the story. By the end of the morning, they have shared every moment of Brooke's trip as well as one family's literacy.

Andrew's Story

He digs through the class print box, judiciously discarding print he doesn't like. At last he settles on a brochure distributed by a local hospital. I ask him about it. He says he likes the shape and color and the way it opens. Andrew methodically pastes the brochure into his journal. He sits with a pencil poised against his face for a long time and then begins to write.

Andrew's journal is unremarkable for a first grader. Over time he has grown from random scribbles to lines and marks to real letters of the alphabet. There is no clear sound-symbol relationship to an outside reader, but it has meaning for Andrew. Slowly and cautiously, he shares his print and what he's written about it with me and then with the class. He is proud of his work.

One day, Andrew quietly announces, "I have a sharing." He stands before the class, holding high a white card with a small picture at the top and writing below it.

"Andrew, what is this? What can you tell us about this?"

"This is my mom and dad's wedding card."

No other print receives so much admiration as this announcement. We pass it around so that everyone can see what Andrew's mom and dad looked like when they were first married. Andrew holds his head a little higher. He answers all the questions. Then we retell the wonderful story of Andrew's family.

Andrew pastes his print into his journal as I wander about checking work. He looks up at me. "You want me to read this to you?"

"No, Andrew. I want to read this to *you* . . . 'Mi FMALE i LC Mi FAL [My family. I like my family].'"

Andrew grins in surprise.

"Andrew! Teacher can read your writing!"

"You can write adult words!"

Andrew's journal is passed around the table as each child takes turns reading the adult words that he has written.

"Andrew! You never brought print before. Now you brought your own print and you have a story and you can write about it. You better bring more print."

And he does.

Clearly, part of the power of family literacy is its ability to transform us and our world. It's in the amazed faces of children as we construct the story of a new T-shirt by reading the shirt front and/or back, the neck tags, the company tags, and the register receipt. The print becomes a record of an event in the life of one child. For the other children, shopping for a T-shirt will never be the same.

Implementing family literacy programs in an educational setting requires a shift in attitude. Traditionally, schools and curriculum imparted meaning to children about the community in which they lived. Family literacy is about rethinking the values and relevance of what is learned in school. Family literacy brings the richness of the child's community into the classroom and drives the curriculum toward authenticity and usefulness.

Family literacy is about taking a chance on a piece of print picked up from the playground at recess. It's about believing that it once belonged to a family somewhere. It's about making sense of it by asking questions and creating relationships. It's risky business because teachers never know what direction the curriculum or daily plan will take. It's applying the teachable moment to literacy, and the dynamics of it leave children and their families and their teachers forever changed.

❑ ❑ ❑ ❑ ❑

What Do I Do Here?

JUDY REED
(as told to Sharon W. Smith)

This narrative is based on a conversation Sharon Smith had with Judy Reed, a tutor of an ESL/family literacy group. Judy reflects on some of the students she came to know through her work.

One of the reasons that some of my best students didn't come to all the tutoring sessions was that they had to be at appointments for their children or themselves. When you're poor and you're on welfare, you can't just tell the clinic or someone you can't come because you have to study. You have to go and keep your appointment.

Two fairly young women came who looked to me as though they would be promising students and leaders in the group. But one had a two-year-old. So I took the chance of saying, "Please bring the two-year-old." He came as a regular student for the whole year, until he was old enough for Head Start. If we hadn't done that, she wouldn't have been able to be in the class.

Another woman who came took a long time to light up. I think she was just quiet and knew much less English than anyone else. But talking with her, I found that she had arranged her schedule so that she could take care of her two grandchildren so that her daughter could go to nursing school. So the only times she could go to the classes were when the classes didn't conflict with her baby-sitting.

When I first went in to tutor, I was not too certain about how to decide who should be admitted to my classes. I was told that this was a family literacy program and that the participants would be parents. So into my class walked this guy who was a parent all right, he was also a grandparent, but all his family was in Puerto Rico. I thought, Well, what do I do here? He turned out to be the most superb member of the class.

He was a kind of grandfatherly member of the community. He had lived in the hills in Puerto Rico and helped on his father's farm. A very simple background—he also worked in a pharmacy for many years—and yet he had a very dignified attitude toward people and himself and life and was very involved with kids who lived near him, in helping them out. He had a great deal of pride in his heritage. He was always bringing in different things like Spanish and English forms from the local bank to help the students learn how to use a bank.

My students came from a background where medical help was either very distant or they couldn't afford it. Their mothers had grown certain herbs in the garden, and they treated all these different illnesses in this way. They were really like nurses. These women still had this knowledge and they were able to bring in different leaves and show them to me. We made a chart of all the different things, whether it was headaches or stomachaches. You know, this is the illness, this is the herb, and this is how you use it. There was a great deal of knowledge that really should be respected by people of any level of education and it was provided by people with no education.

I noticed that these students were devoted to the family over the individual, especially the mothers. They were pretty resigned to the fact that maybe there just wasn't that much opportunity for the rest of their lives, to really get that good at English and get that good a job. But they were happy to work for their children's future. There was an unselfishness that I admired and that people who are more educated don't often respect.

❏ ❏ ❏ ❏ ❏

Adults are motivated to learn and participate when they make a commitment to regular attendance and participation. . . . Induction procedures should include initial assessment and counseling and should encourage commitment and goal setting.

—Family Literacy Program Quality Self Study

□ □ □ □ □

A Day in the Life of a Family Literacy Teacher
MARILYN ANTONUCCI

It's on my mind so I must write it. We have three students here eager and willing to read. But it's so disappointing that for so many reasons the other students can't come. I can write out the reasons they aren't here:

- Barry had to go out to look for a car or truck today.
- Carol called and her truck broke down on the highway yesterday. She said they were almost hit by a truck. She is still very shook up by the experience. Her husband is busily working on the truck to get it fixed up and running again.
- Pat is out sick. She's been having health problems and just can't get out.
- Sonja is also not feeling well and has her two kids to take care of. If she is sick, who takes care of her? How hard it is not to have anyone to ask for help.
- Jose just sort of disappeared. We have sent him a few postcards and called his daughter's house, but no answer.
- Cuc didn't get in today. She usually lets us know what is going on.
- Felicia couldn't make it today. She was waiting for us to come out yesterday for a home visit and we were waiting for her to come to a conference. Communication is an art!
- Gladys is also out. I talked to her on Friday and she is still in great pain from her automobile accident. She brought such energy to our classes. She will not be coming back until the training program has an opening for her.

After a year and a half of working with parents, I have learned that despite the many absences that prevent them from attending the center and completing a planned lesson, their literacy learning continues as they work through the hundreds of problems and new situations they face each day. It's just as Mary Anderson has said: Around and around the clock they are using literacy.

□ □ □ □ □

Parents, usually mothers, grandmothers or baby-sitters, drop into the school with their children (infants to six-year-olds). The adults plan their own activities while the children enjoy a play-based program. Information on a broad range of community resources is shared so that families can help themselves to the services they need. Bread-and-butter issues are addressed before parenting issues are dealt with.

—Family Ties

□ □ □ □ □

The Urban Grass-Roots Think Tank: Adult Writing and Community Building

HAL ADAMS, WITH CHARLES CASEMENT

Hal Adams spoke about his urban grassroots think tank at the 1994 Canadian Family Literacy Convention. Charles Casement wrote about his presentation in the conference report.

Hal Adams coordinates the Austin Grass-Roots Think Tank in the Austin community of Chicago, where he teaches writing to parents and other adult friends of children who attend local schools. The program involves two groups, one female and one male. All the participants are African Americans. Their writing, containing their reflections on their personal histories and everyday experiences, is published in two journals, *The Journal of Ordinary Thought* and *Through the Eyes of a Villain*. The former consists predominately of the writing of the women's group, the latter has contributions exclusively from the male group. The journals appear three or four times a year and are distributed in the community. *The Journal of Ordinary Thought* is also used in the schools.

Austin is a community on the far West Side of Chicago and is one of the poorest areas in the city. About 98 percent of the residents are African American, and over 90 percent of the children in school are on school lunch programs and come from families on public aid. Unemployment is high.

The women's group, which is based in a local school, was the first to be formed. The group is made up of the mothers and grandmothers of children in the school. The women came to the program because they thought it would help their children. They stayed on because they were writing about their own lives and this was a source of support and encouragement for them. The men's group was subsequently formed when men in the community approached Hal and asked him to help them put out a journal of their own. For many of the participants, rap had been a primary means of expression. In publishing the two journals, the Grass-Roots Think Tank has given members of the Austin community a new voice.

The Philosophy of the Program

The program is founded on the propositions that every person is a philosopher, that expressing one's thoughts fosters creativity and change, and that taking control of life requires thinking about the world and communicating those thoughts to others. Through the program, participants gain an opportunity to develop their ability to interpret their world. They become more conscious of the issues and challenges in their lives and are able to think more clearly about them. Literacy is thus seen as a means to self-development, not job development.

The program creates an awareness among the participants of the role of writing in the community. They come to see themselves as thinkers and as activists. Their writing is not just an individual activity but also a social activity; this is reflected in the group sessions, in which participants develop their writing together.

The Group Sessions

The group sessions are run as writing workshops. Participants write about things that are on their minds. Some write their stories down themselves, some say them aloud while someone else writes for them, and others tape-record them. Hal comments on the stories and distributes them among the class. The group discusses the stories in terms of their content—what they say about life in the neighborhood—and this discussion helps them develop further ideas for their writing. The stories are then looked at in terms of the writing itself.

The women's group and the men's group view the world differently. The men vocalize their anger and dreams. The women write about their children, social support, health care, etc.

Results of the Program

The program has demonstrated the positive relationships of literacy to community building in a number of ways:

- Participants have become more active in the schools; some have run for a seat on the local school board.
- Participants took joint action on a dangerous abandoned building next to the school playground. This involved going to court and obtaining a demolition order. The owner of the building subsequently got the court to issue a stay but did agree to secure access to the

building and post a security guard, so this was regarded as at least a partial victory.

- Participants have given talks in the community and on a nearby university campus about their writing and their life in their neighborhood, as well as monthly library readings in a neighboring area.

❏ ❏ ❏ ❏ ❏

Family Treasures

JEAN BRUCE

Family Treasures™ is a research-and-discovery project that brings family heritage to life for schoolchildren through the excitement of a treasure hunt. The Canadian Museum of Civilization in Hull, Québec, Canada, developed the project to link students to museums. At school, students discover how much family "treasures" can tell them about their family heritage, their community, their country, and the world. The museum connection emphasises the importance of preserving our joint heritage and making it accessible.

The Family Treasure Hunt

In any Family Treasures™ project, the word *treasure* is broadly defined so that every student can find an object of great personal significance to an older family member. Monetary value is irrelevant. A family treasure is valuable because of the story attached to it. An interview with the treasure's owner sets the object in context and brings it to life.

What child would be interested in Great-Grandfather's battered old geometry set until it's explained how vital it was to him as a sailor in wartime? When his ship was torpedoed, Grandfather swam for his life, carrying his geometry set between his teeth! Or what about that brass mortar and pestle above the fireplace? It's just another ornament until a child discovers that Great-Great-Grandmother brought it with her from Russia at the age of eleven, when her family sent her to North America to escape a pogrom.

Family treasures are taken to school, if possible, so students search for small, portable objects that are not easily damaged and have little if any monetary value. A handmade quilt, a set of tools, a war medal, a Bible, a photograph album, a ring, or a fossil—if it's treasured, it qualifies. If an object is too precious, too fragile, or too large, a student can draw it or bring a photograph. In the event that no object is available, an oral history of an event, a place, a person, a song, or a recipe becomes the "treasure." Many teachers compile class treasure books, using children's written accounts of their oral history research and drawings or photographs of the treasures. Sometimes there's a video or audio record, too.

Family Treasures™ was developed and piloted at the Canadian Museum of Civilization for use by museums and schools anywhere—in cities, towns, or rural communities. The 1990 pilot program showed that the project works well in both urban and rural areas, in places where families have strong local roots as well as in places where recent immigrants come from diverse backgrounds.

Project Growth
Word about the project's success spread rapidly across Canada through teachers' networks and media publicity. In response to many requests for information, the Canadian Museum of Civilization made basic project guidelines available in 1991. In 1992, more than sixteen hundred students from many regions participated in the second Family Treasures™ book display at the Canadian Museum of Civilization.

Since 1991 the Family Treasures™ project has developed its own momentum. The Welland Historical Museum, the Bruce County Museum, and the Cumberland Museum, in Ontario; the Manitoba Children's Museum, Winnipeg; and the Surrey Museum, British Columbia, have launched their own projects. In 1994–95 the city of Montréal involved six *maisons de la culture* with local schools in a citywide project developed by the Centre d'histoire de Montréal.

The Canadian Museum of Civilization has received requests for information about Family Treasures™ from several countries, including the United States, Great Britain, Australia, and New Zealand. The Manawatu Museum in North Palmerston, New Zealand, has done the project twice, in 1993 and 1995. Six hundred families participated in the 1995 project.

❑ ❑ ❑ ❑ ❑

A *Letter from Kathy Day*

Dear Denny:

It has been difficult to choose from the stories produced by students during our Family Treasures™ project. Carole Goodreau, coordinator for the project, and I have mulled over each one. As we revisited the stories, Carole commented that there are some wonderful lines and some sad ones in them, but revisiting them brought back great memories.

Arnold Nelson

Photographs
Arnold Nelson

My family treasure is the photograph, which is shown here, taken in the fall of 1954. The picture was taken by my mother outside our home in Pincher Creek. My sister, two friends and I had gone to the backyard where we cut hay and loaded it on our wagons. We pretended we were successful ranchers bringing hay to feed the cattle through winter.

My father built our house two years before this picture was taken. The propane tank with its unique cover over the regulator to protect it from the elements is eye-catching. The propane was used in the cook stove. I find the bedsteads very intriguing—why were they there? Had I slept in the crib? Whatever became of them?

My mother had prepared a photo album of my childhood. She gave it to me after I was married. This snapshot is the most precious to me.

Arnold, a student in the Read/Write adult literacy (tutoring) project, went far beyond the factual in thinking through the value of his family treasure. Arnold gave up his annual hunting trip with his sons to be present at the final reception and display of stories and treasures because, his wife Edna said, it was public proof that he had recognized his own literary limitations and had done something about them by becoming a literacy student. He could now share something of great value to himself and could celebrate his accomplishments publicly. Edna said he would be honoured to have his name in print. Carole and I were impressed that a family who seemingly had so little in terms of material things had so much as a family and that Arnold's mother had seen fit not only to record their life on film but to preserve it in a gift album to him. His tutor was Erna Greenly, a lady who herself had gone back to complete high school while her own children were still in school.

The Baby Cradle
Jonathan (Jonty) Walters

In my family we had a special treasure. It was a baby cradle. It had leather underneath and boards on the sides. It hung from the ceiling on ropes and went up and down. It was made in the Colony by one of the carpenters years ago. It was first used by my great-grandmother. It was painted a dark red, almost brown.

My mother used it for all my family. We have seven children in my family. I was the last one to use it when I was a baby. Most of the time my mother used it in the daytime, like when she was sewing or when I was sick. She only used it at nighttime when she didn't have very much room for a big crib.

A few years ago she sold it to an antique dealer. Now she wishes that she had never sold it. I didn't know much about it before I started this story. I wish my mother would have another baby and we'd still have it to use, because now I know how important our cradle was.

Jonty, a Hutterian Brethren child from a local colony, recognized and talked poignantly about an item of importance not only to his family but to his cultural heritage. The curator of the Glenbow Museum of Calgary supplied Jonty with a photograph of a cradle from their collection that exactly matched the one he remembered. Jonty and his parents and his tutor, Pat Ness, and her family braved a forty-mile round-trip in a blizzard to attend the reception for Family Treasures™. The first thing they wanted to see upon arrival was his story in print, in our Family Treasures™ album. Jonty's mother said they would be pleased to have his story published.

The Rocking Chair
Randy Evenson

The rocking chair is in the corner of the playroom. My sister rocks in it a lot. It's too small for me now. It was built for little kids to rock in. When I was little I liked to sit in it and rock and look at a book. When we grow up I think my mom should have it so her grandchildren can rock in it.

Before there was TV my grandma said all the little kids used to sit in it while the grownups talked. My grandma thinks about 50 kids in our family have rocked in the chair over the years

Randy's mother and grandmother got involved in the project as well, as his story indicates. At the potluck supper that kicked off the project, Randy's grandmother stood up and although obviously very stressed at having to speak in front of everyone, with pride showed us a beautiful tartan pleated skirt. It was, she told us, the last garment her grandmother, a dressmaker to King George V, had made. Later in the evening, another grandmother got up to speak, drew all the children around her, and described what it was like to go to a country school in the early years of this century. She described how each school day began with the children singing "God Save the King"—in honour of King George V. This gave added value to the story of the skirt in everyone's eyes, including Randy's grandmother's. The rocking chair had been in Randy's family for a long time; the first telling of the story was a historical accounting of who made it and who had used it—obviously not Randy's story. With gentle questioning, Randy was able to express his own feelings about this little chair. He was really pleased with his grandmother's solution as to how to share the chair. It was also good to see that he, a primary grade student in our PAL student literacy project, related the value of the chair to his memories of having sat in it while reading. His grandmother has confirmed that it is fine to have Randy's story and these anecdotes published, along with his name.

My Grandfather's Chaps
Denver Finley

My Grandfather, Raymond Harley Finley, lived in Stirling, Alberta. He made his own chaps—from sheep's wool and leather. Now they are a sandy white color, with brownish-grey leather.

When my Grandfather died on November 7, 1970, the chaps were passed down to my Dad. Dad was lucky to get them because they could have gone to my Dad's brother, Lee, in California.

Now, they have been passed to me. They are a little big for me now but with a belt, they will fit fine. They have been in our garage awhile and could use some repairs. I'm sure the rip in the back can easily be fixed with a belt and some hand-stitching.

My chaps are too special to wear. They are going to hang up in the garage for now.

Denver was/is a painfully shy young boy, who was referred to our PAL project because he needed to participate more in class and read more. Choosing these chaps to write about stirred something in him; he got his dad (also very shy) to join him in a videotaped interview about them. The look of pride and excitement in Denver's eyes when his dad told him he could try them on in front of the camera was priceless. Later, his mom, Chris, told me that Denver always sat in the backseat when the family went anywhere, never saying a word. The weekend after the final Family Treasures™ reception, when they were traveling to the family farm, Denver asked if he might sit in the front between Mom and Dad. She said he never stopped talking the whole way there. Denver's family home caught on fire shortly afterward; fortunately the chaps were in the garage. Denver's mom has given her permission for his story and anecdotes to be used and for his name to be in print.

Sincerely, Kathy Day

□ □ □ □ □

Libraries and Family Literacy
JUDITH ROVENGER

The connection between family literacy programs and libraries is a natural one. The tradition of libraries as "the people's university" is a cherished cornerstone of the public library movement in America. Generations of families have availed themselves of the cultural and educational opportunities afforded, without cost (as long as local communities provide tax-dollar support), to those who would make use of them.

However, the role of libraries has the potential to expand from supporting family literacy goals to becoming a full partner in the family literacy movement. The institutional nature of libraries—their physical plant and facilities, and their credibility and permanence in their communities—makes them an ideal partner for grassroots initiatives that involve families, neighborhoods, and literacy.

While federal, state, and even private dollars look ever more elusive, it is clear that the formation of partnerships, collaborative efforts, and alliances are the best bets for winning a share of the pie. The time is ripe for the family literacy movement to claim even fuller attention from libraries.

While all libraries do not deliver the same level of service, the predominant national attitude, as evinced by the American Library Association and the Association of Library Services to Children, articulates a strong commitment to families and their information and literacy needs. Libraries' story-hour programming and their advocacy for multicultural literature demonstrate the predisposition of libraries to honor families as they are. In light of the activities and services that public libraries already provide to family literacy, it seems logical to take the next step and begin looking at more formal ties. These ties would start with the acknowledgment of the services that libraries offer and develop into expanded and innovative services jointly fostered by true collaborations and alliances, beginning with national organizations and extending to the local community level—where public libraries and family literacy truly live.

□ □ □ □ □

Learning Through Play at the Public Library
SANDRA FEINBERG

In today's stressful world, many young families, newly isolated from their extended families and old friends, are seeking companionship, support, and the opportunity for their young children to socialize and learn with other children. They are also in need of information on childrearing, child development, and early education. They need a local place to go, one that is supportive and relaxing, where they can meet other families, exchange ideas, get information, and play with their children. Why not the public library?

How does the parent/child workshop serve the needs of families in public libraries?

The strength of the parent/child workshop, a specially designed library-based program for parents and toddlers, rests on the principles that learning for young children takes place within the family context, that parents are a child's first teachers, and that it is through play that the young child learns. The librarian facilitates family interaction and learning by organizing the setting, providing appropriate materials, communicating with the parents and children, and connecting the families to outside resources and community supports. The parent/child workshop turns the library into a family-centered environment and recognizes the family's critical role in the development of a literate community.

What are the basic requirements for the workshop?

There are four requirements to conduct the workshop successfully: a community room or special area set up with developmentally appropriate materials, a willing and trained staff, access to community resource professionals, and some financial support for initiating and continuing the program. The workshop is conducted one day each week in one-hour-and-fifteen-minute sessions (either early morning or mid-morning) for five consecutive weeks. The number of families registered depends on the size of the room.

How is the room set up for parents to play with their children?

The room design is carefully constructed and contributes to smooth interaction among the various participants—parents, children, librarian, paraprofessional, and resource person. It is organized into three simultaneously functioning activity areas.

In the *resource materials area* circulating materials and a multitude of free handouts are displayed. Different aspects of parenting are featured each week in coordination with the topic presented by that week's resource professional. Also included in this area are audiovisual materials, books, and puzzles specifically aimed at infants and toddlers.

The *toy and game area*, which covers at least two thirds of the room, contains books, puzzles, musical instruments, blocks, toys, dolls, puppets, dishes, hats, and gross motor equipment. These materials, arranged on tables set flat against the walls of the room and on some low shelves, are easily accessible to the children. Since there are no chairs, parents sit on the carpeted floor with their youngsters and are encouraged to play and interact with them and with the other parents.

The *art activity area* provides materials and instructions for a simple art project for parents and children to complete together. Two collapsed card tables are arranged in an L-shape with a canvas drop cloth underneath. A paraprofessional (a clerk or an early-childhood education student) arranges the table for one of five weekly art activities: coloring, pasting, cutting shapes, making play dough, and finger painting.

Who runs the workshop?

Every workshop requires a librarian, a paraprofessional, and a resource person. The librarian's main function is that of a facilitator: to familiarize herself or himself with the families, to encourage them to borrow materials and make full use of the wide range of services and programs available for them, to introduce the resource person, to maintain a comfortable and consistent flow of activity, and to conclude the workshop with finger plays and songs in a circle.

The paraprofessional staffs the art activity area and supports the role of the librarian. The paraprofessional encourages participation, keeps the art activity area organized, and interacts casually with parents and children. Some training and knowledge about early childhood development will enhance this person's effectiveness in communicating with the parents, children, and librarian. In libraries with smaller community rooms, the art area does not require a paraprofessional and is simply designed as another station for independent parent/child interaction.

Who are the community resource professionals?

The community resource professionals, qualified individuals knowledgeable in areas such as speech, play, child behavior, nutrition, and physical fitness, are an essential ingredient to the workshop. They generally represent a local agency or organization that works with families. Their goal is to interact with the participants, either one-on-one or in small groups. They encourage parents to ask questions, speak freely about their concerns for their children, and communicate whatever anxieties and fears they have as parents.

In addition to working directly with parents, the community professional forms a relationship with the librarian and begins to view the library as a family support institution. This relationship provides a foundation for other cooperative programs and networking opportunities.

How does this program build community partnerships?

As a result of the workshop, librarians build relationships with the community resource professionals, including mental health and social service professionals, educators, public and private community-based agencies, youth counselors, parents, and interested citizens. These people can band together to:

- Share information, ideas, and resources.
- Plan cooperative programs and services.
- Advocate for children and parents.
- Educate professionals and the public about topics related to children and families.
- Demonstrate the ways in which working together can make professionals more effective family support agents.

How can libraries with few resources provide the workshop?

It is important to be flexible depending on the resources available. Some suggestions for libraries with minimal resources include:

- Acquire donated toys and other play materials from families. It's important to consider developmental appropriateness, safety, and durability. Good-quality used toys are acceptable.
- Cull the existing library collection for books and other materials for young children as well as materials for parents to bring into the workshop. Send for free materials from national and local agencies.
- Look for local funding sources and apply in partnership with another agency for start-up funds. This program has a lot of popular appeal.
- Ask the resource professionals to provide their service at no charge. This workshop is a great opportunity for them to meet with the community.
- Team up with a local early childhood center to provide the workshop at their site.

Can other agencies offer the workshop?

The workshop is adaptable for any agency that has space, professional staff, and materials. In some cases, the agency that wants to offer the workshop can take the initiative and contact their local library to work in partnership to develop the program. The workshop can be set up in a alternative site such as a local school, church, or day-care center.

References

FEINBERG, SANDRA. 1985. "The Parent/Child Workshop: A Unique Program." *School Library Journal* (April):38–41.

FEINBERG, SANDRA. N.d. "Parents, Children and Libraries." *Family Resource Coalition Report* 5(2).

FEINBERG, SANDRA, and KATHLEEN DEERR. 1995. *Running a Parent/Child Workshop: A How-To-Do-It Manual for Librarians.* New York: Neal-Schuman.

❑ ❑ ❑ ❑ ❑

Starting Together: A Community Partnership
PATRICIA A. CHIARELLI

Starting Together is a relatively small local initiative that began in Stony Point, a town on the Hudson River less than an hour from New York City. It has been effective in providing resources to families of young children because it is small and also because it was founded on a solid belief in the empowerment of families. When Starting Together was just an idea, I tried running workshops for parents on how and what to read to their children. Extensive research tells us parents reading to their children is the key to their literacy. Well, nine parents out of the hundred invited came to the workshop, and they already had been reading to their children for years. Inviting parents to workshops on topics predetermined by me was not going to work.

During the spring of 1993, I started doing some research into programs around the country (Chiarelli 1994). There were federal initiatives, such as Even Start and the Fund for the Improvement and Reform of Schools and Teaching (FIRST), but grants were few and the competition enormous. State initiatives in New York seemed to be involved in setting up prekindergarten programs that did not have a clear literacy component. There were several excellent university–school district liaisons and a few community-based programs for families from low economic areas. None seemed to fit a mostly middle-class town like Stony Point. It soon became clear that I wasn't going to find a program that could fit our area.

Awarded a summer grant by the Haverstraw–Stony Point School District to continue researching possibilities, I visited the Center for Family

Resources (CFR) in Mineola, New York.* CFR is an educational, training, and consulting organization that helps professionals and communities serve families in comprehensive family-centered and supportive ways by advancing policy, program, and practices that build family strengths. Its Family Literacy Institute promotes family support projects and has the most extensive library of materials in the area. It was there that I learned about the importance of formulating a philosophy that would guide the formulation of programs.

Guiding Principles

Starting Together is a communitywide partnership that empowers families to help their children develop intellectually, emotionally, and socially. This partnership is open, dependable, bridge building, relevant, practical, nonintrusive, nonevaluative, and based on the needs of families. Our core values are respect and belief in family knowledge and caring; we believe parents care.

I abandoned my vision of every family in our community reading regularly to their children. I started listening. I made phone calls to individuals or agencies that have a stake in the health of our families—parents, preschools, child-care providers, school personnel, and clergy—and gathered enough data and interested people to have a general meeting. On July 15, in a large room filled with setting sunlight and lots of comfortable chairs, fifteen people—two principals, three members of the clergy, three teachers, six parents, and the parenting program director of the Rockland Teachers' Center—gathered to discuss the needs of families.

All participants were eager to describe their concerns: the isolation of parents from one another, the increased loneliness of children, a diminished sense of responsibility, economic difficulties that lessen family time spent with children, a general confusion about parenting issues, and children who lacked imagination, self-esteem, and the ability to participate in activities. There were no comments that supported a deficit model, nor was there any discussion about program; we agreed that discovering what parents felt they needed was the effective approach. We did not have the answers but we knew the community should do more to help families of young children. Four of us volunteered to develop a needs assessment.

Needs Assessment

Out of twelve thousand residents (1990 census) there were approximately one thousand children age six and under whose families would be the target of our programs. We identified seventeen sites at which to disseminate our as-

---

*The Center for Family Resources is located at 22 Jericho Turnpike, Suite 110, Mineola, NY. The telephone number is 516 873-0900.

sessment questionnaire: preschools, libraries, the elementary school, and some churches. Each site was contacted by phone, sent a cover letter with suggested instructions, and given a number code. Those sites at which we could ask families to fill out the questionnaire immediately obviously produced a better number of returns. Families of school-age children filled them out during meet-the-teacher night, as did parents who brought their children to preschool story hour at one of the libraries. We received fewer returns from preschools that handed the questionnaire to parents as they were leaving with their children. Approximately one third of the over eight hundred questionnaires disseminated were returned, which we considered sufficient to generalize about the needs of families in our community. The most popular topics were child development, child discipline, ways to boost self-esteem, and ways to increase academic achievement, topics that have remained the top choices during subsequent assessments. Families preferred to receive information by attending evening meetings, and there were few requests for child care and almost none for transportation; they also wanted the opportunity to borrow reading and viewing materials. They were not interested in home visits.

We received some valuable advice from a county legislator, who suggested that we start with the people "at our doorstep," those we could reach easily, then implement a small but successful program that would prove our initial worth and the promise of our endeavors. The participants "at our doorstep" happened to be at the Rose Memorial Library. Marylu Perchak, a certified teacher, had been running story hours for preschoolers on Tuesdays. There was always full enrollment, ten three-year-olds for each of the two morning sessions and fifteen four-year-olds for each of the two afternoon sessions. Marylu invited a language specialist to speak to the parents while they waited for their children. The response was overwhelmingly positive and parents left the sessions wanting more time and more sessions. An informal question-and-answer format was used and parents submitted questions in advance. As far as we could determine, this session was the only service ever provided to families of young children in Stony Point. Since it was attended by fifty parents, we already had a workable formula to start planning some programs, put together a budget, and acquire funding.

Our First Year

On a limited budget of $2,000, Starting Together was able to provide twenty-seven meetings for families during 1995. We continued the sessions at the library story hours, in which a consultant meets with parents while their children attend a story hour with a preschool teacher. On Saturday mornings, two- and three-year-olds listened to stories and participated in activities together with their parents. Evening sessions just for parents allowed more time for discussion than the forty-five-minute story hour at the library. Having decided to extend our programs to kindergarten and first-grade parents, we had several sessions at the school geared toward academic achievement. Early winter weather caused postponements, and an outbreak of the flu, poor attendance. When only six parents attended a session for which twenty-three had registered, we learned to schedule well before Thanksgiving and not until after January. For sessions not at the school, we charged a two-dollar registration fee because we discovered that families are more committed to attend when they have to pay for the service.

We adhered to the same procedure of having the families predetermine the topics through questionnaires or informal surveys, and still used a question-and-answer format. (The one time we set the topic was the one time only one parent came; it seemed that families in this community did not need information about how to choose quality day care.) One parent's statement sums up the feelings of most participants: "I found I had a little of everyone's problem, that I'm doing okay, but best of all, I know I'm not alone."

Continuing to Grow

During our 1996 program, we will also set up resource centers at each of the town's two libraries. Each will consist of a separate display or shelves of materials (including books and videotapes) that can be borrowed by families. (CFR's library will again help us with selection.) Special programs will extend the school's kindergarten orientation in the spring beyond a one-night session so that families will have an opportunity to meet together and discuss their concerns more fully. Our programs are now reaching families with children ages two through six, or the first grade. We are advertising our program through fliers disseminated in many well-traveled sections of town—real estate offices, stores, restaurants, doctors' offices. Since we now have state funds, we are able to invite families from other towns to the sessions.

Now that we have provided programs for the families "at our doorstep," it is time to think about those families who don't know the questions to ask, the families who don't attend story hours with their children. How do we reach them? Marylu Perchak again provided a key to a program for such families. She began tutoring a first grader this year and after sessions with the child, she would stay and talk to the parents about the kinds of things they could be doing with their younger three-year-old. For example, they thought that three years of age was too young to be read to. Marylu brought puzzles and books from her own home and helped the parents learn how to use them with their children. A program idea now being discussed is providing subsidized tutoring for school children in their homes and then extending the session to include parents. The first needs assessment we conducted indicated that families did not want home visits, but they might accept tutoring for their children who are having difficulty in school.

The goal of Starting Together—to provide resources for families to help their young children develop intellectually, emotionally, and socially—may not be realized for years in terms of hard data, such as a decrease in students needing remedial services. Other variables, such as school curriculum and changing population, would also affect outcomes. However, as each parent leaves a session or borrows some materials that provide a few ideas to lessen the difficulties of parenting, to help them react more successfully to their children's needs, we are being successful. Programs developed from partnerships of family, school, and community that take the time to assess thoroughly the needs of families and implement programs with careful attention to feedback will always be successful.

References

BERGER, E. H. 1981. *Parents as Partners in Education.* St. Louis, MO: CV Mosby.

CHIARELLI, P. A. 1994. "Early Intervention Strategies for Family Literacy." In N. J. Ellsworth, C. N. Hedley, and A. N. Baratta (Eds.), *Literacy: A Redefinition*, pp. 233–46. Hillsdale, NJ: Lawrence Erlbaum.

HENDERSON, A. T., C. L. MARBURGER, and T. OOMS. 1986. *Beyond the Bake Sale: An Educator's Guide to Working with Parents.* Washington DC: National Committee for Citizens in Education.

NATIONAL ASSOCIATION OF SCHOOL BOARDS. 1991. *Caring Communities: Supporting Young Children and Families.* Alexandria, VA: NASB.

POLICY INFORMATION CENTER. 1992. *America's Smallest Schools: The Family.* Princeton, NJ: Educational Testing Service.

principles for policy makers

All public policy regarding families and literacy should begin with the shared understanding that families have a right to define themselves.

❑ Family literacy programs should not be restricted to programs for "undereducated mothers and their young children."

❑ The rhetoric describing families that is used to obtain funding should be critically appraised. Negative propaganda and scare tactics should automatically exclude a proposal from funding consideration.

Families and communities have the right to voice their concerns, influence policy, and set agendas at local, national, and international levels.

❑ Finances and other resources must be committed to ensure the inclusion of voices that typically are not represented in the debate among academics, policy makers, and program developers.

❑ Constitutional frameworks guarantee equality in education. Deficit models should therefore be rejected, because they infringe on the rights of individuals within communities.

❑ Proposals for programs should recognize the contributions of families. Proposals should be written locally with the active participation of the families who would benefit from the program.

❑ National and international programs that have no local relevance should be automatically rejected.

❑ World organizations can provide funding and "technical assistance," but it is essential that decisions about family literacy initiatives be made locally.

Language and literacy development goes beyond the demands of economic development.

❑ Literacy for life means rejecting the dominant belief in unidirectional progress.

❑ Supporting literacy development supports families, helps develop strong communities, and celebrates life.

❑ When policy makers recognize the importance of local literacies, and when they support the development of programs that empower families to use their languages and literacies to express themselves, to manage the adversities in their own lives, to solve the social and economic problems that confront them, to participate in the communities in which they live, and to live personally satisfying productive lives, then all families benefit.

❑ Similarly, bilingualism, which is often considered a major cause of illiteracy, can actually enhance the literacy opportunities of families. Speaking a second language should not be regarded as a problem. To the contrary, bilingualism can be thought of as knowing twice as much. In many cultures a person knowing only one language is considered uneducated.

Policies regarding family literacy programs do not eradicate the needs of families for adequate housing, food, and jobs.

❑ The question arises whether the focus on family (il)literacy programs by policy makers is another attempt to revictimize families by shifting public attention away from societal problems, such as homelessness, lack of adequate housing, limited educational opportunities, and lack of jobs, that afflict family life.

❑ ❑ ❑ ❑ ❑

What About the Wider Social, Economic, and Political Factors?

LUCILLE FANDEL

The way I see things here in the United States, there is a cultural struggle going on within the field of education, and family literacy is one of the arenas in which it is being played out. As evidence, I cite the materials handed out at a training session our entire Even Start team was required (by the Massachusetts Department of Education) to attend in 1994. The trainers were from the National Center for Family Literacy in Louisville, Kentucky. The center is not a federal institution, but as far as I can see, it speaks what is federal policy. The "overview" set forth the NCFL's public policy agenda regarding family literacy. Under the heading "The Promise of Family Literacy" the materials state:

Family literacy has roots in and supports several movements in America: efforts to strengthen the family and provide early childhood education, school reform, and economic development through adult literacy. . . . [It] is a way to address our critical national needs to support the family, improve the skills of children and adults and strengthen our economy. (NCFL 1994, p.3)

As I read this I asked myself, What about the wider social, economic, and political factors that besiege families in this society? Aren't family literacy programs about our naming those factors and exercising our power for change? Later, in the same "overview," under the heading "Public Policy Defines Family Literacy," the authors write:

Another way of defining family literacy is to review the public policy initiatives that are embracing family literacy as a strategy in achieving the goals of separate but related public policy programs. Since the overall goal of family literacy is to break the intergenerational cycle of dependency that is created by low educational achievement, any public policy with a goal of self-sufficiency and educational achievement for the low socioeconomic population is related to family literacy. Federal initiatives that embrace family literacy include Even Start, Head Start, Chapter 1, the National Literacy Act of 1991, Welfare Reform, and the Bureau of Indian Affairs Early Childhood Initiative.

The above statement does not reflect the "overall goal" of the Springfield (Massachusetts) Even Start Family Literacy Program!

❑ ❑ ❑ ❑ ❑

Family Literacy and the Politics of Literacy
BRIAN V. STREET

This article draws on the writings of Brian Street that appear in Immigrant Learners and Their Families, *edited by G. Weinstein-Shr and E. Quintero.*

Viewing from a distance—as a British social anthropologist and as a literacy researcher—the growth of interest in "family literacy" in the United States, there seem to me to be two basic approaches or philosophies of education involved in the movement. One of these, and the dominant one until recently, has been the *cultural deficit* model; the other is the *culturally sensitive* model.

Within the cultural deficit model, educators, politicians, programme directors, and funders have seen the family—and links between generations in the family—as a way to achieve educational goals that schools were unable to accomplish. At its most extreme this involved using family literacy schemes to infiltrate schooled and middle-class values and forms of literacy into diverse homes. These homes were seen as lacking the qualities of educational support and cognitive skill required of formal schooling, which was taken to be why so many children from them "failed" in the school system. The solution was to take the school to the home, to teach parents how to be proper teachers of their children, to read to them in approved ways, and to inculcate the ways of learning, speaking, reading, and writing valued in mainstream education.

The endeavor has all the hallmarks of many third-world literacy programmes in which the same assumptions about cultural deficit have been made and in which the assumed superiority of first-world, "advanced" societies led to a missionary spirit for transferring "our" advantages and truth to "them." In the case of third-world campaigns the vast failure of most to attract so-called illiterate learners to classes or having persuaded them into classes, to keep them there, or having seen them through several literacy-learning thresholds, to help them maintain that literacy in contexts where it was not required, has led to radical rethinking about the nature of literacy and of the programmes intended to deliver it (Verhoeven 1994).

Similar rethinking has not always been so prominent in industrialised societies as they encounter the growing number of people who have literacy difficulties. Instead, top-down assumptions about delivering and imparting particular literacy practices to the "illiterate" and stereotypes about sad, empty "illiterates" living in darkness and awaiting the light of middle-class schooled literacy continue to dominate media representation: the "crisis of illiteracy" remains rooted in an assumption of a single homogenous society and a single homogenous literacy required of its members. As with representations of life in poorer countries, the assumptions about life among non-mainstream groups in industrial countries such as America and the United Kindgom—whether new immigrants, minority groups, poor sectors of urban society, etc.—fail to see the richness, complexity, and diversity of "other" people's lives. Educational programmes, particularly those focused on "literacy," are particularly prone to this myopia and so instead of building on what is there already—the complex uses of different literacy practices in everyday life now evident from research on different cultural groups—they continue to purvey a single, narrow definition of "literacy" and attempt to impose it on their subjects. It could be argued that the single major cause of continuing school "failure" and literacy difficulties lies in this cultural misunderstanding between those offering literacy instruction and those on the receiving end.

In recent years, however, recognition of the significance of cultural misunderstanding and the problems it raises has increased, fed partly by the continuing "failure" of mainstream programmes and partly by the increased knowledge obtained through research (whether by academics or by teachers and facilitators) into the lives, cultures, and varied literacy practices of different groups of people.

The culturally sensitive model (Villegas 1991) underpins *Many Families, Many Literacies* and points forward, I believe, to a new partnership in education not only across generations but across cultures and classes. According to this model, people with literacy difficulties in some parts of their lives nevertheless already have some knowledge of literacy and live in cultural settings where various kinds of literacy are valued. The problem for mainstream teachers is that these forms of knowledge and life are not always apparent. Precisely because they involve cultural beliefs and practices and not just formal technical skills of the kind teachers are used to dealing with in literacy classes, they are not easily recognised.

Once it is recognised that people from nonmainstream backgrounds do not come *tabula rasa* to the education system, that they come bringing trails of their own cultural heritage and that this is frequently why they have difficulty "seeing" what the mainstream teacher takes for granted, whole new possibilities for learning and teaching, for the design of literacy projects, and for informed inquiry are opened up. Instead of frustration or even scorn at the inability of their students to do things that seem straightforward enough to them, these culturally sensitive educators start by building upon what is already there. This involves, as Auerbach stresses elsewhere in this book, listening to what their students have to say. It also involves finding out about the lives and cultural meanings not only of the students who come to classes but also of those students' families, their children and grandchildren, their parents and grandparents. This, then, is where family literacy takes on a new and richer dimension than it does in the dominant culture-deficit approach.

"Immigrant" and minority groups are often targeted in the standard family literacy projects, but from the broader culturally sensitive perspective they represent only one dimension of the larger issue: namely the recognition that all learners, "mainstream" as well as minority and those from diverse cultural backgrounds, carry with them cultural assumptions about what and how they are learning and about what is appropriate in their "ways with words" as Heath (1983) famously describes the speaking, listening, reading, and writing they all engage in, and that therefore teachers need to become cultural anthropologists, alert to signs of difference and to where students are coming from and equally self-conscious about their own assumptions and how those assumptions might be viewed by students.

This self-consciousness, moreover, extends beyond the classroom. The focus needs to shift from the classroom to the wider cultural setting. The discovery of variation and diversity that this broadening involves is one of the major strengths of the culturally sensitive approach.

A significant principle is that this cultural sensitivity has to be learnt not only by the teachers, who often (though not always) come from different cultural and class backgrounds than their students, but also by the learners. Just because someone comes from a particular cultural background is, it seems, no reason to assume that she or he understands and values that culture. Many young people in immigrant families are so concerned with fitting in with their host society, learning American English and the American life-style, that they may be cut off from their home language and culture. Ironically, this very focus on the American way of life may be a source of difficulty in coming to grips with it: by abandoning their home language and culture these young people also cut off links with the older generation, links that mainstream students can by and large assume. They thereby lose the support, both emotional and educational, that is crucial to their own learning.

Sociologists have often described a pattern in which third-generation immigrant children who have lost touch with their parents' language and culture begin to search for their "roots" and to look for way to maintain their cultural heritage. Current research (Weinstein-Shr and Quintero 1995) suggests that this process may now be speeding up: first-generation children are losing touch with their background but some are already beginning to see the disadvantages of this and to attempt to rebuild their linguistic and cultural knowledge. The culturally sensitive approach shows the ways in which this intergenerational collaboration can be assisted by sensitive educators and the educational and cultural gains of doing so.

Seeing literacy as not just a single unitary phenomenon attached to formal education but as a variety of social practices is such a new and challenging approach that researchers and practitioners working from these new positions have found themselves subject to intense critical scrutiny. This is partly because any new view that shifts the epistemological ground is open to both misunderstanding and resistance: old views persist, perhaps unrecognised, as we try to make sense of the new, and there are vested interests that depend on the old views for their legitimacy and their access to resources.

References

HEATH, S. B. 1983. *Ways with Words.* Cambridge, UK: Cambridge University Press.

VERHOEVEN, L. (Ed.). 1994. *Functional Literacy: Theoretical Issues and Educational Implications.* Amsterdam/Philadelphia: John Benjamins.

VILLEGAS, A. M. 1991. *Culturally Responsive Teaching.* Princeton, NJ: Educational Testing Service.

WEINSTEIN-SHR, G., and E. QUINTERO (Eds.). 1995. *Immigrant Learners and Their Families.* McHenry, IL: Center for Applied Linguistics and Delta Systems.

The advancement of written communication is also a universal movement. The national and international contexts are as tangible as the local contexts. The recognition or not of cultural differences, the multiplication or the confinement of local initiatives, the decentralisation or the standardisation of the programmes, depend also on the way literacy is being dealt with at the national and international level. Too many national and international interests are involved to consider literacy only as a local reality. In fact, it is for that reason that community literacy leaders are attempting to create links and facilitate exchange with other experiences at the national level, or at the international level. Indeed the revindication of learners and the alternative projects of many literacy workers cannot be sufficiently sustained without advocacy work that reaches the national and international arenas.

—Paul Belanger

□ □ □ □ □

Partnerships with Linguistic Minority Communities
ELSA AUERBACH

During presentations and focus group meetings at the National Coalition for Education Activists Conference in Boston, August 1995, the following strategies were mentioned as being especially successful in establishing or maintaining partnerships. All examples are activities mentioned by conference participants.

- *Review school budgets and secure funding allocated for partnership activities.* Often parents and teachers are told that there is no money for activities or initiatives that would enhance school-community partnerships. When school personnel are expected to reach out to parents and communities on their own time, it very often doesn't get done. However, open budget reviews (which may be requested by parents or parent organizations as well as by teachers) may show ways in which funding can be secured. This is a priority strategy, since many of the other strategies listed below require financial support.
  - Pay teachers for time spent working and communicating with parents.
  - Use citywide in-service funds for partnership activities like workshops with parents or community organizations.
- *Make sure all communication from the school is in a language and medium that parents can understand.* Often parents are bombarded

with flyers that they cannot read because of their own English or literacy limitations. It is the school's responsibility to make sure that there are translations, phone calls, and bilingual meetings. Relying on children to do the translating is problematic for many reasons: it shifts family roles, may lead to selective translation, and may create tensions within families. In addition, schools should not take for granted that parents know what school policies and procedures are (an open house, a bilingual program, etc.).

- Identify (and pay) community residents or school staff to act as translators and community liaisons.
- Provide FYI (for your information) sheets or handbooks about specific issues and school policies in all the languages of the students; include attendance policies, discipline policies, information on parental rights to privacy, suspension policies, bilingual contacts, information on how to communicate with teachers, explanations of procedures and activities, etc. *They should be written simply (not in bureaucratic language) and presented in an inviting format.*

- *Go to the communities and the families.* Often parents are expected to come to the school to communicate with teachers and participate in school activities; however, parents may be intimidated or uncomfortable doing so. Time and transportation may be further obstacles. When educators go to the communities of the families, they send a positive signal about two-way communication and wanting to meet parents on their terms. (Caution: Teachers need to be sensitive to community/family norms for home visits: in some cases, they may be seen as a sign of caring and commitment; in others, they may be seen as intrusive.)
  - Have monthly family nights at a community site (e.g., in a housing development or at a community center).
  - Ask teachers and administrators to participate in community-sponsored events (cultural events, meetings about community issues, neighborhood councils).
  - Ask teachers to make selected home visits (after checking beforehand whether it is appropriate).

- *Work with community-based organizations (CBOs).* School personnel should identify key organizations within the communities of the learners (Mutual Assistance Associations, cultural groups, legal rights and advocacy groups, etc.) and consult these groups, collaborate with them, and involve them in providing training and services. The relationship should be two-way, so that CBOs are part of planning and organizing school agendas, events, activities. (Caution: Schools should not assume that a particular CBO is representative of a particular community but should investigate the range of CBOs and their standing in that community.)

- Organize teams of CBO representatives, school personnel, and parents and have them meet regularly as well as plan specific activities.
- Collaborate with community-based organizations to organize workshops, meetings, retreats, etc.
- Work with community representatives and YMCA staff to set up after-school activities in response to parental need.

- *Communicate with families regularly about curriculum, students' learning, and students' needs.* Instead of communicating with parents only when there is a problem, teachers should establish regular rituals for communication that both inform parents about what is going on in the classroom and invite parents to provide input about their children's needs, interests, and special circumstances and about their own concerns as parents.
  - Write monthly newsletters in relevant languages and send notes and make calls to families about *positive* student accomplishments.
  - Invite parents to share their perspectives on children's needs and to give input on curriculum matters (through community or school-based meetings, consultation with representatives, home visits, etc.).

- *Actively seek community participation and knowledge in curriculum development.* Bringing community knowledge and community practices into the classroom and curriculum shows students and their families that their culture and knowledge is valued. This can be done by working with community members as part of curriculum planning teams, training teachers to research culture-specific practices in the communities, inviting community members into the classroom, and creating learning tasks that connect home, community, and school.
  - Research household funds of knowledge and invite community members into the classroom to discuss their community involvement.
  - Ask students to keep home-school journals.
  - Have students conduct research projects on community literacy practices, language use, cultural practices, etc.
  - Consult community liaisons about curriculum issues/development.

- *Create contexts for parents and children to learn from each other.* Projects or activities in which parents and children work together to explore themes or community issues can provide a concrete way for parents to become engaged with their children's educational development and for children to learn from their parents' cultural knowledge. These projects can be either school-based, bringing parents into the classroom, or community-based; they may involve storytelling, reading, art, cultural practices, and/or book making. In school contexts, they provide the additional benefit of teaching the teacher about family culture.

- Ask parents and children to coauthor books around community themes.
- Use children's literature with parents and children.
- Encourage parents and children to participate in traditional cultural activities.

- *Involve parents in setting the agenda for meetings/activities.* When parents determine what they want to focus on, either in meetings or in more general planning, they are more likely to want to participate than when someone else has decided what they "should" know or do. Likewise, when parents participate in setting the time for meetings, they are more likely to attend. (Caution: Parents may be reluctant to attend school-based meetings that focus on drugs, violence, etc., because attending them may imply that their child has a problem. These topics may come up naturally in the course of meetings or when parents raise them.)
  - Invite parents to voice concerns or issues at the beginning of meetings.
  - Schedule meetings on parent-selected topics.

- *Address parents' own needs and concerns.* Parents may be unable to participate actively in their children's schooling because they are so immersed in their own struggles (related to work relationships, finances, housing, health, etc.). Parent meetings or organizations that focus on their needs and support them in dealing with the issues they face may attract their participation more readily than those focusing only on schooling (or "how to be a better parent"). In one parent's words, "I'll go to any meeting that's going to lift me up."
  - Invite parents to community-based meetings on safety, day care, health, etc.
  - Set up native language literacy or ESL classes for parents if that's what they want.

- *Train parents in skills needed to advocate for kids.* Often parents are not familiar with the culture of schooling in the new country, are intimidated by power differences with school personnel, or come from cultures where parent participation is minimal. Training can help them develop the skills to ask questions, interact with school personnel, and organize for specific changes when necessary. This training is often most effective when it comes from community organizations (rather than from school personnel). Programs set up by schools to train parents to conform to school expectations often meet with resistance or disinterest. Teachers who themselves feel unable to effect change for institutional reasons may find that referring parents to advocacy organizations and supporting those efforts will push the change process forward.

- Encourage community-based organizations to train parents in their rights and responsibilities, in asking questions, and in organizing for change.
- Provide information about local parent organizations or CBOs to parents.
- Help parents contact parent advocacy organizations.

- *Provide information about citywide resources.* Although there may be a range of services and resources for parents, they may not know about them. Listing all the agencies or resources available in the neighborhood, community, or city is a direct benefit that schools or community groups can provide.
  - *Provide a directory of tutoring resources, with location, language, cost, phone number, contact person, etc.*
  - *Provide a directory of services related to other problems (counseling, drug problems, etc.).*

- *Involve all school personnel (from administrators to mainstream teachers to custodians and bus drivers) in issues relating to language-minority students.* Often the issues relating to ESL students are left to the teachers of those students. The principal of the school should be the principal of *all* the children, taking an active interest in language-minority students. Likewise, all school personnel should be educated and involved in activities related to language minority children. Cultural events at the school should involve the whole school and be seen not as entertainment but as education.
  - Organize workshops or retreats for school administrators, community representatives, teachers, and the parents of students in a given cultural group to discuss parental concerns, curriculum, and cultural issues relevant to that group.
  - Request that the principal attend neighborhood council meetings.
  - Encourage the principal to attend classroom-based multicultural events/activities.
  - Invite custodians, lunch monitors, and bus drivers, as well as educators, to activities, workshops, and training events.
  - Involve ESL teachers in parent meetings with mainstream teachers (to act as advocates for ESL students).
  - Accompany cultural events with discussions, background information, and question-and-answer sessions.

- *Integrate a parent- and community-education component in teacher education.* All prospective teachers should have extensive exposure to the communities of the students they will be teaching and should be taught how to research their students' communities.

- Require community immersion internships in which prospective teachers work in an agency in a language-minority community.
- Invite parents into teacher education classes to share stories.
- Include a component on integrating parent, community, and cultural knowledge into the curriculum.
- Include a teacher-research component in which prospective teachers learn how to do ethnographic and action research on community and classroom cultural/literacy practices.

❏ ❏ ❏ ❏ ❏

Debating Intergenerational Family Literacy: Myths, Critiques, and Counterperspectives
Audrey N. Grant

The emerging debates about intergenerational family literacy education in Australia, the United States, and the United Kingdom entail far more than disagreements over appropriate teaching methods or program delivery. Rather, there are fundamental differences between two groups of arguments, the first group premised on individualised, simplified, deficit notions of the family and of literacy, the second group built on social notions of the family and of literacy and the recognition of collaborative strengths and complexities. The first group can be termed *autonomous* notions because they treat key ideas as if they are neutral and context free, independent of any value judgements and disembodied from any social or cultural context. By contrast, the second group draw attention to the ways key concepts are *embedded in social and cultural contexts*, and assume ideological contests over meaning, value, and power (Street 1984). By referring to the beliefs associated with deficit, autonomous theories as *myths* and their social alternatives as *critiques and counterperspectives*, I am making my own values apparent. Nevertheless, I have attempted to be evenhanded by wherever possible using prevalent expressions of the deficit, autonomous perspectives as exemplified by their exponents rather than their critics.

1. Primary Focus and Language: Disabling or Enabling
Myth: *It is essential to focus on and diagnose the deficiencies. This demands a language of deficit and accountability.*

The argument here is that the deficiencies that beset many families must be emphasised in order to be addressed. Negative family environments place children at risk, in danger of neglect, abuse, ignorance, poverty, and illiteracy.

There are many parents and children who can't read or write, and the illiteracy rates in Western countries are national scandals. These are the realities.

What is worse, if family literacy programs are not funded, if agencies do not intervene, if accountability is not prescribed, if evaluation does not measure outcomes . . . what chance is there of ever breaking the intergenerational cycle of illiteracy and its consequences of poverty, low education, family break-up, alienation, marginalisation, you name it?

Moreover, hasn't the public a right to demand that their governments guarantee a cost-efficient return on tax dollars, that community and charity agencies be held accountable and prove their worth by openly and successfully competing for limited funds and resources?

Hence the need to launch campaigns that wage war on illiteracy and other social disadvantages, so that illiteracy and poverty are eradicated and standards of education are measurably higher and homes and communities are improved places.

Critique and Counterperspective: *It is crucial to focus on strength and to foreground potential. This enables a language of promise and possibility.*

I cannot agree with an approach that concentrates primarily on what's wrong with families. I'm not denying the grim realities of many people's lives. In every metropolis or rural district there are many families battling to survive, to get through the day. There are the brutalising effects of poverty, neglect, abuse; there is the alienation and despair of a new generation of young people. Australia has the highest suicide rate of young males in the world. These are indeed national scandals, and it is only right to insist that they are intolerable and need to be addressed and redressed. My concern is that the deficit approach to naming and identifying the problems makes things worse.

We are all familiar with the language of deficit and deficiency commonly applied to a supposed decline in literacy standards during times of economic recession, the scapegoats being school teachers and school dropouts. The same discourse of deficit is now applied to families, parents, and children, to illiteracy and its unmitigated disastrous consequences, to an intergenerational cycle of disadvantage, and is again counterproductive. It's inaccurate as well, as sociological and historical studies indicate (Graff 1987; Green, Hodgens, and Luke 1994). Wherever the language of deficit and deficiency is promoted—whether through public advocacy, advertising, grant proposals and conditions, accountability guidelines, or mission statements—it creates new problems, masks and misdiagnoses existing ones, and reduces genuine possibilities for collaborative action and transformative change.

To put it bluntly, the deficit model has a really nasty side: it mistakes symptoms for causes, blames the victim for the failings, salves the conscience of the advantaged (like you and me), renders the work of would-be helpers patronising, and is powerless to expose or address the structural evils, the corporate sins, and the broader social injustices. Instead, a counter-perspective offering an alternative vision is needed to *focus on collaborative action and transformative change—a language of promise and possibility.*

2. Reform Agendas: Economic or Social Solutions, Individual and/or Community Responsibility

Myth: *National interests are best served by economic reform and market deregulation. Social problems have individual solutions: "It is the changed conduct of individuals which can reshape society for the better"* (Howard 1995).

According to this perspective, government economic and social security policies must render the welfare sector cost-efficient by cutting back or streamlining welfare services and "safety nets," targeting the "truly needy" and the "deserving poor" in our society, motivating and retraining the dole bludgers to reenter the labour market, and engaging the able-bodied in productive work and citizenship. We need policies and programs that target the needy individuals and the poor families in our communities and bring to them the training, education, or discipline they and especially their children have missed out on, perhaps through no fault of their own.

Critique and Counterperspective: *Because human beings are primarily social not economic beings, social visions must inform reform agendas. "Society shapes individuals . . . and individuals shape society. . . . We are responsible for each other as well as ourselves"* (Cox 1995).

The makers of economic rationalist reform agendas, currently coming from the political right and left alike, are criticised above all for focusing on the markets to the exclusion of the social. Political visions for reform are thus rendered barren and simplistic, socially destructive, and spiritually bankrupt (Wallis 1994).

Alternative, social reform agendas are recast into positive grounds for action and for rebuilding a cohesive society. Eschewing the limited vision of economic rationalists and market reformers, social visionaries build their reform agendas on such strengths as the generation of social capital through trust and cooperation, quality-of-life indicators of progress and well-being, the redistributive role of government, a supportive family perspective in policy making, and reciprocal community responsibilities for addressing social problems. Fundamental to a social vision is a belief in society.

3. Versions of the Family: Private and Public Spheres, Targeting Poor "Disadvantaged" Families or Valuing Family Life

Myth: *Disadvantaged families should be targeted with training programs on how to manage their lives and how to utilise incentives for full participation as economic beings in the community. Blame is associated with poor parenting: "poor parents" must be motivated to assume responsibility.*

This myth is implicit in many one-time intervention or "fix it" projects, as well as in established institutional programs and education systems. Terms such as *disadvantaged, poverty, standards, quality, and motivation,* common in analysis and policy statements, often construct the "other" unquestioningly as "deficient." Such constructions of "others" seem to be made most readily where the cultural and social backgrounds of various stakeholders differ (when authorities are dealing with low-income parents and their children, for example). The myth is stated more blatantly as material factors or circumstances become overlaid with gender and class-specific attributes and cultural preferences, and their assumed connections are taken to be transparent, self-evident.

Powerful research evidence of this myth comes in the shaping of deficit versions of the "disadvantaged" families and normative or "ideal" versions of "advantaged" families. One major example, an Australian research study of "literacy practices in and out of schools in low socioeconomic urban communities" (Freebody, Ludwig, and Gunn 1995), found that for school personnel the types of families whose children attended the local school, as well as the types of communities, "were nearly always distinguished in terms of socioeconomic status." "Poverty" was understood in far more than financial or material terms:

> In the descriptions and explanations given by the educators interviewed . . . poverty, as a group attribute, brings with it a complex and confidently drawn mosaic of associations to do with much more than material resources. A heavily weighted baggage of moral, intellectual, social, physical, cultural and motivational dispositions is readily attached to poor people. Educators, like all of us, are members of a classed society. (p. xxxi and Vol. 2, p. 204)

Critique and Counterperspective: *All families are part of a broader society and need broad-based support, not "fix it" programs."Families are a public as well as a private matter and support for their well-being must be shared, not pushed into the narrow framework of 'the needy' or left to private means alone"* (Edgar 1988, pp. 2–3).

Constructs and stereotypes of poor parents, at-risk children, and the "disadvantaged" family and community often occur in tandem with solutions that assume a "we know what's best for you" and a "fix it" mentality. But what of poverty, unemployment, and the commonly assumed concomitant problems of low education and "illiteracy"? How can they be fixed without paying attention to social responsibility and structural evils? It is ironic that as long as solutions to the societal, structural problems are limited to retraining programs that target individuals, there will be no attempt to review the effects of the radical and rapid commodification and globalisation of work practices currently underway, or of the downsizing of large corporations. Far from creating employment, multinational corporations are ripping jobs out of major cities.

What then are the *alternative starting points* for socially cohesive family perspectives and policies offering correctives? One is *to recognise and try to deal with the "discursive disadvantaging" of the "other" and the "cultural reproduction"* in which we are all implicated. At one level this requires attention to the words we use and the social discourses we live through, which construct and limit the realities we can know and address and shape what does and can go on in professional contexts (Connell, Johnstone, and White 1992; Freebody, Ludwig, and Gunn 1995). Hence our need to choose sensitive terminolgy, avoid "deficit" labeling, and attempt to make visible our cultural assumptions. At a deeper level, the deconstructing of "disadvantaging discourse" requires that we reposition ourselves and open up spaces for others, especially in relation to power.

A second, related basis for constructive family policy is *"to reassert the value of family life."* Edgar regards this as

> the key to understanding and assessing policies and programs that claim to be for the family. . . . Family life is of central importance to the creation and maintenance of every individual and of society itself. . . . The family is both producer and consumer, the primal motive force for all productive activity. (1991b, p. 32)

Key starting points for valuing family life outlined in an American Assembly report are to build on the personal resources of people, the community, and support partnerships; to focus more on "what families do for the rest of society" (and less on "what is done for families"); to call for "broad-based universal programs . . . widely supported by the public but designed also to assist [those] most disadvantaged" by others; and "to include the poor as citizens, and not as dependents" (*The Future of Social Welfare* 1989, as cited in Edgar 1991b, p. 33).

Clearly, if policy deliberations are to reengage mutual responsibility and partnerships and to reassert the value of family life rather than to marginalise or "pathologise" many, they must encompass the central place of the family:

> We do believe that the family unit is central to society because it is the place in which social behaviour is constructed, interpreted and transmitted from one generation to another. . . . The family is both individual and societal at one and the same time. . . . The family is an active crucible in which personality and society are forged, in which we hammer out in constructive real-life action how our lives will be led, given the resources and constraints that limit our control, and given the wider sources of change that compel us to accept, adapt or resist. (Edgar 1991a, p.2)

A social definition of the family also includes a reciprocal understanding of rights and responsibilities: *"The community as a whole is the 'parent' for every child. Parenthood is a social act, not a private one, and parental rights derive from their responsibility, on behalf of the community, to raise children towards effective adulthood"* (Edgar 1993a, p.3).

4. "Family Literacy": Blame or Respect, Compensation or Access

Myth: *"Illiteracy" is the fault of poor parents and disadvantaged families.*

The Australian newspaper of 30 May 1995 reported the study by Freebody et al. under the headline, "Illiteracy blamed on poorer parents." This imputation of blame, together with the processes of marginalisation and exoneration, has become entrenched by the consistent tendency of school personnel to tie low literacy achievement to poverty.

Often those who take an autonomous, supposedly objective stance assume a diagnostic epidemiological metaphor of illness or disease, of difficult treatment and compensatory approaches. If illiteracy is the problem, treat that; if "these" families and their illiteracy are the compounded problem, fix them with literacy programs and parenting skills.

Critique and Counterperspective: *"Without a focus on social relationships and persons-in-activities, it is easy for outsiders (educators) to underestimate the wealth of funds of knowledge available in working-class households. Funds of knowledge are available regardless of the families' years of formal schooling or prominence assigned to literacy"* (Moll and Greenberg 1990, p. 327).

While critical of blaming individual families and students, I am not suggesting shifting the blame onto particular school personnel and schools as an alternative. The point is to depersonalise blame and to shift the focus away from individuals—as if they are sole agents—and onto the effects of institutional structures and issues of access and support (Green, Hodgens, and Luke 1994).

Keys to successful family literacy are sharing personal strengths and partnership and community resources. Compensatory programs are likely to be limited by providers' attempts to impose programs on those who are deemed to need them. When providers work with and alongside parents and community agencies, sharing the power and the resources and collaborating on decision making, they are repositioned to allow the families (their clientele) to identify their own and their children's needs and desires in relation to literacy. Families' preferred ways of thinking and being (in contrast to the culturally dominant ones of "discursive disadvantage" and blame, marginalisation, and exoneration [Freebody, Ludwig, and Gunn 1995]) might then be listened to and enlisted to bring about family literacy programs that are successful from the participants' point of view.

5. Constructs of Il/literacy and the Literate: Mechanical Skills or Social Practices, Naive or Critically Literate Subjects

Myth: *"Literacy is the mastery of the basic skills of encoding and decoding letters and sounds"* (Swallow 1995, p. 12). *Literacy levels are alarmingly low; illiteracy breeds other problems; eradicating illiteracy requires drill in the basic skills.*

Within a deficit model literacy is readily and narrowly defined in terms of technical skills or linguistic abilities, which are assumed to be fixed, neutral, and context free. Literacy and illiteracy are treated as simple factual matters. For instance, "literacy is the ability to read and write and spell correctly." Fixed levels of performance are deemed to separate the "illiterates" from the "literate," and those levels are taken to be unchanging, static, timeless.

Critique and Counterperspective: *Literacy is not a property, attribute, or ability of a person. Rather reading and writing are social practices and cultural ways of making and taking meanings, learnt and contested in everyday use.*

In autonomous models *literacy* is often taken to equal *illiteracy*, and hence to be the problem. Just as *spelling* in popular discourse has become synonymous with *spelling problems*, so too literacy is being constructed as *a problem*. Even our enlightened Commonwealth Government's International Literacy Year publicity in Australia conveyed this message, through a snappy white poster with large blue and fine black print:

literacy
the problem is bigger than you think.

Strictly speaking, of course it is *illiteracy* that is taken to be the problem, and even if that loaded term is avoided the connotation is still there. That's a subtle way in which a deficit discourse takes over, so that in the end there are few if any positive associations generated in popular parlance by the use of the word *literacy*. The same is now happening with the concept of *family literacy*.

This reductionism rules out attention to other explanations. It strips away the wider contexts, decontextualises the phenomena so that the wider social, economic, political, and structural factors, difficulties, and arenas are overlooked, except again at an individual level. So "poverty" is treated as *that* family's problem or a cluster of low-income families' problem or part of the "illiterates' cycle of disadvantage," an *other's* problem, so there are two classes of people—those with the problem and those free of the problem.

In addition, the problem—whether defined as il/literacy, poverty, injustice, broken family relationships—is not inquired into as an issue of institutional access or as a societal or structural evil, bound up with dominant economic and political values, policies, and developments. Examples of policy developments or social changes that are obviously having adverse repercussions on families and communities but that are ignored by context-free explanations are the policies of economic rationalism of the 1980s, the philosophy of managerialism and commodification of the "new fast capitalism" of 1990s, the "counterrevolutionary" dismantling of social welfare provisions and services, the exercising of legislative power in favour of the wealthy, and the extent of "white collar" crime and corporate greed and profit.

When "illiteracy" or the lack of literacy is deemed to be the problem, the solution is set prescriptively by the terms of the diagnosis—a top up of "literacy" for individuals, families, work forces, adult populations, is prescribed, in the same way a reskilling of the work force may be prescribed. Wider structural factors can remain unaddressed, because they are rendered invisible by both the diagnosis and the treatment. This is a Band-Aid approach, itself impoverished by a simplistic analysis and uninformed by a social vision.

Literacy may be necessary, but it is not sufficient for success in our society, let alone for achievement in the school system. Nor is a literacy program, however good, sufficient to guarantee low-income families recognised credentials or access to better jobs. What counts as successful reading and writing has changed over time, as has language usage; what counts is fundamentally a question about social practices and constructions. It is also a political question.

Conclusion

The above arguments in favour of social perspectives contrast major alternatives rather than discuss policies and strategies implicit in implemeting a social vision. I would like to conclude by suggesting five key considerations to policy makers concerned with intergenerational family literacy:

1. *By using the language of promise and possibility we can change the discourse of debate and the focus of policy.* Talking about "opportunities to rebuild society with greater equity" instead of "problems to be remedied" is a way of renewing hope, of "keeping alive the possibility of transforming our lives and society" (Wallis 1994) and brings with it a related policy change from crisis management to preventive action. Policy initiatives providing for broad-based but locally accessible support services and strong social netwerks will create social capital (Edgar 1987, 1991a).

2. *By implementing redistributive policies on our behalf, governments can greatly improve the lives of people with low incomes.* Nongovernment policy makers also have a key role to play in engaging public responsibilities and community resources and in reversing the current shortsighted trend to dismantle welfare systems.

debating intergenerational family literacy ············223

3. *By reengaging the social "contract of mutual obligations" between families and the wider community, policy makers can provide a sure foundation for collaboration.* Specific policies for co-opting various community groups, churches, welfare agencies, and other intergenerational resources are important if the exciting collaborative vision of providing parents and children mutual access to literacy is to become a reality.

4. *By adopting a family perspective, policy makers can make "family well-being the goal for every social policy choice, not just a suitable rationale to disguise some other objective"* (Edgar 1987). Giving priority to family concerns would bring about a restructuring of labour market programs, child care, and community-based welfare support programs. Family literacy programs could then adopt participatory approaches that respect the wealth of knowledge existing in households and communities and that share power and resources instead of furthering the status quo.

5. *By recognising that there are many literacies and cultural ways of being, policy makers can take into account the social and political place of family literacy programs.* Literacy programs stemming from this premise will legitimise and support home languages and local literacies, offer families greater access to dominant powerful literacies, break down entrenched institutional barriers to access, information, and equity, and increase quality of life without falsely promising employment and economic security.

To prevent the autonomous myths from prospering in the fertile ground of intergenerational family literacy policy and provision requires "changing the subject." We need to articulate comprehensive alternative perspectives, including visionary social strategies for pursuing policies that value family life. We need to connect human action to its social significance through social and cultural perspectives. We need to institute comprehensive and practical social reform that makes a substantial difference in the lives of families. We need to reposition ourselves as professionals so that we can be compassionate in our interactions. These stances and answers open up spaces for others (in relation to power especially), primarily those who, marginalised by the dominant ethic of competition, have known scant access to economic, social, and cultural capital.

References

CONNELL, R. W., K. M. JOHNSTONE, and V. M. WHITE. 1992. *Measuring Up: Assessment, Evaluation, and Educational Disadvantage.* Belconnem, Australian Capital Territory: Australian Curriculum Studies Association.

COX, EVA. 1995. "A Truly Civil Society": 1995 Boyer Lectures [1–6]. Audiocassettes: Sydney: Australian Broadcasting Corporation. Sydney: ABC Books.

EDGAR, DON. 1987. "Director's Report: Will a Real Family Policy Please Stand Up?" *Family Matters* 19(October):1–4.

EDGAR, DON. 1988. "Director's Report: Children Need Pride of Place in Family Policy Debate." *Family Matters* 20(April):1–7.

EDGAR, DON. 1991a. "Director's Report: Family Values or Valuing the Family?" *Family Matters* 29(August):2–3.

EDGAR, DON. 1991b. "Valuing Children and Parents: The Key to an Australian Family Policy." *Family Matters* 29(August):32–34

EDGAR, DON. 1993a. "Director's Report: Parents at the Core of Family Life." *Family Matters* 36(December):2–3.

EDGAR, DON. 1993b. "The Development of Competence." *Family Matters* 36(December):20–25.

FREEBODY, PETER, CHRISTINE LUDWIG, and STEPHANIE GUNN. 1995. *Everyday Literacy Practices in and out of Schools in Low Socio-economic Urban Communities.* Vols. 1 and 2. Brisbane, Centre for Literacy Education Research, Griffith University and DEET.

GRAFF, HARVEY J. 1987. *The Labyrinths of Literacy: Reflections on Literacy Past and Present.* London, Falmer.

GRANT, AUDREY. 1986. "Defining Literacy: Common Myths and Alternative Readings." *Australian Review of Applied Linguistics* 9 (2):1–22.

GRANT, AUDREY. 1993. "Perspectives on Literacy: Constructs and Practices, an Overview." In Susanne McConnell and Aileen Treloar (Eds.), *Voices of Experience, Book 2: Positions on Literacy Theories and Practices*, pp. 2–11. Canberra: Commonwealth of Australia, DEET.

GREEN, BILL, JOHN HODGENS, and ALLAN LUKE. 1994. *Debating Literacy in Australia: A Documentary History, 1945–1994.* Melbourne, Australian Literacy Federation.

HOWARD, JOHN. 1995. "Fair Australia." Address delivered to the Australian Council of Social Services (ACOSS) Congress, 13 October, Sydney.

MOLL, LUIS, and and J. GREENBERG. 1990. "Creating Zones of Possibilities: Combining Social Contexts for Instruction." In Luis Moll (Ed.), *Vygotsky and Education: Instructional Implications and Applications of Sociohistorical Psychology*, pp. 319–48. Cambridge, UK: Cambridge University Press.

STREET, BRIAN. 1984. *Literacy in Theory and Practice.* Cambridge, UK: Cambridge University Press.

STREET, BRIAN. 1993. *Cross-Cultural Perspectives on Literacy.* Cambridge, UK: Cambridge University Press.

SWALLOW, GAVIN. 1995. "What Is Literacy?" *Score* 3(3):11–12.

WALLIS, JIM. 1994. *The Soul of Politics: A Practical and Prophetic Vision for Change.* London: Fount (HarperCollins).

i want to ask a question: family members speak out

At the International Forum on Family Literacy held in Tucson, one of the working groups focused on understanding family literacy programs from the participants' point of view. They developed the following set of questions. Their message: participants in such programs should be given the opportunity to speak out, to question the status quo, to protect their own rights, and to make sure the program is in their best interests.

Do you understand how the program works?

Does the program sound like a quick fix?

Does the program promise you the American dream?

Does the program sound too good to be true?

What is the evidence for the claims that are made?

Does the program feel like a sales pitch or a medical diagnosis?

Does the literature blame you?

Does the program talk about undereducated parents and say they are to blame if their children are having trouble learning to read and write?

Does the program depend on the age of your child?

Is the program only for parents of very young children?

Does the program empower parents to be strong advocates for their children?

Is there respect for what your kids already know?

Who is sponsoring the program?

Where is the money coming from?

What's in it for the program organizers?

How much money is actually spent on the parents who are participating in the program and how much goes to the provider?.

How much money is spent on assessment? (This is also money that goes to the provider.)

Do parents who have participated in the program help run it?

Does the program build on how you use print in your everyday life?

How is the program connected to other community programs?

Is the program flexible?

Are there worksheets and meaningless exercises? If so, why?

Are the activities open-ended?

Can you use your life experiences when you participate in program activities?

Can you ask questions about the content of the program?

Have you been invited to participate in the development of the literacy activities that are used in the program?

Does the program use your family as a resource and encourage you to share your experiences?

Can the instructor speak to you in your own language?

Does the program value the language that you speak?

Does the program value your life and how you live it?

Does the program challenge or devalue parents?

Does the program make you feel as if you have to change your life, the way you speak, or your culture?

Is the program an indoctrination into another culture?

Does the way the program is run cause difficulties for you with other members of your family?

Does the program make you feel insecure or less confident?

Does the content of the program build on what you know?

Is the content of the program value-laden?

Is the content of the program relevant to your everyday life?

Does the content of the program acknowledge parents as experts?

Does the program recognize that reading and writing are complex and that there are many ways to be literate?

Does the program present reading and writing in bits and pieces?

Do you get to work with real texts?

Who's in charge?

Do parents help decide what kinds of activities take place?

Do parents share responsibilities in the program?

Do parents get to participate when decisions are being made?

Are the materials respectful of the families in your community?

Are all the materials from one publisher?

Were the materials advertised on TV? Do they cost over two hundred dollars and come from an 800 number?

Does the program take training to use?

How much time is spent on assessment?

Are the program organizers assessing you or the program? If they are assessing you, why?

How is the assessment used?

Does the assessment acknowledge that parents have a lot of knowledge and skills that need to be taken into consideration?

Does the assessment have something to do with what's happening in the program?

Do you get an opportunity to assess the program?

Does the assessment build on your strengths?

Does the assessment empower you to move to your next level of accomplishment?

Question! *Question!* **Question!**

Bibliography of Quotations

AGNIHTRI, R. K. "Campaign-Based Literacy Programmes: The Case of the Ambedkar Nagar Experiment in Dehli." In David Barton (Ed), *Sustaining Local Literacies.* Clevedon, Avon, UK: Multilingual Matters, 1994, p.53.

AUERBACK, ELSA. Speech to the International Forum on Family Literacy, Tucson, Arizona, October 1994.

BARTON, DAVID. "Globalisation and Diversification: Two Opposing Influences on Local Literacies." In David Barton (Ed), *Sustaining Local Literacies.* Clevedon, Avon, UK: Multilingual Matters, 1994, p. 4.

BELANGER, PAUL. "Literacy and Literacies: Continuity and Discontinuity." In David Barton (Ed), *Sustaining Local Literacies.* Clevedon, Avon, UK: Multilingual Matters, 1994, pp. 89, 90.

BRANDT, DEBORAH. "Accumulating Literacy." *College English* 57(6)(October 1995), p. 651.

DARLING, SHARON. *Family Literacy: The Need and the Promise.* Louisville, KY: National Center for Family Literacy, 1992, p. 3.

Family Ties. The Newsletter of the Family Literacy Group, Ontario, Canada. April 1993 (Issue 2).

GADSDEN, VIVIAN. "Understanding Family Literacy: Conceptual Issues Facing the Field." *Teachers College Record* 96(1)(Fall 1994), p. 80.

GEROULD, KIM. Speech to the International Family Literacy Forum, University of Massachusetts at Amherst, June 1995.

HEATH, SHIRLEY BRICE. "Questioning at Home and School: A Comparative Study." In G. Spindler (Ed.), *Doing the Ethnography of Schooling: Educational Anthropology in Action.* New York: Holt, Rinehart, and Winston, 1982.

LIMAGE, LESLIE J. "Lessons from International Organizations on Language Issues and Literacy." In David Barton (Ed), *Sustaining Local Literacies.* Clevedon, Avon, UK: Multilingual Matters, 1994, p. 95.

Literatura Infantil: Helping Parents and Children Learning Together. Watsonville, CA: Watsonville Migrant Education, 1991, Dr. Paul Nava, Director.

MARTENS, PRISCA. *I Already Know How to Read: A Child's View of Literacy.* Portsmouth, NH: Heinemann, 1996, p. 79.

National Center for Family Literacy. *Family Literacy Program Quality Self-Study.* National Center for Family Literacy, 1994.

National Center for Family Literacy. *Family Literacy Program Rating Scales.* Louisville, KY: National Center for Family Literacy, 1994, pp. 8, 15.

National Center for Family Literacy. *Spreading the Word and Planting the Seed.* Louisville, KY: National Center for Family Literacy, 1991, pp. 7 and 8.

POLAKOW, VALERIE. *Lives on the Edge: Single Mothers and Their Children in the Other America*. Chicago: The University of Chicago Press, 1993.

RIVERA, ANNA. In *Teacher Research on Funds of Knowledge: Learning from Households*, by N. Gonzalez, L. C. Moll, M. Floyd-Tenery, A. Rivera, P. Rendon, R. Gonzales, and C. Amanti. Santa Cruz, CA: National Center for Research on Cultural Diversity and Second Language Learning, 1993, p. 14.

RIVERA, KLAUDIA. Speech to the International Forum on Family Literacy, Tucson, Arizona, October 1994.

SCRIBNER, SYLVIA. "Mind in Action: A Functional Approach to Thinking." *The Quarterly Newsletter of the Laboratory of Comparative Human Cognition* 14(4)(1983), 103–9.

SHANNON, PATRICK. "A Lot of Money, That's What I Want." Unpublished essay.

SHOCKLEY, BETTY, BARBARA MICHALOVE, and JOBETH ALLEN. *Engaging Families: Connecting Home and School Literacy Communities*. Portsmouth, NH: Heinemann, 1995, p. 96.

SMYTHE, S. "Intergenerational Literacy in an Early Learning Centre: Implications for Abet in South Africa." A presentation to the Southern African Literacy Forum, Gordon's Bay, July 26–30, 1995.

SOARES, MAGDA BECKER. *Literacy Assessment and Its Implications for Statistical Measurement*. Federal University of Minas Gerais, Brazil, for the Section of Statistics on Education Division of Statistics, March 1992.

SOLSKEN, JUDITH W. "Who in the Family Supports Children's Literacy Learning and at What Cost?" Unpublished paper.

STREET, BRIAN. "Sociocultural Dimensions of Literacy: Literacy in an International Context." In *The Future of Literacy and the Literacy of the Future: Report of the Seminar on Adult Literacy in Industrialized Countries*. Hamburg: Unesco Institute of Education, 1991.

TAYLOR, DENNY. *Family Literacy: Young Children Learning to Read and Write*. Portsmouth, NH: Heinemann, 1983, p. 93.

TAYLOR, DENNY, and CATHERINE DORSEY-GAINES. *Growing Up Literate: Learning from Inner-City Families*. Portsmouth, NH: Heinemann, 1988, p. 195.

WHITON, LINDY. Presentation at the Family Literacy Forum, University of Massachusetts, Amherst, June 1995.

participants in the international forum on family literacy

TUSCON, ARIZONA, 1994

Authors who participated in the International Forum are marked with an asterisk.

JoBeth Allen has been an active research partner with Betty Schockley and Barbara Michalove since 1988. Her own children (Rachel, Luke, and Paul) have been her best teachers.

Patricia Anders is a professor in the department of language, reading, and culture at the University of Arizona. She is the proud mom of three children, Karen (twenty-six), Joel (twenty-three), and Paul (sixteen).

Cheri Anderson is a doctoral student at the University of Arizona and also a resource teacher with Tucson Unified School District's student and staff development. She is the designer and director of visual literacy and aesthetic literacy projects.

*Elsa Auerbach teaches in the English department and bilingaul/ESL graduate studies program at the University of Massachusetts, Boston. She is the parent of two teenagers, who in their earlier years were "victims" of family literacy (her own preoccupation with their literacy development).

Eileen Barry lives in Massachusetts with her husband, Kevin, her son, Michael, and her dogs, Bailey and Buddy. She teaches in an adult literacy project and is a doctoral student at the University of Pennsylvania.

*David Barton teaches in the linguistic department at Lancaster University, England. He is one of the founders of the Research and Practice in Adult Literacy (RAPAL) group, which aims to link researchers and practitioners in the field of adult basic education.

Barbara Bernard currently works as a teacher in the curriculum and instruction department of the Anchorage School District. Hans (thirteen) and Steffan (nine) continually serve to inform their mother and her practice as she works with families and schools.

David Bloome is professor of education at Peabody College of Vanderbilt University in Nashville, Tennessee. He is a former secondary English and reading teacher. His recent research has focused on reading and writing in communities, families, and schools.

*Elizabeth Cantafio has been working with homeless people for more then ten years. Currently she teaches in a "developmental" program and is a doctoral candidate at the

University of Pennsylvania. She is granddaughter of Michael G. Sabol, daughter of Betty and Tito, and sister to Diana Louise and Tito Michael.

*Jennie DeGroat, a Diné (Navajo) from Mariano Lake, New Mexico, is the daughter of the late Harry and Hazel DeGroat, is married to Kenneth Henry, and has three sons, Keyah, Kin, and Niya. She is a doctoral student at the University of New Mexico.

Esteban Diaz is a professor at California State University, San Bernardino. Rosa Diaz is the principal of Wilson Elementary in San Bernardino, California. Their children are Sonia, Xochitl, and Esteban. They have two grandchildren, Christina and Joshua.

Catherine Dorsey-Gaines, associate vice-president of Kean College in New Jersey, is a professor of early childhood and family studies. She is the coauthor of *Growing Up Literate: Learning from Inner-City Families*. She is a wife, the mother of two sons, and the grandmother of four.

*Tomás Enguidanos works in San Francisco as a Spanish bilingual special education teacher. In his travels to Cuba and Venezuela last year, he met and started loving someone who he hopes will help him create a literate family of his own.

Richard Figueroa is a professor of education at the University of California at Davis. He, his wife, Professor Nadeen Ruiz, and their two children, Roberto and Elena, have been personally involved in the issues affecting the education of special children.

*Bram Fisher, the family literacy project coordinator for the Movement for Canadian Literacy, lives in Kinsgston with his wife, Bryn, and their two youngest sons, Casey (seventeen) amd Willie (fifteen). Their "family literacy" now primarily takes place when their eldest son, Jeremy (twenty-one), drops by for some conversation over dinner.

Barbara Flores is a literacy/biliteracy scholar-activist who was primarily shaped by the lessons told by her elders about social justice and by religious upbringing about the importance of leading a virtuous life based on respect for others and courage to fight for human dignity and justice.

Alan Flurkey is a teacher in the Phoenix area, where he has been involved in elementary education since 1982. Alan and his wife, Jane Flurkey, have three young children—Ian, Zachery, and Hillary.

*Michele Foster, a professor at the Claremont Graduate School, grew up in an extended family—mother, grandmother, and grandfather—in Massachusetts in a house built in 1857 by her great-great-grandfather, a runaway slave. Her son, Toure, the sixth generation of her family, now occupies the house.

Dana Fox comes from a family of educators. Her mother, Emogene, teaches at the University of Central Arkansas, and her father recently retired as director of the Arkansas Migrant Educational Cooperative. Dana currently teaches reading and writing courses at the University of Arizona.

*Ken Goodman is a practical theorist, researcher, and teacher-educator whose work has changed our understanding of literacy processes. His sociopsycholinguistic transactional theory of the reading process is the most widely cited in the world. Ken is married to Yetta Goodman.

*Yetta Goodman is a professor of education at the University of Arizona. She is a major spokesperson for whole language and in her extensive writing shows concern for educational issues with a focus on classrooms, students, and teachers. Goodman is a mother of four daughters and a grandmother of six grandchildren.

*Audrey Grant teaches and researches literacy and adult literacy education at La Trobe University, Australia. Audrey's older sister, brother, sister-in-law, and a nephew live in Australia; two married nephews and one great-nephew live in America.

Terry Greene is a recent Ph.D. graduate of the University of Arizona. As the daughter of a career Air Force officer, Terry spent most summers in the back seat of the car, reading her way from state to state. Many additional hours were spent writing to those friends left behind.

*Jerome "Jerry" Harste is a children's author, a father, a teacher, and a language researcher. The difficulty his own children faced with regard to formal schooling led to his extensive research into what children know about literacy prior to coming to school and how instruction may be built from this base.

Debra Jacobson is happily part of many families. She and her dog feel rooted in Tucson, Arizona. She has worked in several schools over the years and is currently on leave and studying education at the University of Arizona.

Angela Jaggar had parents who were supportive, wonderful first teachers—her maiden name is Maestri—so it is easy to understand why she become a teacher. Currently she is a professor of education in the department of teaching and learning at New York University.

*Judy Kalman lives with her husband and their two children in a house overlooking a park at the southern end of Mexico City. She is a researcher at the Departmento de Investigaciones Educativas, Centro de Investigaciones y Estudios Avanzados (DIE-CINVESTAV), where she pursues her interest in literacy.

Dorothy King grew up in a family that cherishes literacy. A favorite childhood memory is of retreating to the hayloft during a thunderstorm and finding *Ivanhoe* and *Robin Hood* in the eaves. She works with literacy programs in schools serving American Indian children and their families.

*Susan Lytle, who is interested in the literacies of women and teaching, is an associate professor of education at the University of Pennsylvania. She has two daughters, Sarah and Jenny, who read and write "as if their life depended on it."

*Teresa McCarty grew up in Columbus, Ohio, where her extended family still lives. She is currently an associate professor of language, reading, and culture and codirector of the American Indian Language Development Institute at the University of Arizona in Tucson.

*Dan Madigan has written extensively both collaboratively and by himself about significant literacy events that evolve in the home as a result of stories that emerge through written, oral, and visual forms.

Prisca Martens is an assistant professor in language education at Indiana University, Indianapolis. Prisca and her husband, Ray, an artist, have two children, Matthew, who is ten, and Sarah, who is eight. A book she has written on her daughter's literacy has recently been published by Heinemann.

Janelle Matthis received her Ph.D. from the Universtiy of Arizona and is presently an assistant professor at Northern Illinois University. Her husband and two teenage daughters are constant reminders of the complexity and diversity of "funds of knowledge" even within one family.

Judy Nichols Mitchell is a professor of language, reading, and culture at the University of Arizona. Her principal interests in literacy instruction and assessment center around the study of readers' oral and/or written retelling of stories and other texts that they have read.

Luis C. Moll has conducted educational research with language-minority students for the past fifteen years. He has examined literacy instruction in English and Spanish and studies how literacy takes place in the broader social contexts of households and community life.

Joanna Morasco's mother and father entered the United States from Italy via Ellis Island. Currently a doctoral student at the University of Arizona, Joanna received an M. Ed. from Trenton State College in 1992. She's lived most of her life in Greenwich Village, Manhattan.

*****Theodora Niemeijer** is a first-generation United States American and grew up in a miltilingual family. Valuing the richness of this personal experience and the importance of family, she chose to work in the area of family education.

*****Maryann Nuckolls** is a teacher in the Tucson Unified School District, Tucson, Arizona. She has worked with community print in both adult education and public schools for more than twenty years. Presently she is documenting family stories for a newly adopted daughter.

Pat Rigg's major interests are English as a second language and adult literacy. Her latest book, co-authored with Francis Kazemek, is *Enriching Our Lives: Poetry Lessons for Adult Literacy Teachers and Tutors* (IRA, 1996).

*****Klaudia Rivera** is executive director of Programa de Educacion de El Barrio in New York City, which implements a participatory, student-centered philosophy. Rivera holds a doctorate from Columbia University and is on the faculty of the City College of the City University of New York.

Pamela Rossi is interested in the role of the arts in the cultivation and celebration of whole literacies for the whole child. She is exploring new paradigms in reading and literacy theories. Her work is dedicated to educators and to her life companion, Robert.

*****Judith Rovenger** is the youth services consultant for the Westchester Library System (NY). She has taught at Columbia, Rutgers, and Lesley College (Boston). She is a reviewer for *Sesame Street Parents* and received a Distinguished Achievement Award for Excellence in Education Journalism (1994).

Kathy Short has focused her work on children's literature, curriculum as inquiry, and collaborative learning environments for teachers and children. She teaches courses at the University of Arizona, where she is an associate professor.

Debbie Smith is a doctoral student in language, reading, and culture at the University of Arizona. She is presently working with fifteen high school teenagers who are members of gangs or tagging (graffiti) crews or who are associated with gang culture.

Judith Solsken is a professor of education at the University of Massachusetts, Amherst, where she teaches courses in literacy education. She and her grown-up daughter continue to share literacy learning by recommending books to each other.

Julie Spreadbury has a Ph. D. in family literacy from the University of Queensland, Australia, where she focuses on the transition from the child's preschool year to the end of the first year of formal schooling.

*****Denny Taylor** is an ethnographer and writer who has spent more than twenty years working with families, communities, and schools. Her latest book is *Toxic Literacies: Exposing the Injustice of Bureaucratic Texts*. In the summer of 1996 she participated in a family literacy project with her mother and wrote a children's book set in Garn-yr-erw, the coal-mining village in South Wales where her mother was born and where Denny spent much of her childhood.

Shirley Thornton is a retired Colonel in the United States Army Reserve. She has served as Director of Public Education for the State of California, California's State Director of Special Education, and Deputy Superintendent of the Specialized Program Branch of the California Department of Education. She is a strong advocate for equality and excellence in education for *all* children.

Jesse Patrick Turner, a whole language teacher, teaches reading and writing at a community college. He is currently enrolled as a doctoral student at the University of Arizona. Jesse and his wife, Carolyn, have a six-year-old daughter, Erin-Beth, who loves to dance and get lost in books.

Eleanor Vargas, after all her children were in school full-time, returned to the University of Arizona and worked in a lab for severely disabled preschoolers. Watching children participate enthusiastically in their own learning and grow in their love of reading has changed her own views on education.

Rita Weisskiff, a writer and educator, directs the development of curriculum for *Ghostwriter*, a Children's Television Workshop multimedia project. Rita's three grandchildren are too young to watch *Ghostwriter*, but her husband, Steve, and their two sons and daughters-in-law do. And everybody reads.

additional contributors

Maria Acosta was a student at and a part-time employee of the Bob Steele Reading Center (Hartford, Connecticut) for many years. When her husband was fired recently after many years with the same company, Maria took two jobs. She is unable to continue her education at this time, but her dream has always been to be a social worker.

Hal Adams is a visiting associate professor in the College of Education at the University of Illinois at Chicago. He is founder and coordinator of the Family Writing Program, which conducts adult writing workshops in poor neighborhoods in Chicago.

Kai Allen is a survivor of the Philadelphia streets currently living peacefully with her daughter, Luna, and son, Jared.

Mary Anderson is married to Willie Anderson and has three children (two boys and a girl) and six grandchildren. She started to attend Read/Write Now in order to get her GED. Now, she's in the Even Start program of Read/Write Now, together with her granddaughter Latasha.

Marilyn Antonucci lives in western Massachusetts with her husband, Frank. She has two sons, Anthony, a sophomore at Bard College, and Michael, a graduate student at Emory University. She is a family literacy teacher in the Springfield Even Start family literacy program.

Elaine DeLott Baker began working with communities in Mississippi in 1964 as a field worker for SNCC (Student Nonviolent Coordinating Committee) and CORE (Congress of Racial Equality). She has lived in Colorado since 1969 with her husband and two children. She is currently pursuing her doctoral degree.

Mary Benton is the language arts coordinator at the Deerfield Community School in Deerfield, New Hampshire, where she supports the literacy development of children age six through fourteen. In addition, she has been involved in many state and regional projects that focus on adults' understanding of policy issues and teaching practices that impact children.

Steven Bialostok, a doctoral student at the University of Arizona, is the author of *Raising Readers: Helping Your Child to Literacy* and *But What Will They Read? Helping Parents Understand Whole Language*. The most important person in his life is his son, Ethan, who as an infant was adopted by Steve, a single father.

George Brice grew up in Jamaica, left school, moved to England, and then to the United States. He has three children, two who live with him here and one who lives in England. He formerly had a printing business and is currently working as a carpenter.

Jean Bruce is a social historian at the Canadian Museum of Civilization, a national museum with a strong commitment to bring heritage to life. Jean believes that pride in material heritage begins at home, with stories about family "treasures" and their significance.

Trevor Cairney is professor of education and Pro Vice Chancellor for Research at the University of Western Sydney, Australia. He has led twenty funded research projects in his twenty-five years as a teacher and educator. He has and written seven books and more than one hundred and twenty articles in the field of literacy.

Sonia Carrasquillo was born and raised in Puerto Rico, where she studied theatre and drama. As a teenager, she appeared regularly on several daytime television shows. She came to the United States two years ago. She has a daughter, six, and a son, four.

Charles Casement is a freelance writer specializing in the field of education. An illness in early childhood played a significant part in his own literacy development. During his prolonged stay in bed, his mother read to him every day. He has had his nose in a book ever since.

Olivia Milagros Chabran is a daughter of the wind, born from the soil of the Americas and Africa, recovering from homelessness and heroin addiction. She is wandering the planet with her daughter Melina and sister Alicia and learning to live with HIV.

Patricia Chiarelli, founder and coordinator of Starting Together, teaches at Stony Point Elementary School and at Manhattanville College. She lives in New Jersey with her husband, Jim, and her son, Scott. Pat's life in teaching has been most influenced by a father who loved learning and a mother who taught her how to follow her heart.

Kathy Day a literacy worker in Southern Alberta for twelve years, Kathy helped organize the original Family Treasures Project as part of the Partnership Approach to Literacy (PAL) school based literacy project and the Read/Write Adult Literacy project. She now works on contracts related to literacy and community development. Kathy believes that literacy development must support the dignity and learning strengths of individuals, and their need for strong attachment to community.

Galena Sells Dick grew up in the Navajo community of Rough Rock, Arizona, where she lives with her husband, Ernest, five children, and four grandchildren. She currently directs Rough Rock's K–3 Navajo bilingual/bicultural program, a key component of which is parent involvement.

Elaine Douglas was born and grew up in Spanish Town, Jamaica, with two sisters and three brothers. She is a nurse's aide, having recently graduated from the nurse's aide program at a Hartford-area (Connecticut) community college. After her daughter recovers from a recent illness, Elaine plans to continue her education.

Randy Evenson, at the time he wrote "The Rocking Chair," was a student at his local primary school. He was very shy. Randy no longer lives in the community, but his grandma still lives there.

Lucille Fandel is a family literacy instructor in the Even Start program in Springfield, Massachusetts. Her work is done with the hope of contributing to a more just society in the United States.

Sandra Feinberg, devoted to public library service for the past twenty-five years, is an adjunct professor at the Palmer School of Library and Information Science, Long Island University. She lives in Stoney Brook, New York, with her husband and two sons.

Denver Finley was a grade-three student when he participated in the Family Treasures™ project. He was so shy that he spoke very little at home or at school. Today Denver is in grade six; although life has not been easy for him, he is more outgoing both at school and at home.

Margaret (Margie) Gallego is an assistant professor at Michigan State University currently on leave as a visiting scholar at the Laboratory of Comparative Human Congition at the University of California, San Diego. Her husband is Jeff, her daughter, Esme.

Brenda Hall grew up in Hartford, Connecticut. She remembers a childhood virtually free of the problems she now encounters when she visits her old neighborhood. In addition to continuing with her tutors at the Bob Steele Reading Center, she wants to become a nurse's aide.

Marla Hensley traveled extensively as a dependent of a government employee. She has a B.A. in early childhood education from Hood College, Frederick, Maryland, and has taken graduate courses at the University of Maryland and the University of Arizona. She has been involved with the Funds of Knowledge Project at the University of Arizona as a teacher-researcher, and she continues to incorporate the talents of her students' parents within her kindergarten classroom at Cavett School in Tucson, Arizona.

Bill Hughes spends a great deal of time and energy photographing the families in the Springfield (Massachusetts) Even Start family literacy program. These photographs appeared in a recent publication made up of stories by sixty-four students, *Believe in Yourself: It's Never Too Late.*

Helen James is Deputy Headteacher at Bangabandhu Primary School, London Borough of Tower Hamlets. She was previously an advisory teacher with the Centre for Language in Primary Education in London.

Nan Jiang, former teacher of English in China and author of numerous published articles on issues of teaching English as a foreign language, is currently studying at the University of Arizona in a Ph.D. program. He is married and has a daughter attending an American kindergarten.

Aimee Johnson attended a community college to enhance her effectiveness as a case worker for a local social service agency. She is a supportive caregiver for her children and grandchildren and has provided extensive external educational support (such as tutorial services) for both her grandchildren.

Peter Johnston is a professor at the State University of New York at Albany. He and his wife, Tina, have three children, age eight, twelve, and thirteen. They regularly trade books with one another and decorate their bathroom walls with provocative articles from newspapers and magazines.

Jo-Anne Wilson Keenan is a teacher in the public schools of Springfield, Massachusetts, and also the project director of the Springfield Learning Community Collaborative. Jo-Anne lives with her husband, John Keenan, and her son, Noah Wilson.

Lillian Lancaster is one of nine children and attended segregated, all-black schools in Haskell, Oklahoma. She graduated from Langston University, a historically black institution in Oklahoma and then taught briefly in Cleveland, Ohio. For several years, she taught high school English in the Orange County, Florida Public School System, where she currently works in the Office of Training and Development Services.

Hope Jensen Leichter is the Elbenwood Professor of Education in the Department of Institutional and Transcultural Studies at Teachers College, Columbia University. Her books include the seminal text *The Family as Educator* which was first published in 1974 by Teachers College Press.

Elvira Souza Lima is a researcher and educator who divides her time between the United States and Brazil. She and her husband, Marcelo, an artist and university professor, are both involved with cultural and educational projects with minorities and the working classes. They have two children who have many times participated in their projects.

Ray McDermott is a professor of education and anthropology at Stanford University. A former grade school teacher turned cultural anthropologist, he is interested in the history of writing systems and their use in different cultures. He has been working for twenty-five years on the difficulties of learning to read in American schools. For the past two years, he has been codirector of the Stanford Teachers Education Program.

William Marten is a survivor of a life of particular hardship, including a difficult childhood spent helping his mother make a living as a sharecropper. For over four years, William has attended small group tutoring classes at the reading center and has worked with a tutor one-on-one; he is one of the center's most persistent students. His dream is to leave the Northeast and buy a house back home in the South.

Letta Matsiepe Mashishi is the coordinator of the English language programme based at the Centre for Continuing Education of Wits, Johannesburg, South Africa. Her research interest is in the role of parents in the educational development of primary school children.

David Moses was born and grew up in Guyana with his two sisters and his brother. Soon after arriving in the United States, he enrolled in a program at the Bob Steele Reading Center in Hartford, Connecticut, and in 1992 he was chosen student of the year. David and his wife have one child.

Sharon Murphy teaches at York University in Toronto, Canada. During her childhood in Newfoundland, a regular family literacy event was the after-Sunday-dinner at-the-table debate about controversial issues in the local newspaper.

Arnold Nelson feels very good about his literacy skills and is a very strong community advocate for literacy. He does not hesitate to share his love of learning and life with all who will listen.

Gretchen Owochi is a recent University of Arizona graduate specializing in literacy development play and early childhood education. She lives in Tucson, Arizona, with her husband, David, and two spunky yellow labs, Dash and Comet.

Pat Peguese was born in Durham, North Carolina. She is the mother of one daughter and the grandmother of three children. She loves to write and bake and cook with her granddaughter, Shatoria. She has a big family, six sisters and three brothers. She thanks God for her life and her family.

Judy Reed is a writer and painter who is currently working on a biography of her great-great-great-grandmother based on a memoir chronicling the hardships of her life in the second half of the eighteenth century. Judy has been an ESL/family literacy group tutor at Literacy Volunteers of Greater Hartford, Connecticut.

Gladys Rios has one daughter, Patricia. After her separation from her ex-husband, Gladys decided to go back to school and was accepted at the Even Start program. Today, she is employed at Springboard Technology, in Springfield, Massachusetts.

Elsie Rivera was born in Westfield, Massachusetts, and has a husband and three children. She was so determined to be in school that she only missed one week of class during her last pregnancy. That baby is now a year and a half old.

Jan Robinson is an Aborginal woman who was born and raised in a small rural community but who currently lives in a major Australian city. While she only completed one year of high school, she has recently undertaken several adult literacy courses and participated in several family literacy programs. She is an active participant in her children's education.

Sarah Rodgers, born in St. Kitts, West Indies, moved to Puerto Rico and then to the United States. When the eldest of her four children reached school age, she began working with a tutor at the Bob Steele Reading Center in Hartford, Connecticut. Within two years, she was able to find work that she enjoys, enabling her to provide for her children.

Jenny Ruge is a senior research assistant who has worked with Trevor Cairney for the past four years. She is currently working full-time on a national Australian children's literacy project that focuses on community literacy practices. She is also a former primary school teacher .

Sharon W. Smith is a graduate student in the reading and writing program at the University of Massachusetts, Amherst. She is married, has two children, age sixteen and twenty-four, and feels fortunate in these difficult times to be part of a large, close, and still growing extended family.

Brian Street is a senior lecturer in social anthropology at the University of Sussex and visiting professor of education at the University of Pennsylvania. He is best known for his book *Literacy in Theory and Practice*. He lives in Brighton with his three children, Chloe (seventeen), Alice (fifteen), and Nicholas (twelve).

Antonia Tapia left school after the third grade and is now in her second year with the El Barrio Popular Education Program, where she studies Spanish, English, computers, and video. Her goals are to improve her comprehension in English and to obtain her high school equivalency certificate.

Adele Thomas is an associate professor on the faculty of education at Brock University, St. Catherines, Ontario, Canada. She works with preschool teachers and collaborates with the participants in a high school family literacy program in Niagra Falls, Ontario.

Lucia Vega has completed two years of study with the Programa de Educacion de El Barrio. She learned to read and write in the program and is in the second level of basic education in Spanish; she also studies English, computers, and video. Her writing included here is from her first year in the program.

Jonathan (Jonty) Walters has a lifestyle very different from his contemporaries, by virtue of his membership in the Hutterian Brethren Springpoint Colony. Family and community life are front and center.

Melanie Uttech is a doctoral candidate in language, reading, and culture at the University of Arizona and the coordinator of a United States–Mexico student exchange program at the University of Guanajuato, Mexico. Her dissertation, an ethnographic study of a rural school and community in the state of Guanajuato, received the National Security Education Program award for international research.